MW00613415

MUHAMMAD II

THE HAREM

Inside the Grand Seraglio
of the Turkish Sultans

N. M. PENZER

DOVER PUBLICATIONS, INC.
Mineola, New York

Bibliographical Note

This Dover edition, first published in 2005, is an unabridged republication of *The Harem: An Account of the Institution As It Existed in the Palace of the Turkish Sultans with a History of the Grand Seraglio from Its Foundation to the Present Time*, originally published by J. B. Lippincott Company, Philadelphia, in 1936. In the Dover edition, we have changed the placement of several illustrations and made corresponding changes in the List of Illustrations. We also have reduced the size of four illustrations that appeared in the original edition as oversize foldouts.

Library of Congress Cataloging-in-Publication Data

Penzer, N. M. (Norman Mosley), 1892–
    The harem : inside the Grand Seraglio of the Turkish sultans / N.M. Penzer.
        p. cm.
    "This is an unabridged republication of The harem : an account of the institution as it existed in the palace of the Turkish sultans with a history of the Grand Seraglio from its foundation to the present time, orig. published by J. B. Lippincott Co., Philadelphia, in 1936"—CIP data sheet.
    ISBN 0-486-44004-4 (pbk.)
    1. Harem. 2. Turkey—Court and courtiers. 3. Women—Turkey—Istanbul—Social life and customs. I. Title.

DR736.P42 2005
949.61'8—dc22

2004064920

Manufactured in the United States of America
Dover Publications, Inc., 31 East 2nd Street, Mineola, N.Y. 11501

TO

THE MEMORY OF

MY FELLOW-TRAVELLER

AND FRIEND

OSWALD WEGUELIN GREENE

PREFACE

THIS work, as the title-page explains, deals with the *ḥarēm* of the Turkish Sultans—but not merely with the *ḥarēm*. It deals also with the Grand Seraglio as a whole. Thus only one palace is concerned, and only one *ḥarēm*. It is necessary to make this clear, because several royal palaces existed in Constantinople, and all of them contained *ḥarēms*. True, the majority of them date from only the nineteenth century, but the first palace to be built by the Conqueror after his entry into the city in 1453 was not *the* Palace, but quite a different one in another part of the town. It might be thought that if the names of the palaces were given all difficulties would be overcome, but unfortunately the same name was bestowed on both palaces at different times. The only palace, with its *ḥarēm*, which this work sets itself to describe is that built by Muhammad II, the Conqueror, on Seraglio Point between 1459 and 1465.

The exact meaning of the various terms employed in its description is given in detail in Chapter I. It will be sufficient here to say that the Italians, the first Europeans to have dealings with the Turks, found it necessary to coin a word which would include the whole of the Royal Palace buildings—the *ḥarēm*, grounds, kiosks, etc. Thus *seraglio* was adopted, and the promontory on which it stood, the site of ancient Byzantium, was known as Seraglio Point. The abbreviated form *serai* simply means 'palace,' and the modern Turkish name for the palace which forms the subject of this work is *Topkapi Sarayi*, or the Seraglio of the Cannon Gate, although both gate and cannon have long since disappeared.

My grateful thanks are due to the following: to the Director of the *Topkapi Sarayi* Museum, Tahsin Öz, who, besides allowing me to carry out an extensive and thorough inspection of the Seraglio, gave me much valuable information while the work was passing through the press, and personally corrected the plan of the Seraglio, adding matter that it would have been impossible to include otherwise; to

5

my friend Captain H. Burton, of the Norfolk Regiment, for several introductions in Istanbul; to Dr K. L. Scott, Principal of Robert College at Istanbul, who very kindly put his valuable library at my disposal and helped me in several other ways; to the Director of the University Library of Istanbul, for allowing me to reproduce the illustrations facing p. 157 and p. 213 ; to the various departments of the British Museum, from whom I received every possible help; to the staff at the Brighton Public Library (strong in works on costume); to my friend Miss Frances Welby, for her great help in translating some of the more difficult Italian manuscripts and texts; to Miss Heath (Mrs Ahern), who so patiently drew the plan from my manuscript notes and rough drafts; and to Miss W. Rawlinson, who voluntarily undertook the typing of the manuscript.

N. M. P.

CONTENTS

7

ILLUSTRATIONS

ILLUSTRATIONS

THE HAREM

CHAPTER I

INTRODUCTORY

It would probably be impossible to think of any Eastern institution that is more familiar by name to the whole of the Western world but less understood in actual fact than the *harem*. From early childhood we have heard of the Turkish *harem*, and have been told that it is a place where hundreds of lovely women are kept locked up for the sole pleasure of a single master. And as we grow up but little is added to this early information. We perhaps realize the difference between wives and concubines, and appreciate their position in Muhammadan law. We may even discover that very few Turks ever had more than one wife, and that few could afford to keep more than a negro cook as maid-of-all-work. But most of us still imagine that the Sultan is—or, rather, was—a vicious old reprobate, spending all his time in the *harem*, surrounded by hundreds of semi-naked women, in an atmosphere of heavy perfume, cool fountains, soft music, and over-indulgence in every conceivable kind of vice that the united brains of jealous, sex-starved women could invent for the pleasure of their lord.

There are perhaps two main reasons why such false ideas have lingered so long in the Western mind. In the first place, so great has been the secrecy which has always surrounded the Imperial *harem* that first-hand and reliable information was seldom forthcoming. In the second place, the dividing line between fact and fiction, as far as the *harem* was concerned, was very thin and ill defined. After all, it had only been popularized in Western Europe early in the eighteenth century, when Antoine Galland first published the *Arabian Nights*, and the public were much too intrigued by the novelty and fascination of the tales themselves to entertain any desire to question the *mise en scène* or seek to dissipate the clouds of romance and hyperbole that hung so heavily over this newly discovered creation of the Orient.

The vague, and sometimes conflicting, descriptions of travellers that followed, the meagre accounts of English governesses and

13

companions, the letters and diaries of ambassadors' wives or secretaries, were the sole sources of information. But even so the number of the intelligent reading public was small, while many of the more important first-hand accounts still remained in manuscript, and had long since found their resting-place amid a host of dusty archives or on the shelves of some State library uncatalogued and forgotten. Thus all kinds of misunderstandings, exaggerations, distortions, and occasionally deliberate fabrications, have merely tended to add confusion to the indifferent and scanty accounts of the *harem* already existing.

It is not only in the more intimate details of Court etiquette that misconceptions have occurred, but even in generalities, the appreciation of which is absolutely necessary to the understanding of the whole *harem* system. For instance, it is still quite widely believed that *harem* rule was coeval with the great days of the Ottoman Empire—with the first Murad, Bayezid, Muhammad, Selim, and Suleiman the Magnificent—whereas in reality the *harem* must not be connected with the Ottoman power at its height, but should be looked upon as the beginning of its decline and fall. To the early rulers of Turkey the *harem* was unknown; it was unwanted. They were much too busy overcoming their numerous foes and establishing an empire to find time to indulge the appetite for a sensual life that only follows in the wake of security, well-filled treasuries, and abundance of leisure. Yet it must not be imagined that the *harem* system was solely responsible for the ultimate fall of the Ottoman Empire. It was not the system that was wrong, it was those in charge of it. So far from being a palace of women lazing about marble halls awaiting their master's pleasure, the *harem* was a little world of its own, governed with the utmost deliberation and care, not by a man at all, but by a woman. Every member of it had her exact duties to perform, and was forced to comply with all the rules and regulations that in many respects were as strict and rigid as in a convent.

No one knew the etiquette of the *harem* more than the Sultan, and once it was respected all would be well. Even if that great lady the Sultan's mother and the Grand Vizir were placated he still had the janissaries to reckon with. A Sultan could go so far, but no farther: deposition was certain and death probable.

And yet it is hard to lay all the blame on a man who may have spent his whole life locked up in a room in the Palace, suddenly to find himself set free and hailed as Sultan. No wonder excesses often followed, with dire results to all concerned. A chain is only as strong as its weakest link. A nation born and bred in slavery and dependent on slavery for its very existence is safe only so long as the machine runs smoothly, but as soon as a single cog ceases to function the whole mechanism may be affected. At the same time the machine may be well worth a close inspection, and here and there we may come across a part that will hold our interest, and perhaps even teach us something as well.

For instance, the enormous activities of the Palace seem to have almost entirely escaped general notice, and while idle curiosity has always centred on the *harem*, the fact that the Palace contained a great military School of State, over a dozen mosques, ten double kitchens, two bakeries, a flour-mill, two hospitals, and various kinds of baths, storerooms, sports fields, etc., is almost wholly ignored.

It is impossible to understand the *harem* unless we consider it merely as a single unit in a large and highly complicated system.

As the work proceeds the *harem* will appear in its right perspective; it will no longer be a vague term used as synonymous with Seraglio, but will be clearly defined as regards its scope, and described as fully as possible with the aid of a detailed plan and occasional photographs. And here it is necessary to be quite clear as to the real meaning of words such as *harem* and *seraglio*. Let us take *harem* first. The word is borrowed from the Arabic *harām*, and means ' that which is unlawful,' as opposed to *halāl*, ' that which is lawful.' Thus the whole region for a certain distance round Mecca and Medina is *harām*— that is to say that certain things allowed elsewhere are not permitted there. Consequently, owing to the sacredness of those holy places, the word also signified ' holy,' ' protected,' ' sacred,' ' inviolate,' and lastly ' forbidden.' In its secular application the word was used in reference to that portion of a Muslim house occupied by the women, because it was their *harām*, or sanctuary. The Turks softened the word into *harēm*, and added to it the termination *lik*. Thus the correct Turkish word for the woman's part of the house is *harēmlik*. The suffix when added to substantives denotes place, and the ' place of sanctuary' exactly expresses that portion of the house allotted to the wife, her children and servants.

The abbreviated form *ḥarēm* is more correctly applied to the *personnel* of the *ḥarēmlik*, although the shorter form is now almost universally adopted with all its various meanings. But in the case of the word *selāmlik*, which signifies the domain of the husband, no change has occurred. This could not well be otherwise, as *selām* simply means 'greeting' or 'salutation,' and the one place in the house where guests could be received was naturally the *selāmlik*.

Relations with European Powers soon gave rise to the coining of a word that would embrace not only the *ḥarēmlik* and the *selāmlik*, but the entire Royal buildings as a whole. By a curious Italian adaptation of a Persian word the term *seraglio* was introduced, and came to be generally accepted by both Europeans and Turks. Its etymological history is interesting, and helps to explain its exact meaning. The modern *seraglio* is directly derived from the Italian *serraglio*, 'a cage for wild animals' (Latin *sera*, 'a bar,' with *aculum* added as suffix), and was adopted owing to its chance similarity with the Persian words *sarā* and *sarāī*, which originally simply meant 'a building,' and particularly 'a palace,' and which are familiar to us in the word 'caravanserai' (Persian *karwānsarāī*), 'a (halting) place for camels,' and so 'an inn for travellers.' In its proper sense of 'a building' or 'a palace' *sarāī* was largely used by the Tatars, from whom it was borrowed by the Russians, who degraded it to mean merely 'a shed.' But in the language of the Levantine Franks it became *serail* and *serraglio*. It was at this point that a mistaken 'striving after meaning' with the Italian *serrato*, 'shut up,' etc., connected it with the private apartments of women. But as the old idea of 'palace' was still recognized in both *serail* and *seraglio* (spelled now with one 'r') they were universally adopted to mean the entire Royal Palace on the hill of the ancient Byzantine acropolis. In fact, the peninsula itself became known as Seraglio Point, and is still so called to-day.

The adoption in recent years of the Western alphabet and phonetic spelling has caused many curious-looking words to appear, and it is with difficulty that some of them can be recognized at all. The tourist of to-day on getting into a taxi in Pera and wishing to go to the Seraglio should ask for the *Topkapi Sarayi*, and he will at once be understood. As mentioned in the Preface, the meaning of the phrase is ' the Palace of the Cannon Gate,' and refers to an old gate that once stood at the very tip of Seraglio Point, and which was protected by several pieces of cannon now in the arms museum in the ancient church of St Irene. The 1933 Turkish guide-book to the Seraglio calls itself *Topkapi Sarayi Müzesi Rehberi* (*Guide to the Museum of the Cannon Gate Palace*).[1] But in spite of this the terms *seraglio* and the abbreviated *serail* or *serai* are in general use, especially among foreigners.

Yet the visitor may be perplexed when the hotel guide asks him if he has yet visited the Old Serai, or *Vieux Séraï*, especially if he already knows that the Old Serai, or *Eski Serai*, was pulled down long ago and the site first occupied by the *Seraskerat*, or War Office, erected in 1870, and then, since 1924, by the University.

But the reference is really to the Seraglio. The explanation is as follows: after Muhammad II had taken Constantinople he built a palace on the Third Hill in 1454, and when between 1459 and 1465 the larger palace on the First Hill superseded it the former was known as *Eski Serai*, or Old Serai, while the latter was called *Yeni Serai*, or New Serai. Among European writers, however, it was usually referred to as the Grand Seraglio.

Now when the *Yeni Serai* was abandoned in 1853 it immediately was called the Old Palace by Europeans. The Turks, however, preferred to call it the *Top Capu* (now spelled *Topkapi*) *Sarayi*.

Even so that is not all, because in 1709 Ahmed III had started building a summer palace near the Marmora on Seraglio Point. This palace was also known to the Turks as *Top Capu Sarayi*, but to us merely as the Summer Palace. It was totally destroyed in 1862–63. It will thus be seen that there is plenty of justification for the visitor to be confused by the redundance of names. I find it clearest to refer to the 1454 palace as the Old Serai or Old Seraglio, that which forms the subject of the present work as the Grand Seraglio, or simply the Seraglio, and the 1709 one as the Summer Palace. In this way, I think, everything will be clear.

Having now looked at the true meanings of *ḥarēm*, *selāmlik*, and

[1] Istanbul.

17

seraglio, we can appreciate the fact that, whereas the former two must be used only to refer to the apartments of the women and the men respectively, the term *seraglio* can be very conveniently employed for the entire Palace and all its buildings.

As is well known, among all Eastern nations the gate was most important both architecturally and politically, whether it was the gate of the city wall, the gate of the palace, or the gate of a private dwelling. We have just noticed that the Seraglio itself is known by the name of a gate; the seat of Ottoman Government was named after a gate—the *Bab-i-Humayun*, or Sublime Porte. So also the divisions of any large building were regulated by its gates. I shall have a good deal to say about gates later; here I am merely anxious to stress the importance of gates not only in the understanding of the plan of the Seraglio, but in giving their name to the court into which they lead, and in some cases to the buildings surrounding or in the vicinity of that court.

Thus in the case of the Seraglio, although the *ḥarēmlik* and the *selāmlik* were the two main divisions of the buildings which formed the private apartments of the Royal household, there were other buildings beyond the famous Gate of Felicity, or *Bab-i-Sa'adet* as it was called. Hence all that unknown part of the Seraglio beyond that gate was known as the House of Felicity.

As we shall see in a later chapter, the semi-public First Court was bounded on its inner side by a thick wall pierced by a gate known as the *Ortakapi*, past which admittance was limited to those seeking audience at the Divan. Only the Sultan was allowed to proceed past this gate on horseback. From the Second Court access was gained to the House of Felicity only through the Gate of Felicity, and only members of the Sultan's own household were allowed entrance.

With these few details we are in a much better position to understand the early descriptions of the Seraglio that have come down to us, and from what direction attempts to view the Palace were made, and how far the would-be sightseers got.

During the whole period over which the Seraglio continued to be the Royal residence the number of people who claim with good justification to have seen any part of it past the Gate of Felicity can be counted on the fingers of one hand. Even if we include men who at one time were actually employed in the Inside Service of the Seraglio itself, the total still remains under a dozen.

In considering these early accounts we must differentiate between these two groups. But even when we have read what ex-pages of the Seraglio have to tell us we realize more than before how segregated the various units of the Palace system were, and how any information about the *harēm* was still trivial and unreliable, if, indeed, any was forthcoming at all. Thus the first three accounts, those by Angiolello (1470–81), Bassano da Zara (*c.* 1530–40), and Menavino (*c.* 1545), deal almost entirely with the Palace School. Bassano da Zara, however, discourses on the general manners and customs of the Turks as well, and I shall have occasion to refer to his work again.

The first definite account we have of the *harēm* is contained in a description of Constantinople by one Domenico Hierosolimitano, entitled *Relatione della gran città di Costantinopoli* [1] (*sic*), a manuscript which we shall consider in due course. The author occupied the unique post of physician at the Court of Murad III (1574–95), and this alone could account for knowledge of the quarters of the *harēm* shown in his writings. But so secret and jealously guarded was the *harēm* and all that happened inside it that nothing of any consequence whatever was definitely known (let alone seen) until after the deposition of Abd ul-Hamid II in 1909. And even since that date the number of people who have visited any of the closed rooms is a mere handful. As these early accounts have a distinct historical value I shall devote the next chapter to a more detailed discussion of them. True, after 1853, when Abd ul-Mejid had changed his residence to the more airy shores of the Bosphorus, certain 'show rooms' were open to privileged foreigners, but the *harēm* still remained the place of mystery it ever was.

In 1615 the well-known traveller Pietro della Valle had told his readers that nothing could be learned about what existed beyond the Gate of Felicity. And as recently as 1926 we find such an authority as Sir George Young telling us the same thing, only in an even more emphatic way. "Up till now," he says,

the Seraglio Hareem and the Hirkai Sherif Odassi [Chamber of the Holy Mantle] remain two of the very few places on earth that no

[1] 1611.

19

Anglo-Saxon or American foot has as yet trod. As the Pole used to be for explorers—as Everest still is for mountaineers—so have the Sultan's Hareem and the Hirkai Sherif been for tourists.[1]

The secret of the *ḥarēm* was well kept, and even in recent years when Yildiz housed 370 women and 127 eunuchs in the service of Abd ul-Hamid II nothing was really known until after the fall of the Sultan.

It was here that the end of the *ḥarēm* came, for, although the deposed Sultan was allowed to take a few favourites into exile at Salonica, the *ḥarēm* system definitely ended in 1909. There are many accounts of its dispersal and the first and last public appearance of the women. Perhaps the best version is that given by Francis McCullagh:

> One of the most mournful processions of the many mournful processions of fallen grandeur that passed through the streets during these days was one composed of the ladies from the ex-Sultan's Harem on their way from Yildiz to the Top-Kapu Palace [the Seraglio]. These unfortunate ladies were of all ages between fifteen and fifty and so numerous that it took thirty-one carriages to convey them and their attendants. Some of them were sent to the Old Seraglio in Stamboul, but this old palace of the early Sultans had fallen into such a state of disrepair that it was found to be unsuitable for them and they were sent back again to Yildiz. Finally they were all collected in the Top-Kapu Palace in connection with one of the strangest ceremonies that ever took place even there. It is well known that most of the ladies in the harems of the Turkish Sultans were Circassians, the Circassian girls being very much esteemed on account of their beauty and being consequently very expensive. As Abd-ul-Hamid's Seraglio was no exception to this general rule, the Turkish Government telegraphed to the different Circassian villages in Anatolia, notifying them that every family which happened to have any of its female members in the ex-Sultan's Harem was at liberty to take them home, no matter whether the girls had been originally sold by their parents or had (as was the case in some instances) been torn from their homes by force.
>
> In consequence of this, a large number of Circassian mountaineers came in their picturesque garb into Constantinople, and on a certain fixed day they were conducted in a body to the Old Palace of Top-Kapu, where, in the presence of a Turkish Commission, they were ushered into a long hall filled with the ex-Sultan's concubines, cadines and odalisques, all of whom were then allowed to unveil themselves for

[1] *Constantinople* (London), pp. 160–161.

THE ROOFS OF THE SERAGLIO, SHOWING THE SELĀMLIK AND ADJOINING BUILDINGS

the occasion. The scene that followed was very touching. Daughters fell into the arms of their fathers whom they had not seen for years. Sisters embraced brothers or cousins, and in some instances relatives met who had never met before, and were only able to establish their relationship by means of long and mutual explanations.

The contrast between the delicate complexions and costly attire of the women and the rough, weather-beaten appearance of the ill-clad mountaineers who had come to fetch them home was not the least striking feature of the extraordinary scene; and in some instances the poor relatives were quite dazzled by the beautiful faces, the graceful manners, and the rich apparel of their kinswomen. The latter seemed all very glad, however, to get away; and as a rule they lost no time in packing their trunks and departing, sometimes after a very affectionate leave-taking of the other odalisques. The number of female slaves thus liberated was two hundred and thirteen.

Clad in Circassian peasant dress, they are now in all probability milking cows and doing farm work in Anatolia. . . . This joyful reunion in the Top-Kapu Palace had its sad side, however, as more than one of the men did not find the face he sought. Some of the girls had died, some had been put to death by Abd-ul-Hamid, and others of them, after Abd-ul-Hamid's fall, had been brought with him to Salonica by the ex-Sultan or quietly drafted into the harems of imperial princes who had taken a fancy to them. Moreover a good many of the women, especially those who had already passed their first youth, were disheartened to learn that nobody came to fetch them. Apparently their relatives had died or migrated, or did not relish the prospect of bringing back into their miserable mountain huts women no longer young, who had contracted expensive tastes and forgotten the language of their childhood. . . . These unfortunate ladies will probably pine away the rest of their lives in company with the other ladies—remnants of the Harems of the past Sultans—who fill the Top-Kapu Palace and who, in the best manner of the *Arabian Nights*, sigh audibly at the barred and latticed windows and have on one or two occasions dropped roses and perfumed handkerchiefs before good-looking youths passing in the street below.[1]

Sic transit . . . And so passed the *harēm*.

As soon as the few remaining women had been allotted other residences in the town the treasures in the Seraglio were arranged as a museum, and after long preparation it was open for inspection to a selected few. Then gradually other rooms were thrown open, and

[1] *The Fall of Abd-ul-Hamid* (London, 1910), pp. 276–278.

the public were finally allowed to inspect them on payment of a small entrance fee.

Thus in the autumn of 1924 the chief local guide-book afforded the following information:

At the moment one may visit:
> The Bagdad Kieuschk.
> The Moustapha Pacha Kieuschk.
> The Terrace of the Abdul Medjid Pavilion.
> The Museum of Porcelaines.
> The Reception Room or Arz Odassi.

During the next ten years more and more rooms were opened, until in 1933 it was possible to publish an official guide-book and lay down exactly what rooms were open and what closed. This was most necessary, as previously no fixed rule appeared to exist by which a tourist was able to discover what portions of the Seraglio he could see and what portions he could not see. He was merely passed on from one official to another by means of beckoning and pointing. And although this method of direction still obtains to a certain degree, signboards and notices are put up everywhere.

The guide-book, unfortunately, was only published in modern Turkish, but the Director informed me that by the end of 1936 he hoped to have an edition in French or English. At the end of the guide is an excellent map showing clearly the exact itinerary to be followed, while a list of the rooms and courtyards is attached. This list is arranged in two columns. That to the left includes all places open to the public (*Gezilen Yerler*)—forty-two in all—while in the right-hand column are those which are closed (*Gezilmiyen Yerler*)— only thirty-eight in number. Thus at first sight it would appear that the visitor is free to inspect more than half the Seraglio. A closer inspection of the list, however, will reveal the fact that this is not the case, for in the *Gezilen* list several rooms of a single suite are numbered separately, while in the *Gezilmiyen* list they are not. Then, again, there are many places on the map left entirely blank, without any numbers at all. These would swell the 'taboo' list quite considerably.

At the same time the intelligent visitor can get a good idea of the main features of the Palace, and, quite apart from the glories of the Treasury, can obtain first-hand information on the interior decoration of the Turkish, Syrian, Arabic, and Persian schools. But unless he has studied the history of the Seraglio he will go away little wiser than he came, seeing only a jumble of rather tawdry little rooms, not to be compared in size or splendour with others he has seen in palaces in nearly every other part of Europe or the Near East. It is he who will be the loser, for no more interesting or grimly romantic spot exists in the world to-day. It is in the attempt to supply such necessary information, in however small and inadequate a way, that the present work has been written.

Every author writing on Constantinople has endeavoured, some more successfully than others, to give a general impression of the Seraglio as a whole. But excellent as the descriptions may be they can never convey to the reader as much as really good modern photographs. There has always been the greatest difficulty in obtaining photographs, and in the 1933 guide-book it is very definitely stated more than once that no cameras are allowed past the entrance gate, and no photographs whatever may be taken.

Certain parts of the Palace and most of the exhibits in the Museum have been reproduced for public sale by the official photographer, but even he is allowed very little scope, and his activities are restricted by the immutable decisions of the Museum authorities. It is impossible to obtain a view of the whole Palace unless you mount the Divan Tower and climb out through the topmost windows to a perilous perch on the parapet. But the results more than compensate for the trouble involved, and the view of the *harēm* roofs is really most extraordinary, as I trust my readers will agree from an inspection of the photographs themselves (see the plates facing pp. 20 and 24).

I am fully aware that I am not the first person to publish a picture of the roofs, but all previous photographs have been taken in one direction only, and so no idea of the *harēm* in its relation to the *selāmlik* has been obtained. It is one thing to photograph the roofs, and quite another thing to identify what rooms the forest of chimneys and domes surmounts. A thorough knowledge of the Palace is necessary for this, so I make no excuse for describing the pictures in

detail. For the sake of future reference or comparison, I may
mention that I took these photographs on September 28, 1934. The
photograph reproduced opposite p. 20 gives us a view of the Palace
buildings that stretch out along the apex of Seraglio Hill towards the
Bosphorus. They include practically the whole of the *selāmlik* and
the quarters to the left of the Hall of the Divan. Low down in the
middle foreground is the roof of the canopy in the courtyard of the
black eunuchs. To the left are the windows and roof of the Princes'
School (No. 36 in the plan at the end of the book), and in the
extreme bottom left-hand corner we can see the beginning of the
roof of the black eunuchs' dormitories (No. 35 in the plan).

In the centre foreground are the apartments of the *ḥarēm* Treasurer
and Chamberlain (Nos. 38 and 39), while to the right are the cupolas
of the Inner Treasury, now the Arms Museum (No. 26). In the very
middle and a little to the left are (respectively) the low and high
cupolas of the Chief Black Eunuch's suite (No. 37). Beyond the
wall to the right is the mosque of the Palace School, now the
Library (No. 98); while stretching away in the distance to a point
where Marmora and Bosphorus meet we can just identify, among
other buildings, the Hall of the Royal Bedchamber (No. 111), the
Pavilion of the Holy Mantle (No. 110), the Hall of Circumcision
(No. 94), the suite of the Princes, known as the Cage (No. 90), and,
finally, the Revan and Baghdad Kiosks (Nos. 113 and 114).

Reference to the plan at the end of the book will greatly facilitate
the identification of the various buildings.

The photograph reproduced opposite was taken more to the west,
looking towards the Golden Horn, and shows us the whole of the
ḥarēm and that part of the *selāmlik* not included in the first picture. In
the bottom right-hand corner is a portion of the parapet from which
the photograph was taken. To its immediate left, and occupying
all the foreground, are the roofs of the black eunuchs' dormitories.
To the left is a tall octagonal tower, below to the right and left
of which can be seen the roofs of the arcade surrounding the
courtyard of the *ḥarēm* girls (No. 44). Farther to the left, continuing towards the trees, are the covered passages to the girls' hospital
and gardens (No. 56), and the suite of the Head Nurse of the *ḥarēm*
(No. 54).

THE ROOFS OF THE SERAGLIO, SHOWING THE ḤARĒM BUILDINGS

Continuing along the outer wall, we notice the suites of the Sultan Validé, mother of the reigning Sultan (Nos. 65–68), and Selim III (No. 83), with a pointed cupola. Farther still can be seen the wall kiosk of Osman III (No. 85). The three square chimney-stacks surmount fireplaces in the rooms of the Sultan Validé nearest the courtyard, while the dome to the left covers her dining-room (No. 67).

The turret to the right with the black top belongs to the Princes' School, and, finally, the large dome and the one behind it are respectively the Throne Room of the *harēm* (No. 77) and the bedroom of Murad III (No. 87).

And here I may be allowed to say, without any boastful intent, that at this moment of writing I know of no person whatever who has seen more of the Seraglio than I have myself. The point is of more interest than it may appear. The student of Oriental history or sociology may go to Istanbul armed with letters to the Director of Public Works, the Curator of the Museum, and so on, and after much palaver and patience be specially conducted over those parts of the Seraglio not shown to the general public. After hours of inspecting rooms, passages, courtyards, kitchens, etc., he will be politely told that he has seen everything. And who is he to say them nay? By this time his mind has become so bewildered by the labyrinthine nature of the place that *as far as he can judge* he *has* seen everything. It is not that the authorities have anything to hide or any wish to deceive, but there are many parts of the Seraglio that, for one reason or another, are not in a fit state to be shown to visitors. And when the authorities say they have shown you everything they mean everything that is in a fit state to be shown, or that, as far as they can judge, could be of any possible interest to you.

Each time I went to the Seraglio I discovered some part I had not seen before. Sometimes it was a connecting corridor that had been passed previously as of no interest; on other occasions it was a small room to which the key had not been found on former visits. Once I came upon a flight of steps of the existence of which I had had no idea. Then, again, my persistence led me one day to a part of the girls' hospital that my guide himself had never seen before, and in front of one doorway the cobwebs were over three feet high, and so thick that we had to get two long sticks to remove them before it was possible to enter. I merely mention all this to show how intricate and misleading the place is, and how difficult it is to attempt to make a plan of such a conglomeration of buildings of all shapes and sizes, erected in different styles at different times, and, worst of all, on different levels.

Even now I am convinced that there are still parts of the Seraglio that I have not seen: some because the condition of the floor is so bad that it is impossible to proceed with any degree of safety; some because they are so full of rubbish, packing-cases, disused candelabra, etc., that entrance is out of the question; and still others which are in constant use by the resident staff, or which for one reason or another I never properly saw. I feel, however, that (with the one exception of the Chamber of the Holy Relics) those portions of the Seraglio that I have not inspected are of little consequence, and a full knowledge of them would hardly affect the plan I have been at such pains to draw as correctly as possible.

CHAPTER II

PREVIOUS ACCOUNTS OF THE SERAGLIO

As already mentioned, the earliest accounts of the Seraglio deal almost exclusively with the Palace School, while other sixteenth-century writers, such as Cantacusino, Giovio, Junis Bey, Ramberti, Postel, Chesneau, Busbecq, Garzoni, Sanderson, and Morosini,[1] limit themselves to a description of the Ottoman manners and customs, religion and government, and refer but briefly to the Seraglio, saying how impossible it is to discover anything about it. There may, however, be a few exceptions to this general rule, but the only sixteenth-century writer who may possibly have seen quite a considerable amount of the Seraglio is the French traveller Nicolas de Nicolay (1517–83).

NICOLAS DE NICOLAY (1551)

Nicolay accompanied Gabriel d'Aramon in his embassy to Constantinople in 1551. He went for the express purpose of making drawings of costumes, and to him we owe the first important collection on the subject, published in his *Quatre premiers Livres des navigations et peregrinations orientales*.[2] He must have had certain advantages by his attachment to the embassy, and, as he tells us himself, made friends with a eunuch who helped him in his work. Although much of his information on the government of the Empire was derived from Menavino he was a keen and careful observer, as his particular hobby necessitated, and he may well have seen that part of the *selāmlik* which he so quaintly describes. I shall have occasion to return to him when discussing costumes in a later chapter.

In chapter xviii he writes as follows:

> . . . this Sarail is inclosed with strong & high walles, being in circuit about two miles, in the midst wherof upon a little hil is to be seen a

[1] For all of these writers see A. H. Lybyer, *Government of the Ottoman Empire in the Time of Suleiman the Magnificent* (Cambridge, Harvard University Press, 1913), pp. 307–322.
[2] Lyon, 1567. Some copies of the first edition are dated 1568.

faire & delectable garden, which beginning on the middest of the
mount discendeth towards the Sea: there are diuers litle houses &
dwelling places, with a gallery, standing vpon columnes after the forme
of a monasterie, round about the whiche are about 200. chambers, &
therabout the great Turk dwelleth for the most part of the sommer,
for that it is a place, both high, of a fresh aire, & abounding of good
waters: in times past these inhabitations haue bin of the dependences
of S. Sophie, but Baiazet the 2. caused them to be deuided: and in the
midst therof caused a principal house, to be builded, within the which
in the lower chambers to eschew the Northeast wind . . . he dwelleth
all the winter. A litle more below, was another smal habitation, al
made of very cleare glasse, ioyned & tyed together with roddes of Tin
in forme of a rounde Hemisphere, vnder which by wonderful artifice
passed a faire & cleare fountain, which sweetly discending by the same
Hemisphere, spreadeth ouer the whole garden. In this place Baiazet in
sommer often went to refresh himself: & pas his sleep ouer with the
sweet noice of the waters: but now the most part thereof being ruined,
the water hath taken his course towards other places. Within this com-
passe is as yet [read 'further' (?); the French merely has *encores*] the
Sarail of Sultana, wife to the great Turke, garnished with bathes most
magnificque [*sic*], & nere vnto the same a place for yong children,
which are pages, being notwithstanding estemed as slaues, are there
nourished, instructed, & exercised aswell in their religion, as to ryde
horses, to shoote, & doe all other warlyke exercises, euen from their age
of eight, niene, or ten yeeres, vnto twentie, the ordinarie number of
these children being commonly about fiue or sixe hundred.[1]

Although this corresponds closely with the earlier (1548) account
of Menavino there is a certain amount of additional information
included, which Nicolay derived doubtless from talks with his
friend the eunuch, or possibly from personal inspection of parts of
the *selāmlik*.

The portion of the Seraglio described corresponds to the area to
be occupied in later years by the Revan and Baghdad Kiosks, the
Pavilion of the Holy Mantle, and the Privy Stables—*i.e.*, Nos. 113,
114, 110, and 20. The "Sarail of Sultana" and the Palace School
may be taken as corresponding roughly to the *ḥarēm* as shown in
our plan, and adjacent portions of the Third Court and black eunuchs'
quarters.

In the seventeenth century several travellers, such as Peter Mundy,

[1] P. 51 and *verso* of the English translation of 1585 (pp. 65–66 of the 1567 edition).

got into the Second Court, but no farther; while others, such as Sandys, Grimstone, Gainsford, della Valle, Tavernier, Thévenot, Grelot, and Chardin, fared no better. Some of the Venetian *Bailos'* reports may contain valuable material, but I confess not to have studied in any detail the eighty odd volumes already published. I have but little doubt, however, that the best of them all is that of Ottaviano Bon, to whom we shall soon return. I can therefore add no new names of claimants to those already given by Dr Barnette Miller.

DOMENICO HIEROSOLIMITANO (*c.* 1580-90)

We now turn to an Italian physician, who was employed in the Palace during the reign of Murad III (1574-95). According to his own account he was one of seven physicians who attended on the Sultan, and ranked third in order of seniority. From him we get the first known account of some of the rooms of the *harēm*, particularly of the Golden Road (No. 75 in the plan). Owing to his unique advantages he was in a position to visit parts of the *harēm* to which access was only allowed to certain of the black eunuchs and the doctors. It was a long time before any further description was forthcoming, and claimants had to content themselves with the inspection of parts of the *selāmlik* and gardens.

Apart from the little that Hierosolimitano tells us of himself nothing seems to be known about him. His account is unpublished, and is to be found in the Manuscript Room of the British Museum.[1] Its abbreviated title, to which I have already referred, is *Relatione della gran città di Costantinopoli*. In addition to the description of the Seraglio some account of the general topography is given, together with notes on the chief mosques, palaces, fountains, markets, hospitals, etc.

> From the above-mentioned piazza one enters a narrow corridor which leads to another court with a garden of various flowers; here on one side are the rooms of the Grand Turk, and when the women wait upon him they pass through high corridors by means of a key to the door which he reserves for himself alone, or his Chief Eunuch.[2]

[1] Harl. MSS., 3408, ff. 83-141.
[2] This extract and the two which follow are taken from Harl. MSS., 3408, ff. 101b–103b.

After referring to the rooms set apart for the mutes and dwarfs he continues:

> On the side where the women are in attendance there are forty-four separate courts with conveniences of baths and fountains in each, so that one does not look into the other, but he [the Sultan] has access by a secret corridor by means of which each can be entered without the others being any the wiser. Communicating with the women's rooms are the suites where the Grand Turk's children—that is to say, the males—are brought up; for the women remain with their mothers, and the boys on arriving at the age of six are taken from their mothers and placed in other rooms allotted to them with the masters who teach them. The aforesaid rooms of the Grand Turk stretch from the side of the men's suites to that of the women's apartments—that is to say, the 40 [44 (?)] suites, each with its hall, chamber and conveniences of baths, fountains, gardens and aviaries, [built] with surprising cunning and ornamented with panels of painted flowers, but not figures, and hung with divers lovely brocades, with carpets on the floors and brocaded mattresses and cushions—the bedsteads all of ivory inlaid with aloes and sandal-wood and large pieces of coral, of which one was sent to Amurat from Hiemen [Hiamen, Amoy, in China (?)] which cost more than 90 thousand *scudi*.

After describing a secret treasury—of which no trace or record exists to-day—built under both the men's and the women's suites of rooms he proceeds to give an account of the *selāmlik* gardens and the kiosk which stood apparently somewhere very near the site to be occupied later by the Baghdad Kiosk.

> Leaving this place, one enters gardens full of perfumes extending to another wall a mile and a half in circumference, and then, passing this other wall, they reach the garden rooms which are situated between the wall of the aforesaid garden and the other one, which is the sea-wall. And in the middle of this garden are many well-designed rooms, but one in particular of six façades surmounting six large columns, and between the columns are slabs of rock crystal so cunningly inlaid the one with the other that as one looks on them they appear to be a single whole, and above is a cupola with a lantern covered with lead, gilded, and damascened. But the lantern has pillars of carved rock crystal, and the top is made of pieces of coral wonderfully put together one piece with another. It shines in the splendour of the sun, dazzling the sight, and owing to the altitude of the building one can see from the rooms every detail of the entire garden from side

to side. And in a third part of the same garden at the back of the women's lodgings is the treasury of the armoury, with horse trappings all set in gems, and there is another just like it behind the rooms where the pages are trained, as already mentioned.

The rest of the account of the Seraglio is taken up with a brief description of the libraries, the dispensary, the mosques, the table and food of the Sultan, the kitchens, and the stables. After this Hierosolimitano describes other parts of the city, especially the arsenal, with its *personnel*, the town mint, and various parts of Pera. The entire manuscript, however, is well worth publishing, and is comparatively easy to read.

The first Christian to describe any part of the Seraglio from personal knowledge, apart from those actually employed in the Palace, was an English organ-builder named Thomas Dallam, and to his account I now turn.

THOMAS DALLAM (1599)

In order to explain how it happened that such a man found his way into the Seraglio it will be necessary to refer very briefly to what was taking place at Constantinople at the time with regard to intercourse with foreigners. As early as the eleventh century the Venetians and Genoese had obtained trading rights (known later as 'capitulations') from the Greek Empire, and after the capture of Constantinople by the Turks followed the Byzantine custom by renewing them.[1] In 1535 they were granted to the French by Suleiman, and the English soon began to obtain similar advantages with the founding of the Levant Company. In 1580 William Harborne, who was to be first English Ambassador to the Porte, obtained such rights for England, and as a result received a commission from Elizabeth, and was sent out again as a representative of the company, which had been officially founded in 1581.

Harborne did his work well, but the expenses of the company were heavy and competition was keen. Although the financial help

[1] See Nasîm Sousa, *The Capitulatory Régime of Turkey* (John Hopkins University, 1933), and A. C. Wood, *History of the Levant Company* (Oxford, 1935), pp. 8–9.

afforded by Elizabeth left much to be desired she fully realized that the Sultan was a possible ally against Spain, and gave Harborne a pretty free hand in organizing the trade of the new company. After various setbacks a new charter was obtained in 1592, and the affairs of the company prospered. In 1588 Edward Barton had been left as agent by Harborne, and succeeded as Ambassador about 1591.

Four years later the Sultan, Murad III, died, and with the accession of Muhammad III it became necessary for the company to renew the capitulations, which meant letters of congratulation and handsome presents from the Queen of England. The former, with Burghley's assistance, were forthcoming, but the latter had to be supplied by the company. This fact was naturally kept a dead secret, and the gifts were offered as from Elizabeth, and nobody was any the wiser.[1] There was, however, a long delay, and they were not dispatched until 1599. By this time Barton had died, and it was his secretary, Henry Lello, who actually presented the gifts.

Chief among them was the elaborate organ that had been especially built by Thomas Dallam. Owing to its highly technical and complicated construction Dallam was sent out with it in order to erect it on arrival and make sure it was in perfect working order.

From this man, then, we have the first account by an outsider, meagre and not very intelligent though it may be, of the Seraglio.

After a voyage lasting nearly seven months Dallam arrived at Constantinople in the middle of August 1599, and when preliminary visits to the ship by the Sultan and his mother were over he was told to set up his instrument in the Seraglio. The job was a long one, and Dallam visited the Palace every day for a month. In view of the opportunities he must have had for a fairly comprehensive inspection of the *selāmlik* the account is disappointing, but certain portions of it are well worth reproducing:

> The 11th. Daye, beinge Tuesdaye, we Carried our instramente over the water to the Grand Sinyors Courte, Called the surralya, and thare in his moste statlyeste house I began to sett it up. . . . At everie gate of the surralia thare alwayes sitethe a stoute Turke, abute the calinge or degre of a justis of the peace, who is caled a chia [*kapici*, gatekeeper]; not withstandinge, the gates ar faste shut, for thare pasethe none in or

[1] See H. G. Rosedale, *Queen Elizabeth and the Levant Company* (London, 1904).

oute at ther owne pleasures. . . . The waye from the firste gate to the seconde wale is som thinge risinge up a hill, betwyxte wales aboute a quarter of a myle and better. The gats of the second wale was also shutt. . . . These gates ar made all of massie iron; tow men, whom they do cale jemeglans [ajem-oghlans, untrained youths, apprentice janissaries], did open them. Wythein the firste wales ar no housis but one, and that is the bustanjebasha [Bostanji-bashi, Head Gardener] his house, who is captaine of a thousande jemeglanes, which doo nothinge but kepe the garthens in good order; and I am perswaded that thare is none so well kepte in the worlde. Within the seconde wales tharis no gardens, but statly buildinges; many courtes paved with marble and suche lyke stone. Everie ode [oda, room or chamber of the pages; elsewhere it means a company of janissaries] or by corner hath som exelente frute tre or tres growing in them; allso thar is greate abund-ance of sweete grapes, and of diveres sortes. . . . Cominge into the house whear I was appoynted to sett up the presente or instramente; it semed to be rether a churche than a dwellinge house; to say the truthe, it was no dwellinge house, but a house of pleasur, and lyke wyse a house of slaughter; for in that house was bulte one little house, verrie curius bothe within and witheout; for carvinge, gildinge, good Collors and vernishe, I have not sene the lyke. In this litle house, that emperor that rained when I was thare, had nyntene brotheres put to deathe in it, and it was bulte for no other use but for the stranglinge of everie em-perors bretherin. This great house it selfe hathe in it tow rankes of marble pillors; the pettestales of them are made of brass, and double gilte. The wales on three sides of the house ar waled but halfe waye to the eaves; the other halfe is open; but yf any storme or great wynde should hapen, they can sodonly Let fale suche hanginges made of cotten wolle for that purpose as will kepe out all kinds of wethere, and sudenly they can open them againe. The fourthe side of the house, which is close and joynethe unto another house, the wale is made of purfeare [porphyry], or suche kinde of stone as when a man walketh by it he maye se him selfe tharin. . . . Thare weare in this house nether stouls, tables, or formes, only one coutche of estate. Thare is one side of it a fishe ponde, that is full of fishe that be of divers collores.[1]

And, except for an interesting account of "thirtie of the Grand Sin-yor's Concobines" whom he saw through an iron grating in a wall (to which we shall return in another part of the work), that is all Dallam has to tell us.

It seems to be almost certain that his "great house," with its two

[1] *Early Voyages and Travels in the Levant* (Hakluyt Society, London, 1893), pp. 61–63.

rows of pillars, is the large L-shaped hall which flanks two sides of the Pavilion of the Holy Mantle (No. 95 in the plan). It must be remembered that at this time neither the Baghdad Kiosk nor the Revan was built, neither was the Hall of Circumcision. The fish-pond is still there, although it was entirely rebuilt after Dallam's day. This L-shaped hall, of which I shall speak more fully later from personal inspection, is in my opinion the finest part of the whole Seraglio, and might easily be described as resembling a church. There is ample room for a large organ to be erected, and also for any number of people to listen to it; the acoustics would be excellent, and it would be difficult to imagine a better place for our organ-maker to show off his "instramente." He correctly describes one side of the house as being open to the winds of heaven. To-day a glass partition has been built, but a moment's inspection reveals its original form. The "litle house" wherein we are informed Muhammad III had his nineteen brothers strangled may be either the reception-room of the *selāmlik* (No. 92 in the plan) or else that which was immediately afterwards to be the Princes' prison—the *Kafes*, or Cage (No. 90).

Thus we see that the first description of any part of the House of Felicity by a person not permanently employed in the Palace deals only with the eastern corner of the *selāmlik*, to which Dallam was conducted from Seraglio Point, and not through the Third Court.

OTTAVIANO BON (1604–7)

The Venetian *Bailo* Ottaviano Bon can be regarded as the first definite claimant, for it must be noted that although Dallam was not actually in the service of the Seraglio he was temporarily employed there, and merely described what he chanced to notice in the course of his duty, while Hierosolimitano was very definitely in its employ.

But in the present case matters were very different. As we shall shortly see, Bon was a diplomatist of considerable experience, and was doubtless anxious to obtain as much information as possible about the Seraglio by the termination of his office in Constantinople. These *Bailos* were originally the equivalent of a consul-general, but from the sixteenth century onward they assumed the rank of a first-class diplomatic agent. They were instructed to send home reports every fortnight, and on their return after three or four years to submit a detailed account of the Court they had been visiting, together with a description of the country, its manners and customs. As can be imagined, these reports contain matter of the highest importance.[1] By some curious chance, however, Bon made no such report, as far as can be traced, but luckily for us he wrote two accounts which are preserved in the Biblioteca Marciana,[2] or Library of St Mark, at Venice. They have been edited by N. Barozzi and G. Berchet, and included in their *Le Relazioni degli stati Europei lette al senato degli ambasciatori veneziani nel secolo decimo-settimo*.[3]

The first of these accounts is on the Seraglio, and constitutes the most detailed and informative account we have. The second one is very brief, and deals with the government and administration of various parts of the Turkish Empire. Before giving a few lines on Bon's life and quoting from his account, which (with the help of my friend Miss Frances Welby) I have translated direct from the Italian, I must refer to a 'discovery' I made only when the translation was completed.

Much of the account seemed strangely familiar, and I was unable to guess why until I remembered the little work by Robert Withers published in 1650[4] as *A Description of the Grand Signor's Seraglio or Turkish Emperours Court*. A comparison of the two at once showed them to be one and the same work. Withers' translation was found in Constantinople and edited by John Greaves, the mathematician and antiquary. He was apparently quite unaware that it had already

[1] Many of them have been summarized, or published *in extenso*. See Marini Sanuto, *Diarii*, 58 vols. (Venezia, 1879–1903); Eugenio Alberi, *Relazione degli ambasciatori Veneti al senato*, 15 vols. (Firenze, 1839–63). For details see Lybyer, *Government of the Ottoman Empire in the Time of Suleiman the Magnificent*, pp. 311–313, and particularly the magnificently illustrated work of Tomaso Bertelè, *Il Palazzo degli ambasciatori di Venezia a Constantinopoli e le sue antiche memorie* (Bologna, 1932).

[2] Cl. vii, cod. 578, 923.

[3] See *Serie V: Turchia* (1866), pp. 59–115. An account of Bon's life appears in *Serie I: Spagna* (1856), pp. 217–222. See also Luigi Lollino, *Vita del cav. Ottaviano Bon, tradotta da G. Marchiori, publ. da Aless. Soranzo* (Venezia, 1854). The account of the Seraglio was also published separately as *Il serraglio del gran signore descritto a Constantinopoli nel 1608, con notizie sul Bon di Gugl. Berchet* (Venezia, 1865).

[4] The British Museum also catalogue a second edition of 1652, but the book has unfortunately been lost or mislaid.

been published by Purchas,[1] and, of course, had never heard of Bon. As nobody else seems to have realized the connexion between Bon and Withers I may perhaps be permitted to discuss the matter further. Little appears to be known of Robert Withers, and I can find no mention of him in any biography. In fact, the only information about his stay in Constantinople that I can trace occurs in Purchas' introduction:

> These [accounts] hath Master Robert Withers collected: after his ten yeeres observation at Constantinople, where he was educated by the care and cost of that late Honourable Embassadour from His Majestie, Sir Paul Pindar, and well instructed by Turkish Schoolemasters in the Language, and admitted also to further sight of the unholy Holies than is usuall.[2]

Now Paul Pindar was Ambassador from 1611 to 1620, having previously been secretary to Henry Lello, Ambassador from 1597 to 1607. When he left for London in 1620 Robert Withers went with him. This we know from the *Travels of Peter Mundy*.[3] Thus, if Purchas is correct in his information, Withers arrived in Constantinople in 1610, and Pindar became his patron and protector, just as he did to Mundy himself. Pindar, previous to his residence in Constantinople, had spent fifteen years in Venice, and was naturally well acquainted with all the *Bailos'* missions to Constantinople. He is most likely, therefore, to have seen Bon's report and to have shown it to Withers. The English translation was made, quite likely by both men, and remained unpublished at Constantinople. John Greaves arrived in 1638, discovered the manuscript, "the name of the Author being then unknown," and, after finding it out later to be the work of Withers, published it in 1650, believing that to be its first appearance. The *Dictionary of National Biography* confuses matters still more by giving the impression that it was an original work by Greaves:

> In the same year [1650] was published his 'Description of the Grand Seignor's Seraglio,' reprinted, along with the 'Pyramidographia' and several other works, in 1737.

Not a word about Withers, let alone Bon!

---

[1] *Pilgrims* (London, 1625), vol. ii, lib. ix, pp. 1580–1611.
[2] In the Hakluyt Society's—*i.e.*, the MacLehose—reprint it is vol. ix, p. 321.
[3] R. C. Temple (Hakluyt Society, 1907), vol. i, p. 42.

That Withers *did* translate from Bon is obvious to anyone comparing the two versions. Withers gives his distances in Italian milage; in places difficult words are ignored—*e.g.*, *búlgaro*, Russia leather—where observations are in parentheses they are seldom in Bon, but additions by Withers, often trivial and in strange contrast with the rest of the text. Finally, when Bon speaks of how he got into the Seraglio through his personal acquaintance with the Chief Gardener Withers omits the whole passage, which looks rather as if he was 'borrowing' the account, merely adding his own trifling remarks! Be that as it may, this account of the Seraglio was neither by Greaves nor by Withers, but by Ottaviano Bon, written between the years 1604 and 1607, and to him alone is the credit of this fine description due.

Yet Withers was not the only one to make use of Bon without acknowledgment, for in 1624 Michel Baudier, historian to Louis XIII, published his *Histoire generalle du serrail et de la cour du grand seigneur*, which ran into many editions in France, and was translated into English by Edward Grimstone in 1635. Although, as a compiler, Baudier used other material his debt to Bon was very great, as a comparison between the two will at once testify.

Born at Venice in 1551, and graduating in philosophy and law at Padua University, Bon became successively Inquisitor at Candia, *Podestà* at Friuli and Treviso, and Ambassador Extraordinary to the Court of Philip III of Spain at Valladolid in 1601. He returned the following year, and in 1604 was sent in the same capacity to Ahmed I. He remained in Constantinople as *Bailo* for three years to the credit of his country. On his return to Venice he became a member of the *Pregadi* (Senate), where he greatly distinguished himself. In 1616 he was sent to Paris to obtain the French King's mediation in the quarrel between Savoy and Venice on the one hand and Austria and Spain on the other. Complications finally led to his recall, but complete vindication followed, and though now old and infirm he was appointed *Podestà* of Padua. He died in 1622.

The value of Bon's account of the Seraglio lies rather in the detail of the description as a whole than in that of any particular room he chanced to see in the *selāmlik*.

The *ḥarēm* proper he never entered, and when speaking of it he merely says:

> ... there is the women's apartment inhabited by the Queen Sultana, the Sultan, and all the other women and slaves of the Grand Signore; and this apartment is like a huge nunnery in which are all the conveniences of dormitories, refectories, baths, sitting-rooms, and every other kind of building that living demands.[1]

After giving some account of the various buildings in the Second Court and of the Throne Room at the entrance to the Third Court he commences to tell us how he managed to obtain a sight of some of the Sultan's rooms in the *selāmlik*:

> On one occasion, finding the King absent on the chase, owing to my friendship with Chiaià, who is the steward of the *Bustangibassi*—that is to say, chief of the King's gardeners—I had the privilege of entering the Seraglio, under his escort, by the sea gate of the Sea-horses, and was taken by him to see the various rooms reserved for the King, several baths, and many other things as delightful as they were curious, both in the richness of the gold-work and in the abundance of fountains. In particular I saw a suite of rooms, in the summer wing, on a hillock, complete with dining-room and other chambers in so lovely a site that it might well be the place and dwelling of so great a king. It was the Divan [not to be confused with the Hall of the Divan in the Second Court. 'Divan' is used in many senses; that employed by Bon is perfectly correct]—that is to say, the hall open towards the east, resting on most beautiful columns looking on to a small lake, square in form, artificially made from thirty different fountains [by the water's being] led off and visible in an aqueduct of the finest marble which surrounded this lake, so that the fountains discharged the water from that aqueduct into the lake. Its water was then drained off gradually to some gardens, thus making the place most delightful. Two men can walk along the aqueduct abreast, and follow it round to enjoy the fountains, which emit a continuous and gentle murmur. On the lake was a tiny little boat into which I was told his Majesty was wont to enter with buffoons to sail for recreation and to divert himself with them on the water, and very often, walking with them on the aqueduct, he would push them in and make them turn somersaults in the lake. Through a window in the Divan I also saw his Majesty's bedroom, which was of ordinary size, the walls, as usual, encrusted with stones—namely, the finest majolica, which displayed patterns and

[1] Barozzi and Berchet, p. 60.

flowers of different colours, producing a splendid effect. Over the door were curtains, as usual, but of cloth of gold from Brusa with a frieze of crimson velvet embroidered in gold and enriched with many pearls.

The bed was like a Roman pavilion, with columns of fluted silver, instead of wooden supports [*pomoli*]. It had crystal lions, and the hangings were of cloth of gold and green Brusa brocade without trimmings, in place of which were lacings made of pearls, showing it to be a work of great value and very well contrived. The quilts were rather more than a hand's breadth from the ground and of gold brocade, as were also the cushions. The floors, both of this room and the others, with their sofas (which are places used for sitting down) about half a cubit from the ground, were all covered with the richest Persian carpets in silk and gold, and the quilts for sitting on and the cushions to lean against were all of the finest brocades in gold and silk.

In the centre of the Divan hung a very large lantern, round in shape, with its drops of silver inlaid with gold, encrusted with turquoises and rubies, the intermediate parts being of the finest crystals, producing a splendid effect. For washing the hands was a minute basin, its ewer being entirely of massive gold set with very lovely turquoises and rubies—a fine sight to behold. Behind the said Divan was an archery ground, where I saw fine bows and arrows, and I was shown marks of former feats of the King's strong arm with the arrow so great that they were scarcely to be credited.

And so ends Bon's visit to the *selāmlik*. This is the last description of the square lake and terrace before the Revan and Baghdad Kiosks were built (1635 and 1639 respectively) and the whole area was remodelled. As I have already mentioned, Bon's account of the Seraglio is valuable as a whole, and consequently I shall have occasion to make several further extracts as the work proceeds.

EDMUND CHISHULL (1701)

The next account of the Seraglio was included in a book of travels by Edmund Chishull.[1] It was published posthumously by his friend

---

[1] *Travels in Turkey and back to England,* by the late Reverend and Learned Edmund Chishull, B.D., Chaplain to the Factory of the Worshipful Turkey Company at Smyrna (London, 1747). For his biography see A. Chalmers, *General Biographical Dictionary,* and the *Dictionary of National Biography.* His numerous manuscripts were purchased by the British Museum, who possess a copy of his *Antiquitates asiaticæ* (1728) full of his manuscript notes.

Dr Mead in 1747. Chishull was born at Eyworth, Bedfordshire, in 1670–71, and went to Corpus Christi College, Oxford, in 1687, where, having received "a grant of the traveller's place," he was appointed to the factory of the Turkey Company at Smyrna. A sermon he had preached to the Levant Company is said to have done much to secure him the post of chaplain.

He left England in February 1698, and arrived at Smyrna in November. After a tour to Ephesus in 1699 he visited Constantinople in 1701, and returned home the same year. His account, then, dates from this time, nearly a hundred years later than that of Bon. It is quite short, and Chishull is not very clear about his itinerary.

It would appear that he made his way through the First and Second Courts, but did not continue past the Gate of Felicity into the Third Court, as we next find him outside in the Palace gardens. It seems clear, then, that he made his exit by some side-door in the Second Court, unless he retraced his steps and made a complete circuit of the grounds outside the main wall. However this may have been, he arrived in due course at the Goths' Column and made his entrance afresh, now closely following in the footsteps of Dallam.

He succeeded in actually seeing the door of the *ḥarēm*, which he probably reached *via* the Golden Road.

In his *Travels in Turkey* Chishull writes as follows:

> By the interest of a Greek, who serves the bostangí bashá as his surgeon, I was admitted in company of Mr. John Philips, an eminent merchant, into the great *Seraglio* of *Constantinople*, where we passed thro two courts, that form the entry of the palace; the first of which has a small arsenal, furnished with arms and ammunition; the second has piazzas on two sides, in which the *janisaries* are wont to eat, and opens at the upper end into the *diván*.
>
> From these two courts we were permitted to walk round the full extent of the garden, on each side of the palace. . . . The whole plot of ground, which they call the gardens of the *Seraglio* is covered with cypress and other trees, thro which are cut shady walks, where *kiosks* are seen of various sorts. . . . Passing thro the extent of the *Seraglio* towards the extreme point, that looks up the Thracian Bosphorus, you observe a Corinthian pillar consisting of white marble . . . near this pillar we were admitted thro a gate, which opens into a green court, and that again into a garden kept in somewhat a regular order. From hence we ascend by a few steps into an apartment of the Grand Signior,

where are two rich *kiosks*, a fish pond, a paved walk, and an open gallery. Here we were shewn the lodgings, where the unhappy princes of the empire are detained prisoners, as also the dark chambers of the *ichoglans*, and the door that leads into the *harēm*. . . .

The above mentioned gallery is rich and splendid, adorned with various gilding of flower work, and supported with beautiful serpentine pillars. In the sides of one of the kiosks are three orbicular stones of fine porphyry, the middlermost of which is curiously polished, and thereby serves to reflect the prospect of the *Seraglio* and adjoining city, in the nature of a looking glass. . . .[1]

The itinerary is easy to follow, as a glance at the plan will at once reveal. The only point of interest is the "open gallery," which I do *not* agree with Dr Miller in taking to be the same as the terrace between the Kiosk of Baghdad (No. 114) and the Hall of Circumcision. Her own plan is so wrongly drawn at this point, with regard to the number and the size and the shape of the buildings and the general proportions of the courts to the buildings, that it is hard to believe that she could have inspected them personally. It seems quite clear that after leaving the "paved walk" near the Baghdad Kiosk Chishull was conducted along the "open gallery" (No. 95)—which is a perfectly good description of the pillared hall open on the western side—into the courtyard of the *Kafes*, or Princes' prison (No. 91). The "dark chambers" are hard to recognize, but as parts of the Royal Road (No. 75) *are* dark, and small rooms *do* lead off, and the road *does* connect directly with the *harēm* door, I think we can conclude that this was the route he followed. We are not told how he got back, but most likely he retraced his steps (as he had not been allowed in the Third Court) and returned through the gardens to Seraglio Point. I can say nothing about the "three orbicular stones," and conclude that they have followed the course of so many things in the Seraglio. But we are still outside the *harēm*. It was destined for a Frenchman to take us inside.

AUBRY DE LA MOTRAYE (1699–1714)

This French traveller and writer, born about 1674, was for many years a religious refugee in England. His travels in Europe were

[1] Pp. 4–6.

extensive, including visits to Sweden, Lapland, Prussia, France, Spain, Italy, Greece, Russia, Circassia, and Turkey. He arrived in Smyrna at the beginning of 1699, and moved to Constantinople in June of the same year. He made it his headquarters until he left for Sweden in 1714. The chief account of his travels was published in London in two volumes, under the title *Travels through Europe, Asia, & into Part of Africa.*[1] A third volume was added nine years later. His biographers[2] describe him as a "voyageur véridique, mais observateur superficiel," which would seem to be a fair criticism. At the same time, he was the first outsider to inspect the interior of several rooms of the *ḥarēm,* although it must be confessed that such rooms as he describes no longer exist to-day. It was only by a series of lucky chances that he was able to see as much as he did. It seems that the regulating of the numerous *ḥarēm* clocks was in the hands of Swiss and French clock-makers who had settled in Galata and Pera. Motraye became acquainted with some of them, and, on learning that an order had been received to mend some pendulums in the Seraglio, prevailed on the clock-maker in question to take him as his assistant.

"I dress'd my self after the *Turkish* manner," says Motraye, "as he did likewise, and (which happen'd very fortunately to gratify my Curiosity the more) the *Grand Seignior* was then at *Adrianople* with all his Court."[3] He entered in the ordinary way through the First and Second Courts. Having reached the Third Court, he apparently turned left in the direction of the first room of the *ḥarēm* leading into the Golden Road. The rooms he describes must have been either adjacent to the courtyard of the *ḥarēm* slaves (No. 44) or else farther west, where the so-called *ḥarēm* hospital now lies (No. 56). Motraye was himself the first to realize how muddled his account was, so that even if the rooms still existed it would be hard to follow his itinerary:

> I found my Head so full of the *Sopha's,* rich Cieling, and in one word, of the great Confusion of fine things so irregularly disposed, that

[1] 1723.
[2] See L. Michaud, *Biographie universelle,* xxix, pp. 434–435, and J. C. F. Hoefer, *Nouvelle Biographie générale,* xxix, p. 275. The name is sometimes spelled 'Mottraye.'
[3] Vol. i, p. 170.

'twou'd be very hard for me to give a clear Idea of them, and I did not stay long enough to make an exact description.

They were handed over to the care of a black eunuch, who apparently volunteered no information whatever.

The Eunuch conducted us into the Hall of the *Harem*, which seem'd to me the finest and most agreeable of any in the *Seraglio*, where an *English* Clock, with a magnificent Case and Stand, wanted his Assistance to rectify it. This room was incrusted over with fine China; and the Cieling, which adorn'd the Inside of a *Cupola*, as well as the rest of the Roof, was the richest that could be with Gold and Azure; in the middle of the Hall, directly under the *Cupola*, was an Artificial fountain, the Bason of which was of a precious Green Marble, which seem'd to me either Serpentine, or Jasper; it did not play then on account of the Womens being absent. . . . There were several large Windows in this Hall, which besides Glass, have Lattices before them: They had also little *Sofa's*, which had some Pieces of painted Callico flung over them to preserve them from Dust, &c. Upon these *Sofa's* the Ladies sit to breathe the fresh Air, and recreate their Eyes thro' the Lattice. After the Clock in the Hall was put in order, the Eunuch made us pass by several little Chambers with Doors shut, like the Cells of Monks or Nuns, as far as I cou'd judge by one that another Eunuch open'd, which was the only one I saw, and by the Outside of the others . . . this chamber was more richly adorn'd with Paintings and Gilding, than the Hall itself; the bottom of the Windows were above the Reach of the tallest Man, with Glass painted of divers Colours, almost like those in some Christian Churches, excepting that there were no Figures of any living Creature.

Then La Motraye adds, as an explanatory parenthesis:

N.B. In comparing the Chambers of the *Grand Seignior's* Women to the Cells of Nuns, we must except the Richness of the Furniture, as well as the Use they are put to; the Difference of which is easy enough to be imagin'd without Explication.

They were then conducted to "a Room that looked upon the Garden," of which no description is given. After crossing "several fine Halls and Chambers, treading under Foot the rich *Persian* Carpets that were spread upon the Ground almost every where," they made their exit through the *selāmlik*, down past the Goths' Column, to Seraglio Point.

JEAN-CLAUDE FLACHAT (1740–55)

We now come to a French manufacturer named Jean-Claude Flachat, who holds the distinction of being the first foreigner to see the whole of the Seraglio, including the *ḥarēm*. As details of his interesting experiences seem to be very little known I shall make no apology for dealing with him rather fully. All biographies are silent about the date and place of his birth, but we can fairly safely put them at about 1720 and at Saint-Chamond, lying in a picturesque valley at the juncture of the Gier and Janon, some twenty-eight miles south-west of Lyons. At any rate, his brother lived in this town, Jean-Claude died there, and a Flachat was *curé* of Notre-Dame there in 1789. As a young man Jean-Claude conceived the idea of making an extended tour of the whole of the Levant and the Indies with the object of trading and learning all he could of the manufacturing methods he might find, and to offer the results to his country. The scheme appeared too ambitious to the French Ambassador, who refused the necessary passport, allowing him only to travel to Constantinople and to make it his permanent headquarters. Consequently Flachat set out, and, passing through Holland, Italy, Germany, Hungary, Wallachia, and Turkey, arrived at his destination in 1740. Here he settled for no less than fifteen years, during the reigns of Mahmud I and Osman III, and by diligent and unremitting labour not only traded on a considerable scale in manufactured goods of all kinds, but taught the Turks how to make and use looms, dye cotton, plate copper, do tin-plating and other similar industrial trades. His friendship with the Chief Black Eunuch, the *Kislar Agha* Haji Bektash, was the main cause of his success. So interested did this Abyssinian become in Flachat's novelties that Flachat was created " Baserguian bachi," or First Merchant of the Grand Signor. He sold all manner of things to the Seraglio, mechanical devices being in special demand. In fact, the bribe that led Haji Bektash to conduct him over the Seraglio consisted of an automaton of a man playing a drum, and others of a French girl and an Oriental slave, together with some diagrams of other machines, of which we are not given the details. Highly important as Haji Bektash was, it was more than his head was worth to show Flachat the Seraglio openly, even

44

though the Sultan was absent. "The gods of mythology," says Flachat, "manifest themselves to humans with less formality; the entrance to Tartarus is not more forbidden." But, as luck would have it, some mirrors sent by Louis XV to Mahmud I were being installed, and Flachat, with the Comte de Castellane, the French Ambassador at the Porte, was introduced among the workmen, and so any suspicions of the other eunuchs were unaroused. In this way practically the whole of the Seraglio was inspected, and Flachat was a keen observer who would have illustrated his account with diagrams had leave been granted. Soon after the death of his benefactor Flachat departed for Smyrna (in 1755), where he devoted much of his time to the study of madder, from the root of which the colouring matter for dyeing Turkey-red was obtained. The methods employed here by the Greeks in dyeing and kindred industries seemed to Flachat so important that on his return home the following year he took with him a number of the workmen. His efforts were rewarded by the King, who, by a decree of the Council of December 21, 1756, granted a title of "manufacture Royale" to his brother's works at Saint-Chamond, expressly stating that Flachat's Greek workmen should be installed there to carry on their work, that workshops would be open to the public to study their methods, and that pupils would be taken.

Ten years later appeared Flachat's story of his fifteen years in Constantinople, entitled *Observations sur le commerce et sur les arts d'une partie de l'Europe, de l'Asie, de l'Afrique, et même des Indes orientales*.[1] The title gives but little idea of the contents, and perhaps for this very reason the work appears to have escaped notice. It is, moreover, of considerable rarity, and no copy exists in the British Museum, the London Library, or any of the leading libraries where we might expect to find it. Unfortunately the book is small in size, and the diagrams of machines, etc., are much too crowded together and minute to be of much practical value. Of the later life of Flachat we know nothing, but imagine that it was entirely taken up with his experiments in his brother's manufactory at Saint-Chamond, where he died in 1775.

But to return to his description of the *ḥarēm*, Flachat made a most

[1] Two vols. (Lyon, 1766).

thorough inspection of the whole Seraglio, and, although it is difficult
to trace some of the buildings he describes, there is much that I have
been able to check, and in all such cases he is entirely reliable. His
visit was very different from those of men like Chishull, being carried
out in a leisurely and determined fashion. Flachat had intended
making plans and sketches of all he saw, but this was too much even·
for his friend the *Kislar Agha*, and so, taking a hint not to abuse the
favours already extended, he put his pencil back into his pocket, and
trusted to his sight and memory for his subsequent descriptions. He
not only deals with the Seraglio court by court, but describes all the
kiosks of the Outer Palace in considerable detail, as well as the Summer
Palace and the outer walls and gates. In fact, he apologizes for his
lengthy discourse, and after telling us of his visits to the underground
chambers and reservoirs leaves us without any account of them. In
the course of the work I shall have occasion to refer to him from time
to time. I shall here confine myself to giving his description of the
quarters of the black eunuchs and some of the rooms of the *ḥarēm*.
Having described the Palace School and gardens, and kiosks in the
Fourth Court, he continues:

You will notice that up to the present I have only spoken of the ex-
teriors of the main buildings, of which it is quite easy to obtain a
description. It is not so of the rooms of which I am now about to
speak.
The room of the *Cas-Odales* [pages of the *Has Oda*, or Royal Cham-
ber] forms the first section of the ground-floor apartments which lie
to the west. It is very large and paved in marble. The only ornament
to this room is a large basin with a jet of water, around which there
burn all night wax candles seven or eight inches in diameter in large
copper candlesticks. The *Cas-Odales* are on guard there night and day.
I shall not repeat again that all the roofs are covered with lead, with a
lantern that gives light in the large dome of each room, and that most
of these domes are gilded. One passes from there into two vaulted
rooms which the black eunuchs inhabit. An inner court separates
them, and each room has stoves at the side for warming in winter. A
long gallery covered by five domes, which stretches to the south, leads
to a large vestibule; it serves as an anteroom to the first apartment of
the Grand Seigneur. One can also reach it by a higher gallery which
joins up with that of the *Kislar Aga*. It is there that they introduce the
chief officers of the Porte who have pressing matters to discuss with

his Highness. A large number of black eunuchs live all round in little rooms.

This apartment has two doors, one to the north (that of the Sultan), and the other to the south (that of the *Kislar Aga*). The door to the north leads to a corridor where the rooms of the *Karem* are situated [Flachat always writes *Karem*, apparently to imply the guttural 'h' in *ḥarēm*]. They are of average size, all built in stone, and look on to a garden shut in by a very high wall. They are light and well furnished. Their furniture consists of tapestries, carpets, *portières*, curtains, mirrors, clocks, caskets which are put in the corner of the sofa that goes all round and on which they remain night and day. I shall give later on a more detailed account of the materials with which this furniture is made.

One passes from this first garden into a second. The two-storied kiosk, which is in the centre, is a lovely place. The Sultan very often goes there with the Sultanas. The main inside court of the Serrail is at the end of this garden. It consists of four blocks of buildings. The Sultan occupies that to the west, and the walls are all adorned with porcelain on the outside. The Sultanas occupy the rest, which are all uniformly built on fine arcades. This court closely resembles the royal square in Paris; it is longer than it is broad. The rooms are warmed by stoves fitted on the ground floor: and owing to this the women do not feel the severe weather when they come out into the court. One reaches the Grand Seigneur's room by a superb staircase. The vestibule is square, the anteroom larger; the room stretches as far as the angle of the court and ends on this side of the Serrail buildings. It is there one can get some idea of the wealth of the Sultans. All is of unparalleled magnificence. The window openings and ceilings are inlaid with flowered porcelain of remarkable finish. Foliage carved in gold covers the stucco which joins the slabs of porcelain. The walls are covered with tapestry of cloth of gold. The sofa is of a material just as rich. The mirrors, clocks, caskets, are all remarkable, and what is extraordinary is that nearly all the *chefs d'œuvre* are the productions of foreign artists who have been employed to decorate the chamber.

One next passes into the gallery where are situated the apartments of twelve Sultanas. They are large and richly furnished. The windows have iron grilles, and look into the courtyard. They have on the garden side *sacnissis*, or little jutting-out gazebos, where they go to sit and see the country and all that happens in the gardens without being seen. In the middle of the northern façade they have built a fore-part, which serves as an assembly room, as you might call it. All the women go there to pay their addresses to his Highness, and try and please him

with a thousand amusements which follow on one after the other, and
to which the inexhaustible fertility of the genius of these women always
imparts the air of novelty. From there one goes to the large bath. It
consists of three rooms, all of which are paved with marble. The
middle one is the most ornamental; its dome is supported by marble
pillars and cut glass is let in to give it light. The rooms communicate
one with the other by glass doors so that all that goes on can be seen.
Each basin has two taps, one supplying hot and the other cold water.
The basins are neither of the same shape nor used for the same purposes.
They have an eye for utility and beauty alike. The women of lesser
rank and the black eunuchs have baths apart, very neat and comfort-
able. On leaving the grand *Karem* one goes down a corridor quite
dark. It crosses the detached building which the eunuchs inhabit and
leads directly to the prison of the Princes, the Sultan's sons, who can
aspire to the throne. This prison is like a strong citadel. A high wall
is built all round it. Osman caused it to be lowered and to have the
windows opened.[1] It is entered by two doors carefully guarded by
Eunuchs both within and without, each having a double iron railing.
The place has a dismal appearance. There is a pretty enough garden,
well watered. The Princes have fine apartments and baths in the
detached buildings which surround the court. The Eunuchs detailed
to their service all live on the ground floor, and there is a large number
of them. They spare no pains to mitigate their hard lot, and to make
their prison at least endurable. For some long time the severity with
which they were treated has been lessened. Women are given them,
although it is a fact that they can no longer bear children, or else great
care is taken to obviate their becoming pregnant. They have all kinds
of masters, and they even encourage them to perfect themselves in all
handiworks that are applicable to their rank. In a word, they leave
nothing to wish for save freedom. They are, however, not limited to
the apartments of the Grand Serrail alone; the Sultan often conducts
them to other Imperial houses, and especially to Besictache [*i.e.*,
Beshiktash, the first station on the left bank of the Bosphorus, just
past the Palace of Dolma Baghtche], where they are shut up in the
same way. These trips, always agreeable, make a welcome change for
them.[2]

Although changes have taken place, and several of the *ḥarēm* rooms
have since disappeared, it is fairly easy to trace the itinerary from the
quarters of the black eunuchs (Nos. 34 and 35 in the plan) into the
ḥarēm, along the Golden Road (No. 75), and so to the courtyard of

---

[1] See also Flachat, vol. ii, p. 64.   [2] Vol. ii, pp. 195–202.

the Princes' prison (No. 91), which is here described for the first time.

And with Flachat our small list of surreptitious visitors to the *ḥarēm* comes to an end.

There now remains but to speak of those who were *openly* permitted beyond the Gate of Felicity. Their number, however, is very small, for, as I have already mentioned, the slight relaxing of rules about admittance to the Seraglio, which occasionally occurred after the Palace had ceased to be a Royal residence, did not extend beyond the Third Court.

SIR ADOLPHUS SLADE (1829)

The first of these is Vice-Admiral Sir Adolphus Slade (1804–77), who reached Constantinople at the end of May 1829, and was included in a tour of the Seraglio made in honour of a visit to Mahmud II by the Admiral of the Mediterranean Fleet, Sir Pulteney Malcolm, in the following September.

Slade's subsequent history was most interesting, for after being employed on several missions to Greece, Constantinople, and the Crimea he was lent to the Porte in 1849, for service with the Turkish fleet. In the next seventeen years he became administrative head of the Turkish Navy, and was known by the name of Muchaver Pasha. His account of the Seraglio[1] is of no great interest to us, but shows just what important visitors (the Sultan thought Malcolm ranked third man in the British Empire, corresponding to his own Captain Pasha) were allowed to see at this period. They entered the Fourth Court by the *Üçüncü Kapi*, or Third Gate (No. 123 in our plan), and went through the courts in inverse order, visiting the Library (No. 97), the *Arzodasi*, or Throne Room (No. 96), the Divan (No. 23), and the kitchens (Nos. 6–17), which were in full activity:

> ... not less than a hundred dinners were preparing, each at a yawning cavern of flames and smoke that might have graced Vulcan's workshop, and hosts of lackeys were going or returning with full or empty dishes.

---

[1] *Records of Travels in Turkey, Greece, etc. . . . in the years 1829, 1830, and 1831*, 2 vols. (London, 1833). See vol. i, pp. 459–470. In the "New Edition" of 1854, in one volume, the corresponding pages are 241–247.

They were then conducted through the gardens, where they met two mutes who surprised them by their good looks and perfect understanding of all that went on.

As far as can be gathered, no inspection of the inner rooms of the *ḥarēm* was allowed, and the itinerary followed was merely that arranged for any such semi-official visit.

MAXIME DU CAMP (1844–45)

The next visitor to the Seraglio was Maxime Du Camp (1822–94), the French *littérateur* and artist, and intimate friend of Gustave Flaubert. He made many trips to various parts of Europe and the Near East, and served with Garibaldi in 1860. His description of the Seraglio dates from his first trip to the Orient (1844–45), and appears in his *Souvenirs et paysages d'Orient*.[1] Having obtained the necessary *firman*, the party entered by the Cannon Gate and, winding round past the Chinili Kiosk, reached the First Court, presumably near the *Ortakapi*, as one does to-day. They inspected the usual show rooms, including the Library, Throne Room, kitchens, and courts. The account is rather journalistic and not worth quoting, except possibly the description of the Chief White Eunuch, which is as follows:

> Il est vêtu d'un splendide costume, et un turban blanc brodé de palmes vertes s'enroule autour de son front. Ses traits fatigués annoncent au moins soixante ans; il est si gros qu'il semble n'avoir forme humaine que parce que sa graisse débordante est contenue dans ses vêtements. Ses joues jaunes et tombantes se plissent de mille rides entrecroisées. Il n'a point de barbe; un duvet d'enfant ombrage ses lèvres épaisses. Son œil doux regarde lentement et paraît s'entr'ouvrir avec peine. Sa main, qui tient les flexibles tuyaux d'un narguileh de cristal, brille à chaque doigt de bagues précieuses. Derrière lui, un jeune nègre fait bouillir le café sur un réchaud portatif; il l'appelle, et sa voix est grêle, criarde et faible comme celle d'une femme.

VISITORS IN THE TWENTIETH CENTURY

During the rest of the nineteenth century few visits are recorded, but any there were consisted merely of a formal inspection of the

[1] Paris, 1848, pp. 197–211.

regular show rooms as detailed above. In fact, there is nothing to report until in 1910 Professor Cornelius Gurlitt was accorded the unprecedented privilege of making a plan of the Second, Third, and Fourth Courts, which was subsequently used by Baedeker[1] and in other guide-books. But he was not allowed to see the *ḥarēm*, and consequently all that portion is left blank in his plan.

It was published in his *Die Baukunst Konstantinopels*, which is such a wonderfully produced work as to call for some description, especially as there is no copy in the British Museum or the London Library,[2] and also as it contains photographs with text of parts of the Seraglio.

It was published in Berlin,[3] and consists of two large portfolios of photographs of all the chief mosques, palaces, antiquities, schools, street scenes, etc., of Constantinople. A text of 112 pages, divided up into thirty-nine sections, with 224 plans and illustrations, was included by way of explanation. The Seraglio is dealt with at pp. 44–47 and 93–96, with fourteen plans and illustrations in all. As regards the plates, Gurlitt published no interiors of any rooms of the Seraglio, having to content himself with plans of the Baghdad Kiosk and the *Arzodasi*. Several photographs of the Chinili Kiosk are, however, included. The numbers of the plates are 12 *a*, *b*, *c*, and *d*.

The plan of the Seraglio is Plate 12 *e*, and until recent years remained the only reliable one in existence. To-day it is valueless, and merely shows that the rooms of the *selāmlik* and the *ḥarēm* were as impossible of access in 1910 as ever they were. Apart from including the usual show places (Divan, Gate of Felicity, Throne Room, Library, and Kiosks of Abd ul-Mejid and Baghdad) it is in reality only a plan of the courts. But the fact that such a plan was allowed to be made at all can be regarded as a surprising concession.

To bring the story up to date we must turn to Dr Miller's *Beyond the Sublime Porte*,[4] where we are told that after the dispersal of the *ḥarēm* by the Young Turks the first person—and, so far as is known, the first Turk ever—to enter the Seraglio was Abd ur-Rahman Shirif Efendi, the historian who subsequently published a series of eight

---

[1] *Konstantinopel* (1914), p. 156.
[2] Copies can be seen, however, at the libraries of the Victoria and Albert Museum and the Royal Institute of British Architects.
[3] 1907–12.   [4] P. 16.

articles (in Turkish) in the *Tarikhi Osmani Enjumeni Mejmu'asi*, or *Turkish Historical Review*.[1] A plan was included in one of the articles, but once again the *ḥarēm* was left blank.

The first foreigner to visit the Seraglio under the new *régime* was (says Dr Miller) the Marchioness Pallavicini, wife of the Austrian Ambassador to Constantinople, who made a 'grand tour' in 1912. Shortly afterwards Mr W. W. Rockhill, the American Ambassador, was admitted, and the party included Dr Miller, who visited it again in 1916–19, when she collected material for her excellent work *Beyond the Sublime Porte*,[2] which included the most detailed plan ever made at that date. The information she collected and the highly important notes and bibliography have been my guide and chief source of information throughout the present work. In 1933 Dr Miller contributed a most interesting article on "The Curriculum of the Palace School of the Turkish Sultans" to the *Macdonald Presentation Volume*.[3]

And so we complete our survey of people who have visited the Seraglio and the accounts they have left us.

It will be agreed, I think, that prior to the present century no full account of the Seraglio existed at all—for the very best reason in the world: nobody knew anything about it. It is impossible to say how long the Palace will stand or what new restrictions political changes may enforce. Thus I inspected it in detail while I could do so, and offer the results, such as they are, to my readers.

[1] Nos. v–xii.
[2] New Haven, Yale University Press. The book was not published until 1931.
[3] Princeton University Press, New Jersey.

CHAPTER III

THE HISTORY OF SERAGLIO HILL,
ITS WALLS AND KIOSKS

1. EARLY HISTORY

BEFORE we discuss the Seraglio Hill in detail as it was when the Turks had crowned its summit with a palace for their Sultans it will be interesting to consider briefly the part played in earlier days by this incomparable promontory. We should do this not only because of the enormous changes that have occurred here, and the almost unique historical importance that attaches itself to this acropolis, but because of the puzzles and obstacles that to-day confront the student or intelligent tourist who critically inspects its slopes and littoral. He will constantly be stumbling against half-hidden ruins, broken marble columns, crumbling arches, bases of ancient walls, filled-in cisterns, disused wells, and so forth. Constantly he will be asking himself what it is he has chanced upon—Greek, Roman, Christian, or Turkish—and what part it has played in the history of the acropolis. It might well be any: in fact, a single wall or tower may contain materials of all four.

The whole district, therefore, can perhaps best be described as an architectural palimpsest. Each conquering people has left its mark here from the earliest times, erecting walls, altering names, pulling down palaces, utilizing the same material to build new ones, or maybe only a new gate—each improving according to its own views, but continually piling up difficulties for the archæologist or historian who tries to read the story of the stones aright and arrange things in their proper chronological order.

It is extremely difficult to identify every ruin we come across. Before the railway, like a poisonous serpent, had thrust its devastating head round Seraglio Point, crushing, maiming, and devouring as it went, it might have been possible for archæologists, employing the modern horizontal method of digging, to make a really detailed survey of the entire promontory and to enumerate all the Byzantine churches and other important buildings that once stood here. But that is out of the question now, and we must be content with the little that recent research has been able to add to the discoveries of such scholars as Du Cange, Paspates, Mordtmann, von Hammer, van Millingen, Gurlitt, and the rest.

From the dawn of history the unsurpassed beauty of Seraglio Point has been proverbial, as the well-known story of the first colonists shows; for when in the seventh century B.C. the Dorians of Megara consulted the Oracle at Delphi as to the best site for a new colony they received the answer, "Build ye opposite the city of the blind!" Undismayed by the vagueness of such a reply, the hardy band of colonists set off and duly arrived at the Thracian Bosphorus, and founded a city on the site of a town called Lygos, to which Pliny alludes, but of which we know nothing. The promontory on which it stood had been selected for its beauty and strategic importance, and now the Oracle was explained, and they fully realized why the colony which had established itself a few years earlier on the opposite shores at Chalcedon (the modern Kadikeuy) had been called "the blind."[1] They named their new city Byzantium, after Byzas, their leader, the actual date of its foundation being variously given as 667, 660, and 657 B.C.

The choice of beautiful sites for their temples and theatres by the early Greek colonists is well known, and whether we turn to Pæstum, Taormina, Segesta, Selenunte, or Girgenti their selective genius at once proclaims itself as we are lost in admiration first at the site as seen from a distance and then at the view from the building itself. But in the case under consideration nature had spoken in no uncertain voice, and we can allow our imagination, with but little fear of error, not only to identify what to-day is known as Seraglio Point with the acropolis of Byzas, but to decorate it with temples and shrines dedicated to Demeter, Aphrodite, Zeus, Poseidon, and Apollo. Some of its fortifications still exist, and, with Turkish repairs and additions, support the steep sides of the Seraglio that face the Marmora. Remains of a Cyclopean wall were discovered near the sea when the railway was made in 1871, and can with but little doubt

[1] See, however, *Cambridge Ancient History*, vol. iii, p. 659.

THE SERAGLIO FROM THE MARMORA, SHOWING PART OF THE OLD SEA-WALLS, THE DEĞIRMEN KAPI, AND THE SMALL MOSQUE

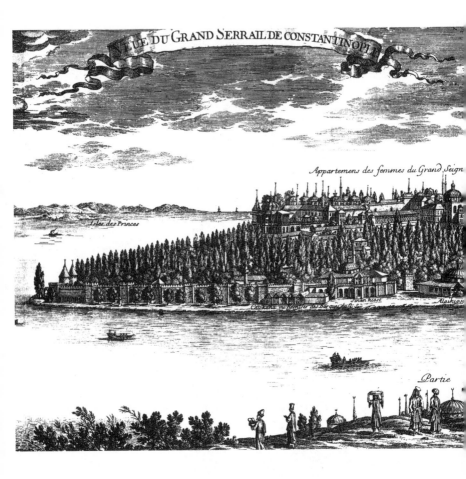

VEÜE DU GRAND SERRAIL DE CONSTANTINOPLE

Appartemens des femmes du Grand Seign

Isles des Princes

Nan Kiosk

Partie

Chambre du Divan

Appartements des Officiers

Entrée du Serrail

Temple de S.te Sophie

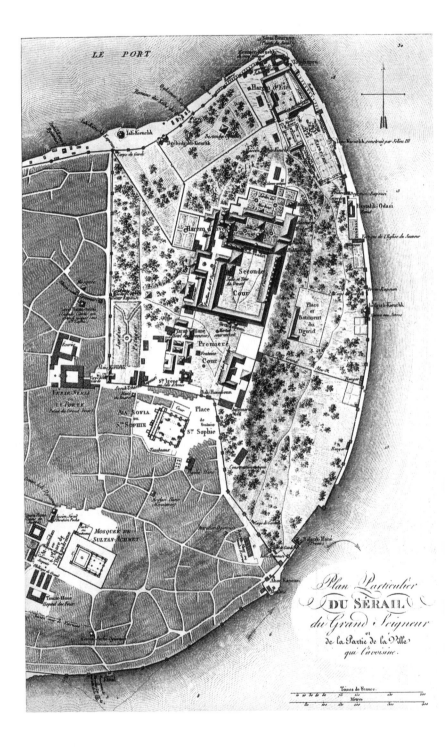

Plan Particulier
DU SÉRAIL
du Grand Seigneur
et
de la Partie de la Ville
qui l'avoisine.

be regarded as part of the outer fortifications of the Byzantine acropolis.

Just outside the Third Gate (*Üçüncü Kapi*) of the Seraglio, in the public gardens which overlook the Marmora, stands an ancient granite column known as the Goths' Column. It is said to have once supported a statue of Byzas. But here was situated the Theatron Minor of Septimius Severus (A.D. 193–211), and in those days the column formed part of the *spina*, or low dividing wall in the middle of the amphitheatre, just as the two obelisks and the Serpent Column once decorated the *spina* of the Hippodrome. In later days it was chosen to celebrate the victories of the Emperor Claudius Gothicus (268–270) over the Goths at Nissa, and has retained the name ever since.

But such a site was soon bound to tempt the invader's hand, and the Golden Horn had already proved itself a true cornucopia. About the year 506 B.C. the settlement was destroyed by the satrap Otanes during the reign of Darius Hystaspes. It was, however, wrested from the Medes by the Spartan Pausanias after the famous battle of Platæa[1] in 479 B.C. A period of unrest followed, Byzantium siding in turn with the Spartans, the Rhodians, and the Athenians. In 340 B.C. it was besieged by Philip of Macedon, and, although the situation was saved by the timely arrival of the Athenians, Byzantium was soon compelled to acknowledge the Macedonian supremacy under Alexander the Great. In succeeding centuries the city withstood considerable losses at the hands of the Scythians, Gauls, Rhodians, and Bithynians. On the arrival of the Romans on the scene Byzantium sided with Pescennius Niger against Septimius Severus, with the result that the city was totally destroyed in A.D. 196, after a three years' siege. Later Severus regretted having done this, and rebuilt the city, adorning it with palaces, a theatre (as mentioned above), a hippodrome, and baths, and giving to it the new name of Antonina. The city, however, never fully recovered

---

[1] The world-famous Serpent Column, still standing in the Hippodrome, or Et-meidan Square, which occupies a large part of the site to-day, is a relic of this battle. Its three heads (one of which is now in the museum on Seraglio Hill) supported a golden tripod, which was a thank-offering to the temple of Apollo at Delphi from the thirty-one Greek towns which were involved in the struggle. Their names, once visible on the coils of the serpents, are now entirely obliterated.

until it became the capital of the Roman Empire under Constantine the Great, who dedicated this New Rome on May 11, 330. The city, now twice the size of ancient Byzantium, was surrounded by a wall, *fora* were laid out, palaces and baths were erected, and the whole was divided up into fourteen Regions. The city was completed by Constantius (337–361), and other additions were made by subsequent emperors such as Valens, Theodosius I, Arcadius, Theodosius II (who built the land- and repaired the sea-walls), Marcian, and Anastasius. And so we come to the time of Justinian (527–565), when Sancta Sophia was built. At this time, too, silk was introduced from China.

The building of the numerous walls continued under Heraclius, Leo the Armenian, Michael III, Manuel I Comnenus, and other emperors.

With the endless sieges of the Huns, Slavs, Arabs, Bulgarians, and Russians we are not concerned. Nor is this the place to speak of the crusades of 1096–97 and 1147.

By the end of the twelfth century the fate of the Byzantine Empire was sealed, and in 1203, or the Fourth Crusade, the Venetian *Doge* Dandolo took Constantinople by assault. The city was sacked, and the damage done to the Imperial palaces, which were robbed of all their treasures, was incalculable. The famous bronze horses of Lysippus still stand over the portico of St Mark's, in Venice. The Latin Empire lasted till 1261, when the city was taken by Michael Palæologus and the Byzantine Empire restored. But its strength had gone, and after resisting the assaults of the Turks in 1398 and 1422 it finally fell on May 29, 1453, to Muhammad II, the Conqueror, and the last of the Emperors of the East, Constantine Dragases, perished heroically on the ramparts.

Even from this hurried survey of the vicissitudes that fell to the lot of Constantinople until it became the capital of the Ottoman Empire it is possible to get some slight idea of the continual destruction and rebuilding that went on in the city: and we can well understand how Seraglio Point would suffer most of all, and appreciate how difficult, if not impossible, it would be for the archæologist to sort out the composite ruins and arrange what remained in its right chronological order.

2. THE WALLS AND KIOSKS

But the story of the ruins is not completed, for we still have the Turkish buildings, restorations, and adaptations to consider. In order to do this it will be necessary to examine the sea- and land-walls, which enclose the whole of the promontory, in detail. The gates and kiosks will also demand our attention, and so in time we shall come to the First Court of the Seraglio itself.

The capture of Constantinople by Muhammad II was merely the climax to a gradual westward movement of the Seljuk Turks and their efforts to establish a capital in Europe.

The first Sultan[1] of the Ottoman Turks, Osman I (1288–1326), died shortly after receiving news of the fall of Brusa, and with it the knowledge that his victorious son Orkhan (1326–59) would make Brusa his capital and continue the career of conquest which he himself had inaugurated. Orkhan successfully carried on the work of his father. Not only had he driven the Byzantines from their last stronghold in Asia, but he had invaded Europe, and opened the way for his son Murad I (1359–89) to transfer the seat of his government to Thrace permanently. This he did after the battle of Maritza in 1363, and three years later Adrianople became the new capital of the Empire. At this period it was the custom of the Sultans to maintain a personal bodyguard recruited from the sons of conquered Christians, and in later days the idea developed into the creation of the corps of the janissaries, destined to play such an important and terrible part in the future history of the Empire. Its foundation has almost universally been attributed to Orkhan, but in the light of recent research we can no longer accept so early a date (see, further, p. 89).

During the reigns of Bayezid I, Muhammad I, and Murad II the European conquests were further extended, until finally Muhammad II took Constantinople itself. Thus, after being at Adrianople for nearly ninety years, the seat of government moved to the shores of the Bosphorus.

Almost at once Muhammad returned to Adrianople to prepare

---

[1] We can call him 'Sultan' for convenience, but actually he styled himself simply 'Emir,' like rulers of several petty states in Asia Minor. Orkhan was the first ruler to assume the title of 'Sultan.'

for his attack against Serbia. But before doing so he looked for
a suitable spot in Constantinople to build a palace which would be
ready for him on his return. For one reason or another none of the
existing palaces was suitable, through either bad state of repair or
unfavourable position. Like Rome, the city was built on seven hills,
and on the Third Hill, which had formerly been occupied by the
Forum of Taurus, or Theodosius, the Conqueror chose to build his
palace. Authorities are not agreed on the date of its completion,
but it was in all probability ready for habitation the following year,
1454, though possibly not completed until 1457. The exact number
of years that the Sultan lived in the Palace is also disputed, but it
would appear to be about ten. During this period it had become
evident that the Palace was not large enough to be used both as a
private and as an official residence, especially with the continual
expansion of the newly formed Palace School. The desire for greater
seclusion was also very possibly a determinative factor. At any rate
a new site was sought where there would be plenty of room for
expansion, where absolute privacy could be assured, and where
strong fortification would be simple. The ideal spot which at once
presented itself was the site of the Byzantine acropolis on the First
Hill.

Work commenced in 1459, and the new palace was completed in
1465. It was called the *Yeni Sarayi* (or *Serai*), or New Palace, in
contradistinction to what was now the *Eski Sarayi*, or Old Palace. I
have already (p. 17) referred to the various names given to the New
Palace at different times and the muddle that resulted from repeated
changes.

The first thing to be done to ensure complete seclusion was to
build a strong inner wall round the apex of the hill which the Palace
itself was to occupy, and cut off the whole of the Seraglio area from
the rest of the city by a high land-wall running right across the hill
from the Golden Horn to the Sea of Marmora.

Protection from the sea—that is to say, on the Marmora coast—
was already well provided for, as the ancient Byzantine sea-walls
ran right round Seraglio Point, past the southern base of the acropolis,
and straight on till they joined the great land-wall of Theodosius at
the Seven Towers. The section of this sea-wall which embraces the

Seraglio was almost entirely built at the time of Septimius Severus, and extended as far as the present lighthouse—that is to say, to a point almost exactly in a line with the great double gate which led into the First Court of the Seraglio itself—the Imperial Gate, or *Bab-i-Humayun*. From the lighthouse the sea-wall was continued westward by Constantine the Great, the last portion near the Seven Towers being the work of Theodosius II. It will thus be seen that as early as the fourth century the whole of the seaboard was fully protected by a strong wall. Particular care was taken to build these walls so near the sea that the waters lapped their bases, thus affording no landing beaches for raiders, and at the same time allowing the strong currents to act as a further protection. Time had proved that sufficient protection to the coast was now acquired, and that the only danger to be constantly feared was from earthquakes and tempests.

The Byzantine emperors were careful to repair the walls whenever such eventualities occurred, and restorations were made by Justinian, Leo the Isaurian, Theophilus, Michael II, and Manuel Comnenus. Thus it can be fairly safely concluded that when Muhammad the Conqueror commenced building his New Palace he found the sea-walls in a comparatively good state of repair.

In 1509, only twenty-eight years after his death, an earthquake occurred, damaging the walls badly. They were, however, immediately repaired by Bayezid II, and again by subsequent Sultans as occasion demanded.

The point on the Marmora where the new land-wall across the acropolis met the ancient sea-wall was in a direct line with Sancta Sophia. It lay almost midway between two gates (to which we shall return later)—the *Balik Hane Kapi*, Gate of the Fish-house, and the *Akhor Kapi*, or Stable Gate.

From here the land-wall runs up the hill in an eastward curve to the Imperial Gate. It has but one opening, the *Kara Kapi*, better known as the *Gülhane Kapi*, as it led towards the hospital of the same name. There are ten towers in this section of the wall. On the far side of the Imperial Gate the wall continues till it reaches the bottom of the hill, where it turns at right angles at the charming little Alai Kiosk, which faces the Sublime Porte (now nearly in ruins) across the road. At the time of its building there were six towers in this section, but only five remain to-day, owing to the sixth's being removed to make way for the gate (leading to the Seraglio park, now open to the public) known as the *Soğuk Çeşme Kapi*, or Gate of the Cool Fountain. This is said to have been built by Sultan Ibrahim about 1645. When the park was ceded to the Prefecture by Muhammad V in 1913 the gate was nearly destroyed by the Prefect in his efforts to allow greater movement of traffic. Luckily this step was prevented, and two small side-gates were opened up to meet the difficulty.

But we must return to the Marmora coast and consider the gates and kiosks in their proper order, beginning at Seraglio Point itself and gradually working round the Marmora till we come to the *Akhor Kapi*, and then continuing over the hill and right round to the Golden Horn, and so back again to Seraglio Point.

As we start at the very point of the promontory the first gate to be considered is that which gave its name, and among the Turks still does, to the Seraglio itself—the *Topkapi*, or Cannon Gate. No sign of it remains to-day, nor of the kiosk which stood next it. But of this I shall speak a little later. As is only to be expected, a gate, of one sort or another, always occupied this most important point. No details, or even the name, of any ancient *propylæum* or gate that must have once graced this site are known. In Christian times there was a gate dedicated to the patron saint of armourers and gunsmiths—St Barbara. Her protection was also especially sought against lightning. It is not known whether it occupied the very point of the peninsula or not, but in Turkish times the *Topkapi* was quite considerably towards the Marmora side. In fact, from the Golden Horn one would only see the tops of the towers among the trees. The date of the building of the *Topkapi* can be roughly given as the middle of the fifteenth century. The gate figures in all the early maps, where it appears as a very simple structure piercing the walls without any towers or other embellishments. It would seem to be the gate referred to by Pierre Gilles (1550) as the one standing "to the North of the Seraglio, towards the Bay."[1]

[1] Dr Miller (*Beyond the Sublime Porte*, p. 144) is surely mistaken when she imagines Gilles to be describing the *Topkapi* at pp. 39-40 of his *Antiquities of Constantinople* (London,

To the north-west it was guarded by the Church of St Demetrius, another military saint, and was therefore sometimes styled by the Greeks, after the Turkish Conquest, the Gate of St Demetrius.[1] Being on the eastern shore of the city, it was also called the Eastern Gate, while in several of the Italian maps it appears as the *Porta de isole*, because it looked towards the Princes' Islands. From the seventeenth century onward it was flanked by two round towers with conical tops, and thus closely resembled the *Ortakapi*, or Central Gate, leading into the Second Court of the Seraglio (see p. 97). In Grelot's time (1680) it had a portico in front right down to the water's edge, as can just be seen in his excellent engraving reproduced opposite p. 54. His description is worth giving. After describing in some detail the "great number of Cannons ready charg'd, and lying levell with the water," he continues:

> In the midst of these great Guns stands one of the four Gates of the *Serraglio*, that is to say, the Gate which belongs to the *Serraglio*, call'd *Bostangi Capi*. It is flank'd with two great round Towers, cover'd each with its proper *Kiosc*, shadowed with two great *Cypress* Trees, that grow without the *Serraglio* by the Sea side. At the foot of these Towers stand two *Bostangi* Centinels, who are the *Capigi's* or Guards of the Gate; so that nothing can be carry'd in or out, without their permission, who do not grant it easily, unless it be to the Officers of the *Serraglio*: Besides, it is through this Gate that the Sultanesses pass, when the Grand Signor carries them forth to accompany him in his pastimes upon the Canal of the *Black Sea*, which he frequently does; or when they go to the *Serraglio* at *Scutari* which stands directly overagainst this Gate.[2]

Thus at one time the gate was known as the *Bostanji Kapi*, or Gate of the Gardeners. This is not at all surprising, as the *bostanji*, to the number of about 400, were employed in all kinds of manual

1729) when he says: "The second [gate] stands upon the Ridge of a Hill: 'Tis very large, has a Porch with an arch'd Roof before it, is gilded, and adorn'd in a surprising manner with *Persian* Paintings, supported with Pillars of Ophitick Marble, and looks into the Bosporus." This sounds more like the Marmor Kiosk, next the *Topkapi*. It might well give the impression of an elaborate gate, especially as several gates, like the Imperial Gate, had considerable-sized rooms built over them.

[1] See Alexander van Millingen, *Byzantine Constantinople* (London, 1899), p. 249.

[2] *Relation nouvelle d'un voyage de Constantinople* (Paris, 1680). This is from p. 73 of the 1683 English translation, and from p. 86 of the French 1680 edition, where we are told further that the guards were "bostangis ou jardiniers."

labour on the shores of the Marmora, as well as merely gardening. Their chief, the *Bostanji-bashi*, was a highly important personage, his powers were considerable, and his favour was greatly sought after. The *bostanji* were all *ajem-oghlans*, foreign and untrained youths, to a large extent recruits for the corps of janissaries. Their employment as guards, gardeners, rowers, wood-cutters, kitchen men, etc., was merely part of the training to strengthen their bodies for their future life in the army, and to make them efficient in some trade useful in time of war. When at its height the corps formed the finest army in the world, and was, moreover, the first standing army known in Europe since Roman times. By the time of Suleiman they numbered some 40,000, but the strictness of the order soon became relaxed, and with the permission of marriage and the acceptance of their sons into the ranks, mutiny, extortion, and other excesses led to an appalling abuse of power not to be crushed until Mahmud II abolished the corps by a wholesale massacre. Of all this more in another chapter. But *revenons à nos moutons*.

In front of the Cannon Gate two Imperial *caïques* were always moored, in which the *bostanji* would act as rowers to convey the Sultan up the Bosphorus, to the Princes' Islands, or on any other pleasure trip he might wish to enjoy. Immediately next the Cannon Gate on the Golden Horn side was the Marble Kiosk, built, according to Gurlitt, in 1518 by the *Defterdar* Abd es-Selam. Although the date is not definite, we can regard this kiosk as the earliest built by the Turks on Seraglio Point for ceremonial purposes. In Melling's drawing[1] it appears as a rectangular building raised on arches or pillars, with two rows of windows and a fairly flat roof without a cupola or other decoration. In the text it is described as being supported by twelve columns of *verd-antique*.

This is very like another description given by Sieur du Loir, who, without mentioning any names, says:

> There is also on the sea-board one of those pavilions which the Turks call *Kiosks*, supported by twelve beautiful marble columns, and enriched with a magnificent ceiling [*Lambris*, which can mean a flat or vaulted ceiling, as well as panelling or dado] painted in the Persian

[1] *Voyage pittoresque de Constantinople* (Paris, 1819), No. 24 in the volume of text, No. 9 in the volume of plates.

style, where the Grand Seigneur comes at times to take the air and enjoy the view of the harbour.[1]

I have been unable to discover the date of its destruction, but it still appears in 1840 maps of Constantinople. It probably underwent considerable alterations when the Summer Palace was built in 1709–1809. As a fire entirely destroyed the whole Palace in 1862–63 and the railway was built eight years later, we can conclude that anything left by the one was entirely eradicated by the other.

A short way round the Point on the Marmora side was a kiosk built for the use of the *Bostanji-bashi*. In Grelot's drawing of it [2]— *i.e.*, in his *other* engraving, of the Marmora side, not that reproduced in the present work—it presents an uneven façade, being broken in the centre by a square tower similar to the famous Seraglio tower, only much smaller. The chief rooms were on the first floor, there being two windows each side of the tower. All this low-lying part of Seraglio Point underwent a great change when in 1709 Ahmed III decided to build a summer palace here. Being so near the Cannon Gate, it was most confusingly called the *Top Capu Sarayi* (see p. 17). It was continued by Mahmud I (1730–54), after which time it was little used. It was, however, renovated and added to by Abd ul-Hamid I (1774–89), and during the reign of Selim III (1789–1807) Antoine Melling made several further additions. We can therefore accept his plan of it as the most correct in existence.

The best account of the Summer Palace is undoubtedly that by F. C. Pouqueville,[3] who visited it under the expert guidance of the Austrian Head Gardener and M. Melling himself. With the latter's plan before us it is easy to follow the description of Pouqueville, from which I herewith give selections. Being admitted by the Mill Gate (or *Değirmen Kapi*, to which I shall refer again shortly), he made his way into the New Garden, laid out on the Schönbrunn pattern by Jacob Ensle, the gardener, or "Jaques," as Pouqueville calls him. The party proceeded along the shore side to the New Kiosk,

---

[1] *Voyage* (Paris, 1654), p. 43.
[2] *Relation nouvelle*, pp. 71–72 of the English edition.
[3] *Travels in the Morea, Albania, and other Parts of the Ottoman Empire*, translated from the French (of 1805) by Anne Plumptre (London, 1813), pp. 324–335. For a long *précis* of the original edition see Boucher de la Richarderie, *Bibliothèque universelle des voyages* (Paris, 1808), tome ii, pp. 242–267.

the three steps in semicircular form which lead to it making a pro-
jection on the garden side.

> Instead of a door, a large painted canvass hanging from the roof like
> a curtain closes the entrance of the Kiosque, giving it in this part the
> appearance of a tent. We put it aside to enter, and I was most agree-
> ably surprised at the elegance of the interior. It is of an elliptical form,
> the largest diameter being thirty-six feet; this runs from the curtain to
> the windows, which look upon the sea. The painting round the sides
> was executed by Europeans; it represents a colonnade, the cornices
> being richly painted, and gilt with great taste; in the intervals between
> the columns are glasses, and some paintings of flowers which seemed
> well preserved. . . . The Sultan's sofa was placed on the side next the
> sea, but had nothing remarkable in it; and there was a fountain of
> crystal, from which flowed very fine clear water, destined for the
> ablutions.

The floor was covered with painted cloth, a new fashion in the
Seraglio, according to Melling. They then traversed a terrace about
fifty feet long and twelve feet broad, ending in a bastion commanding
a fine view of the port as well as the ḥarēm. A staircase in the garden
led to a subterranean kiosk under the New Kiosk, and also connected
with little iron gates by which a hasty escape could be made to the
Marmora. Towards the north end of the garden was the Golden
Gate, leading by a gentle descent to the ḥarēm gate on the right, and
on the left to an iron gate which led to a raised garden terrace looking
down on the larger garden below—i.e., via the "Montée douce" in
Melling's plan. At the end of this terrace was situated a gallery
called "Hassan Pasha's Kiosk":

> It is entirely open to the east, both in its length and height. The
> ceiling is remarkable by the load of gilding, and by glasses which are
> fixed into it in such a way that the surrounding objects are reflected
> on every side.

It was, however, neglected, and the swallows had built their nests
in the cornices.

After a first disappointment Pouqueville got into the ḥarēm. When
he had entered by the ḥarēm gate

> the enormous size of the key and the noise made by the gate grating
> upon its hinges, united with the solitude and sacredness of the place,

seemed at first to strike us all with a sort of awe.[1] Twelve feet away
was a second gate—of wood, and between the two gates was the apartment of the female slaves on the first floor ["Log. des Odalisques" in
the plan]. It is a vast gallery three hundred feet in length, forty-five in
breadth, and twenty in height, with a range of windows on each side,
and divided down the whole length by a double row of closets, painted
some red, some blue, some white, forming two distinct ranges one
above the other, and in these the slaves keep whatever property they
have. Near the windows are little spaces surrounded with a balustrade
three feet high, and furnished with sofas on which the Odaliscas sleep,
in parties of fifteen each.

Provision was made for 300 women in all. A staircase at the end
of the gallery and closed by folding trapdoors led to the courtyard
below. The kitchens were also in this part of the *ḥarēm*. The courtyard stretched in a north-easterly direction, with a colonnade facing
the sea, while the sultanas' pavilions were on the opposite side. At the
farther end of the court were the apartments of the *Kislar Agha* and
the black eunuchs under his control. There was an inner courtyard
connecting at its farthest point with the Marmor Kiosk and the
Cannon Gate. It gave entrance to the rooms of the First Kadin and
the Sultan Validé; "the cornices were loaded with gilding and the
walls with glasses," but most of the furniture had been removed to
the new palace of Beshiktash, on the Lower Bosphorus. The beauty
of the baths made a great impression on Pouqueville. They appear
to have resembled those I shall describe in the winter *ḥarēm* in a later
chapter.

I have given considerable space to the Summer Palace because very
few accounts exist,[2] and that by Pouqueville should be read with
Melling's plan as a guide, and this I have specially reproduced in its
original scale. Besides which the history of the Seraglio would be
incomplete without some account of the Summer Palace.

[1] I fully appreciate his feelings, and experienced them myself after ascending the worn
wooden stairs in the *ḥarēm* proper and standing in silence gazing at the heavily barred
bedroom of the *ḥarēm* girls, a spot so sacred and teeming with such romance that when
I found my voice it was but a whisper.
[2] *Cf.* that by E. D. Clarke, the mineralogist and travelling tutor, in *Travels in Various
Countries of Europe, Asia, and Africa* (London, 1812), Part II, section 1, pp. 13–28. See
also J. von Hammer, *Constantinopolis*, I, pp. 306–321, with conventional plan facing p. 308;
C. Gurlitt, "Der Serai in Konstantinopel" (*Beiträge zur Kenntniss des Orients* (1915), xii,
pp. 31–63).

We must now return to the sea-wall and continue our inspection of the gates and kiosks. I shall also give some description of the recently discovered remains of the Mangana, or Imperial arsenal buildings.

As we have already seen, Pouqueville entered the Summer Palace through the *Değirmen Kapi*, about 300 yards south of it. It is, then, this gate which I shall now describe. It is a small, unpretentious one dating from Byzantine times, but both its original Greek name and the purpose of its erection are unknown. In Turkish times it served a hospital built against the walls for the staff of the Seraglio, as well as a small mosque near by. Both remain to-day, but are in a sad state of ruin, owing to the fact that the railway line has quite cut them off from the rest of the acropolis buildings. Here also was the Imperial mill and bakery, which remained in active use for members of the Seraglio until in 1616 Ahmed I built the one in the First Court, which appears in Melling's interesting drawing reproduced opposite p. 86 of the present work. This gate, then, has been called both *Hastalar Kapi* (also written *Hastalar Capoussou*, *Khastalar Qapusi*, etc.), or Hospital Gate, and *Değirmen Kapi* (*Deyirman Qapu*, *Deïrmen Kapoussi*, etc.), or Gate of the Mill. In order to obtain a satisfactory impression of this stretch of the walls, with the Hospital Gate and mosque as a central point, it is necessary not only to view it from the terrace of the Seraglio below the Goths' Column, but also to inspect it from the sea side in a small boat, which can easily be hired at the New Bridge.

Behind the *Hastalar Kapi* on the land side, in the low-lying space between the walls and the base of the acropolis, was once the Kynegion, the amphitheatre built by Septimius Severus at the end of the second century, and used chiefly for the exhibition of wild beasts, but under later emperors as a place of execution. Thus, with the Theatron Minor, the Byzantine acropolis had two theatres built against its steep eastern slopes, just as the Athenian acropolis had the Theatre of Dionysos and the Odeion of Herodes Atticus built against its southern slopes.

To-day the site of the Kynegion is an allotment, bounded on the seaward side by the railway line.

The next gate, which lies a little farther south, is, in its present form at any rate, a Turkish erection. It seems, however, quite possible that it replaced a Byzantine gate, especially when we consider that we are now approaching the district of the Mangana, or military arsenal, built by Constantine. Not a trace of it remains to-day, and until quite recently its site was little more than a matter of conjecture. But owing to certain excavations carried out in 1921–22 we are able to place it somewhere very close to this Turkish gate, known by the name of *Demir Kapi*, the Iron Gate, which naturally must not be confused with the land gate of the same name that gave entrance to the Seraglio gardens on the west. In his deservedly famous work *Byzantine Constantinople* Alexander van Millingen says that the Mangana must have stood between the Gate of St Barbara and the Hospital Gate. The sole reason he can give is that Nicetas Chroniates (Acominatus), the Byzantine politician and chronicler, says that it faced the rocky islet off the opposite Scùtari shore on which to-day is Leander's Tower. Such deduction is of little value, as we have no idea what Nicetas meant by the expression "faced." It depends on how you chance to be standing and looking. Leander's Tower is not exactly opposite even the extreme point of the Seraglio shore; still less is it opposite the gates farther to the south. But, on the other hand, it is clearly visible from any point on the adjacent coast as far as the modern lighthouse, so that any gate or building in the district could be said to "face" the tower, merely because as one looked out towards the Bosphorus this was the one point that stood out as a landmark. Nicetas tells us further that (in the twelfth century) Manuel Comnenus built two towers, one on the rock and the other on the mainland opposite, "very close to the Monastery of Mangana." The towers were joined by a chain as a protection to the Bosphorus.

The acropolis tower exists to-day close to the *Demir Kapi*, while the site of the monastery, known as St George of the Mangana, was discovered in 1921 a little farther south, just on the landward side of the modern railway. A series of basements and a large cistern surmounted by sixteen cupolas supported by great pillars of masonry were revealed. Bird designs in an adjoining vaulted roof proclaim the work of Byzantine masons. The church, together with a convent at the southern end, was built by Constantine IX Monomacus (1042–1054), and received its name from its proximity to the Mangana.

Immediately to the south of the monastery stood the Palace of the Mangana, of which the foundations were discovered in 1921. They proved to be elaborate, consisting of a large central cistern with thirty cupolas supported by a double row of marble and granite pillars. The unusual depth of these foundations appears to have been necessary to ensure a view of the coast over the high sea-walls. The palace was built by Basil I (867–886) and destroyed by Isaac II Angelus at the end of the twelfth century to obtain material for his own buildings.

But where was the Mangana itself? Having now fixed the sites of the Mangana Tower, Monastery, and Palace, we can surely determine that of the Mangana by studying the map. The only space sufficiently large for an Imperial military arsenal, and fitting in with all recent discoveries, is that lying between the tower and the monastery; and there (with Professor Mamboury) we must place it without hesitation. This also helps to explain the presence of several small closed-up Byzantine gates in the sea-wall near the *Demir Kapi*.

As we continue along the walls a ruinous façade will soon be noticed. It consists of a door with a window above it and a niche each side. This is all that remains of the church of St Saviour, built by Alexius Comnenus (1081–1118). Immediately to the south are the ruins of the kiosk built by Sinan Pasha, the Grand Vizir of Murad III, in 1582. To Europeans it was always known as the Kiosk of Pearls (*Injili Köşkü*).[1] The ruins consist of a substructure built against the exterior of the walls and forming several arcades. Through these buttresses the water of a holy spring ('Aγίασμα) within the city was conducted to the outer side of the walls, and thus rendered accessible to the Christians of the Greek Orthodox Church, who sought the benefit of its healing virtues. This was the holy spring of the church of St Saviour, celebrated as a fountain of health long before the Turkish conquest.[2] Many writers [3] have described the

[1] A good engraving of the Kiosk of Pearls appears in Comte de Choiseul-Gouffier, *Voyage pittoresque de la Grèce* (Paris, 1782–1822), vol. ii, Plate 72. *Cf.* also those of Melling, *Voyage pittoresque de Constantinople* (No. 7 in the text), and A. L. Castellan, *Lettres sur la Morée, l'Hellespont, et Constantinople* (second edition, Paris, 1820), vol. ii, Plate 40.

[2] Van Millingen, *Byzantine Constantinople*, p. 253.

[3] Gilles, *Antiquities of Constantinople*, p. 40; Thévenot, *Travels into the Levant* (London,

curious scenes witnessed on the festival of Transfiguration. The Sultan himself would sometimes view them from a window in the kiosk, watching the sick being buried up to the neck in the sand as a method of cure. To the south of the kiosk, which was destroyed by the railway in 1871, the wall has fallen down by the side of a small gate, the name of which is unknown; inside it is the entrance to a vast basement which constituted the interior passage of this section of the walls. At low tide a walk along the shore will reveal six gates which belonged to numerous convents, the most important being those of St Lazarus and St Mary Hodighitria. A small Turkish fountain built in the reign of Ahmed I bars further progress in this direction.[1] It was in the neighbourhood of St Lazarus that the Topi, remains of a tier of seats (possibly one of the theatres of Septimius Severus), was found. The polo-ground (Tzycanisterion) of the Great Palace was also in the vicinity, and marked the eastern limits of Constantine's palace. Finally, the famous baths of Arcadius and a church dedicated to the Archangel Michael stood near the Topi. Thus the whole area is an architectural palimpsest indeed!

Between the *Injili Köşkü* and the outer walls of the Second Court of the Seraglio it will be noticed in Melling's plan that there is a large rectangular space marked as " Place et Batiment du Dgirid." This was the playing-field for the game of *jerīd*, or wooden javelin-throwing, and stood near the site of the *Nea*, or New Church of Basil the Macedonian. Melling gives an engraving of the game in play, not actually in this particular field, but the one at the archery ground (*Ok-meidan*) near the Sweet Waters of Europe (*Kiat Khānet*), at the far end of the Golden Horn.[2] From this, and other drawings of the period,[3] it will be seen that the javelins resemble in size and shape ordinary wooden broom-handles, about three feet eight inches

---

1687), p. 23; Grelot, *Relation nouvelle*, p. 71 of the English edition; and in more recent times von Hammer, *Constantinopolis*, I, p. 236 *et seq.*, and Constantius, *Ancient and Modern Constantinople* (1868), p. 26.

[1] E. Mamboury, *Tourists' Guide to Constantinople* (Constantinople, 1924), p. 462. See also van Millingen, *Byzantine Constantinople*, pp. 256–257.

[2] *Voyage pittoresque de Constantinople*, No. 24 in the volume of text, No. 17 in the volume of plates.

[3] See, for example, Choiseul-Gouffier, *Voyage pittoresque de la Grèce*, vol. i, Plate 110, and text pp. 170–171; d'Ohsson, *Tableau général de l'empire Ottoman* (3 vols., Paris, 1787–1820), the double plate 171, between pp. 332 and 333 of vol. iii.

in length. With continual practice they could be hurled by a rider (every one was mounted) with perfect aim at the head of the opponent, often causing considerable bodily harm, and sometimes even death. As the drawings show, enormous interest was taken in important matches, and numerous elaborate tents were pitched round the field, and crowds of janissaries and others were in attendance. Grooms, servants, doctors, swelled the throng, and a band of some twenty performers added to the general liveliness. Dr Miller gives us some useful information about the game.[1] It is described as a mock battle in which mounted horsemen threw wooden darts at each other. It was a prominent feature of Royal entertainment in the Hippodrome at least as early as the second half of the sixteenth century, but achieved its greatest popularity during 1650–1700. It was finally abolished by Mahmud II, together with the corps of janissaries, in 1826. A point of considerable interest, not mentioned by Dr Miller, is the connexion that appears to have existed between the Turkish naming of the rival parties in the game of *jerīd* and that employed in the time of Justinian in the old Byzantine hippodrome. In those days the rival parties were known respectively as the Blues and the Greens, and the emperors were affiliated to one or the other.

The Turks took their party names from vegetables—*bahmia*, a green pulpy pod, and *lahana*, a cabbage—the opposing teams being known as *Bahmiaji* and *Lahanaji*. The Sultans also sided with one or the other. Thus Mahmud II belonged to the former, while Selim III was a supporter of the cabbage men.[2] For the thrilling history, with all its political significance, of the Blues and Greens I may refer readers to Procopius.[3]

The Kiosk of Pearls lies almost exactly half-way between the Cannon Gate and the Fish-house Gate, which was situated just inside the Seraglio enclosure, where the land and sea gates meet. As its name at once implies, the Fish-house Gate, or *Balik Hane Kapi*, was so called because it led to the quarters of the fishermen in the service of the Seraglio, whose sheds were built here close to the sea.

---

[1] *Macdonald Presentation Volume*, pp. 305–324. See also William Harborne, *Turkey*, Public Records Office, State Papers, Foreign, vol. i, entry July 25, 1582, quoted by Dr Miller.

[2] C. White, *Three Years in Constantinople* (London, 1845), vol. i, p. 301.

[3] Especially to the fine translation by H. B. Dewing issued (1935) in the Loeb Classics.

In R. Walsh's *Constantinople and the Scenery of the Seven Churches of Asia Minor* [1] there is an illustration by T. Allom of the *Balik Hane*, which shows clearly the fish-stage erected for arresting the shoals of fish. In the foreground of the picture is a boat into which some of the fishermen have dragged, not their nets, but a dead body, this being the spot from which State criminals were thrown. Why the Royal fishing area should be chosen just here is hard to imagine! Quoting from an article by Abd ur-Rahman Shirif Efendi, [2] Dr Miller relates an interesting custom connected with the gate. It was, she says, [3] to this gate that a deposed Vizir, or Chief Black Eunuch, was secretly conducted immediately following his degradation. In the event of a sentence of death there was the very curious practice of a race between the Head Gardener of the Palace, who was also the Chief Executioner, and the condemned—literally a race of life and death. If the Vizir succeeded in arriving at the Fish-house Gate first he was accorded sanctuary within the gate, and the sentence commuted to exile. The last to escape death in this manner was the Grand Vizir Haji Salih Pasha in 1822–23. If, on the other hand, the deposed official found the Head Gardener awaiting him upon his arrival at the gate he was then and there summarily executed and his body cast into the sea.

The *Balik Hane Kapi* has been identified by Constantius [4] with the Postern of Michael the Protovestarius, by which Constantine Ducas entered in 913 on his attempt to usurp the throne. Considerable doubt, however, must be entertained before that assumption can be accepted. [5]

A short way south, and at a distance from outside the land-wall corresponding to that of the *Balik Hane Kapi* from inside the wall, was the *Akhor* (also spelled *Achour, Ahour, Ahir,* etc.) *Kapi,* or Gate of the Stables. Its ancient name is unknown, but as the marble stables erected by Michael III (842–867) were in the vicinity it is at least possible that there was a stable gate here in Byzantine days. The Sultan's mews lay a short distance inland, and are clearly shown in

---

[1] London, 1839 (?), p. 40.
[2] No. v in the *Tarikhi Osmani Enjumeni Mejmu'asi.*
[3] *Beyond the Sublime Porte,* p. 145 and p. 250 n. 31.
[4] *Ancient and Modern Constantinople,* p. 23.
[5] Van Millingen, *Byzantine Constantinople,* pp. 260–261.

Melling's plan. They were known as the *Büyük Akhor*, or Great Stables, in contradistinction to the Privy Stables, in the Second Court of the Seraglio. The number of horses kept here varied between 2000 and 4000. They belonged chiefly to members of the Palace School.

Passing on up the hill, we come to the *Gülhane Kapi* (to which reference has already been made at p. 59), and, continuing along the outside of the wall past seven more towers, we finally arrive on the summit at the Imperial Gate, or *Bab-i-Humayun*. I shall give a short description of this gate when discussing the First Court in the next chapter.

We continue along the walls in a northerly direction, and the main gate leading into the Seraglio gardens soon appears. As already mentioned, it is called the Gate of the Cool Fountain, or Fountain of Cold Water—in modern Turkish *Soğuk Çeşme Kapi*, and formerly written *Sughuq* (or *Souk*) *Chesmeh Kapusi* (or *Kapou*). It was built in the middle of the seventeenth century by Ibrahim, and repaired during the reign of Abd ul-Hamid II. It has no particular architectural importance, and has been very considerably altered in course of time. On entering and turning sharply to the left we find a slope which leads up to the Alai, or Procession, Kiosk. The proximity of this building to the Gate of the Cool Fountain has given it the alternative name the Procession Gate.

The Alai Kiosk is built in the most westerly angle of the Seraglio wall, which at this point turns east towards the Golden Horn almost at right angles. I have been unable to discover the date of the original kiosk built on this site, but there appears to have been one here from early in the sixteenth century similar in size and general construction to the present one, but round instead of polygonal. From inside the kiosk there is an excellent view in all directions, while a stone thrown directly ahead would land in the grounds of the Grand Vizir's Palace—the Sublime Porte as it was at one time. It is indeed a gazebo in its true meaning, and it would be hard to imagine a better place for viewing passing processions. To-day it is put to many practical uses, and when last I visited it an exhibition of modern pictures covered its walls. Many tales are told of the purposes to which it was put in bygone days. Intended primarily as a meeting-place for the Sultan and his *cortège* prior to the weekly visit to the mosque on Fridays, it was used by Murad IV as a vantage point from which to practise his prowess with the arquebus on the passers-by. When popular indignation began to express itself on this particular pastime of the Sultan the Royal 'bag' was limited to ten heads *per diem*!

The kiosk also served for public audiences in emergencies, when the petitioners would gather in the street below, each keeping at a safe distance from the other. Thus in the revolt of the janissaries in 1655 the Sultan was forced to appear at the window of the Alai Kiosk to hear the complaints of the soldiers, and in order to save his own head cast headlong into the street the strangled bodies of the Chief Black and White Eunuchs, while on the following day the bodies of nearly all the other principal ministers were handed to the janissaries as a peace offering by the terrified Sultan.

Dr Miller would credit the existence of another, and earlier, Alai Kiosk "on the shore of the Golden Horn near the angle of the land and sea walls."[1] Her evidence seems to me to be based on misunderstandings of her references, and possibly, with Grelot (see below), the muddling up of *alai* with *yali*, the point being that the very spot she selects for the earlier Alai Kiosk is that occupied in all maps and diagrams by the Yali, or Shore, Kiosk. Let us take the words themselves first. The modern Turkish for 'procession' is *alay*. Other spellings of the word are *alaj, alai, aylai, aylay*.

Now in the case of *yali* there is greater variation. The modern Turkish is *yali*. Other forms are *ialy, iali, jaly, yalli, ialai*, while Melling uses the form "Yaly" in his text and "Iali" in his plan. It will thus be seen how alike the two words have at times become. In a note on the passage in question Dr Miller remarks, with apparent surprise, that in Melling's plan the Procession Kiosk has disappeared and only the Yali Kiosk is shown. I maintain that this latter was the only kiosk built there. She also quotes Grelot, Hill, Du Loir, and Chishull, but not one of these writers mentions an Alai Kiosk in his text. Grelot marks an "Alaikiosc" in his map—an obvious misprint for "Ialaikiosc" or some similar form of "Yali Kiosk." He gives only one other facing Galata: the "Sinan Kiosc." Thus the mistake was only in the name, not in the number of buildings.

[1] *Beyond the Sublime Porte*, p. 147.

So too in the engravings of Choiseul-Gouffier,[1] d'Ohsson,[2] and Melling.[3] Another reliable writer, Comidas de Carbognano, enumerates all the kiosks on the Seraglio promontory, but gives only two, Sinan and Yali, as facing Galata. But when dealing with the 'Alaj,' as he spells it, he is very clear and decisive:

> It forms a tower on a partition wall of the Seraglio, about 100 paces distant from the Porte, whence the Grand Signor watches quite alone the public processions and cavalcades.

Nothing could be clearer or more exact, for the Porte, as the Imperial Gate was called, was only a few minutes' walk up the hill. If, however, by "the Porte" he means the Grand Vizir's Palace across the road, also known as the Sublime Porte, then again the distance given would be satisfactory, for anyone leaving the Alai Kiosk would have to approach the Palace *via* the Gate of the Cool Fountain. I shall return to the Yali Kiosk when we come to it in the course of our circumambulation of the walls. After leaving the Alai Kiosk the walls continue due east towards the Golden Horn. Before the Iron Gate is reached there are two small postern gates that deserve brief mention. The first of these was named after the famous Grand Vizir Sokolli, and the other one is known as the Gate of Sultan Suleiman. This latter was used by Ibrahim, Grand Vizir to Suleiman for thirteen years, when calling on the Sultan. He was strangled by the orders of Roxelana.

The Iron Gate, or *Demir Kapi*, a square massive structure with crenelated top, soon appears at the end of the road. Beyond this gate the wall is destroyed, and we can go no farther, since a modern wall has been built across our path hiding sheds and yards connected with the railway. The Iron Gate was also known as the *Bostanji Kapi*, or Gate of the Gardeners, for just the same reason that the Cannon Gate bore the alternative name—because it led to the Seraglio Garden and was chiefly used by the *bostanji*. It was also used by the ambassadors visiting the Sultan. Coming by boat from Pera, they usually passed through it and continued with their *cortège* to the Imperial Gate, and so to the *Ortakapi*, leading to the Second Court of the Seraglio.

---

[1] *Voyage pittoresque de la Grèce*, Plate 77.   [2] *Tableau général*, vol. iii, Plate 172.
[3] *Voyage pittoresque de Constantinople*, No. 29 in the volume of text, No. 9 in the volume of plates.

At the angle where the land- and sea-walls met was situated the *Yali Köşkü Kapi*, which is on, or near, the site of the Byzantine Gate of Eugenius, the church of St Paul, and the tower of Eugenius. It led direct to the seaboard where stood the *Yali Köşkü* itself. According to engravings and descriptions that have come down to us, it was a low-built, tent-like, octagonal building of white marble supported by many (some accounts say fifty) marble columns with steps leading down to the water's edge. There appear to be some differences of opinion as to the date of its foundation. The building has been attributed to Sinan Pasha (Grand Vizir of Murad III), who, as we have noted, built the Kiosk of Pearls, and its date fixed as 1589. On the other hand, it has been said to date back to the reign of Suleiman the Magnificent (1520–66). We can, at any rate, regard it as a sixteenth-century structure erected as a ceremonial kiosk for the Sultan from which to review the fleet, give audience to his admirals, and for similar functions.

Writing on his voyage of 1610, George Sandys describes the Yali Kiosk briefly as

> a sumptuous Summer-house; having a private passage made for the time of waxed linnen, from his *Serraglio*: where he often solaceth him-selfe, with the various objects of the haven: and from thence takes Barge to passe unto the delightfull places of the adjoyning *Asia*.[1]

In the drawing at the opposite page Sandys shows the kiosk to be hexagonal in shape with a cupola at the apex. There are eleven large arches and rows of steps only a few feet from the water. There is no sign of the Sinan Agha Kiosk, which should have been here at this time. A fuller account of the Yali Kiosk is to be found in a diary of Antoine Galland,[2] of *Arabian Nights* fame, extracts from which have been given by Dr Miller.[3] Almost contemporary is Grelot's account, which reads as follows:

> Yet all these Embellishments in the Sultannesses *Kiosc* [*i.e.*, the Sinan Agha, for which see later] are nothing in comparison to the Great Hall or Room in the other *Kiosc* [the Yali]. There is nothing in the World

[1] *A Relation of a Journey begun An: Dom: 1610* (London, 1615), p. 33.
[2] *Journal pendant son séjour à Constantinople* (1672–1673), *édit.* Charles Schefer (2 vols., Paris, 1881). See vol. i, pp. 186–188.
[3] *Beyond the Sublime Porte*, p. 148.

that can be thought to be more noble and magnificent; whether you look upon the Marble, the Pillars, the Artificial Water-Works, and stately Tapestries, the Galleries round about it, the charming Prospect which appears on every side, or the costly gilded Fretwork of the Ceiling, which would almost raise a mans thoughts to believe it something of Enchantment.[1]

He tried in vain to "take a draught of it."

A little more than a hundred years later it was described by de Carbognano (1794):

> At a little distance from the preceding one [the Sinan Agha] is the fifth Kiosk built in the form of a tent and ornamented on all sides with many columns, as well as in the apex of a beautiful dome. Its erection is likewise attributed to the same Soliman I. The Sultan goes unaccompanied to the Kiosk on the first day of *Bairam* and of *Kurban Bairam*;[2] on the setting out or returning of the squadron of the Captain Pasha;[3] and on the birth of Princes or Princesses of royal blood, especially when there are celebrations at night with fireworks at sea.[4]

Melling gives a similar description,[5] and his illustration resembles those of Sandys and Grelot. According to Constantius[6] it was destroyed in 1861.

Quite close to the Yali was the Kiosk of Sinan Agha, built in the sixteenth century chiefly as a summer-house for the Sultanas from which to view the passing shipping in the Golden Horn and up the Bosphorus.

Once more we can turn to Grelot:

> The first of these *Kioscs* was for the Women, of which he had a good Number. It is somewhat higher rais'd than the other, and the passage to it from the *Seraglio* is such as will not admit the persons passing to and fro to be seen. It is built from Arches all in Length, consisting of three fair Chambers, every one adorn'd with several gilded Alcoves furnish'd with their Sopha's or low Couches, having their *Minders*, or

[1] *Relation nouvelle*, p. 74 of the English edition.
[2] The two great festivals, the first being celebrated at the completion of the fasting month *Ramaḍān*, the second on the 10th of the last month (*Dhū-l-ḥijja*) with sacrifices to commemorate the ransom of Ishmael with a ram.
[3] This is the scene represented in d'Ohsson, *Tableau général*, Plate 71.
[4] *Descrizione topografica dello stato presente di Constantinopoli* (Bassano, 1794), p. 25.
[5] *Voyage pittoresque de Constantinople*, in the text to Plate 9.
[6] *Ancient and Modern Constantinople*, p. 11.

Mattresses and Cushions belonging to them, spread with rich Coverlets of painted Linnen and Cloth of *Tissue*. These Sopha's or Beds are placed near the Windows, wherein are Lattices, through which the Women may see and not be seen; for should they be seen, it might be as much prejudicial to the party discover'd, as to him that made the discovery.[1]

Comidas de Carbognano tells us it is built on eight arches and adorned with a cupola.

I can find no information as to its destruction. Quite close were the Seraglio boathouses, containing many Royal *caïques* and larger boats richly ornamented in gold and elaborate carvings.

Between the Sinan Agha Kiosk and the boathouses was another kiosk, not at the water's edge, but built high on the Seraglio wall, which at this point was a considerable way inland. It was known as the Kiosk of the Basket-makers (*Sepetjiler Köşkü*—the "Dgébedgiler-Kieuchk" of Melling's plan), and was used mainly as a means of signalling to the fleet. It was enlarged by Sultan Ibrahim in 1643, and appears on Stanford's map in Murray's guide[2] as late as 1907, but in 1895 Grosvenor described it as "blackened and indescribably dirty, affording hardly a hint of its former daintiness and importance."[3]

The name of the kiosk calls for some explanation. The word *sepet* means a basket, and is used to denote the baskets seen in grocery, fruit, and druggist shops for storing the merchandise. It also refers to baskets used by workmen for carrying tools and other small articles. They are shaped like our rush game baskets, and are made of split palm or broad flag leaves. Thus they differed from the *zembil*, which were light baskets with a cover and handle used for indoor domestic purposes, and still more from the *küçük sela,* or little baskets used in *harēms* for preserving rice, coffee, sugar, tobacco, cotton, etc. Yet there is no reason to believe that all these varieties were not made by the basket-makers whose former pitch was just below the wall kiosk that was to receive its name for the following reason. It is said that the Sultan Ibrahim diverted himself with basket-making, and consequently protected and granted various privileges

---

[1] *Relation nouvelle*, p. 74 of the English edition.
[2] *Handbook for Travellers in Constantinople, Brûsa, and the Troad.*
[3] *Constantinople*, p. 711.

to the basket-makers' corporation. This called forth corresponding gratitude on their part; so when in 1643 the Sultan rebuilt the kiosk the basket-makers humbly petitioned to be allowed to defray a portion of the expense. It was this fact that led to its bearing their name.[1]

The only other item to mention before we reach the Cannon Gate once again is the small Wood Gate (*Odun Kapi*), just near the north-east end of the boathouses. As its name implies, it was used for the enormous supply of wood needed in the Seraglio for the baths, kitchens, and general heating purposes. The supply came partly from the Forest of Belgrade, stretching as far as the Black Sea, and partly from the Mediterranean. When describing the First Court we shall see where the wood was piled, which, according to Tavernier, amounted to "above 40,000 Cart-loads of wood, every Cart-load being as much as two oxen can draw." According to White[2] it was through this gate that bodies executed in the Seraglio were taken forth and cast into the sea.

A small well and the battery are all that existed along the remainder of this coast, and so at last we arrive again at the point of the penin-sula, the *Serai Bournou*, and Cannon Gate.

Before we consider the First Court of the Seraglio mention should be made of two kiosks in the Outer Palace, in no way connected with the walls—the Chinili and the Gülhane Kiosks. The Chinili, or Tile, Kiosk is perhaps the most interesting of all the kiosks in the Seraglio, as, apart from its archæological and ceramic interest, it is the one existing building that unquestionably dates from the time of Muhammad II. It is situated in the Seraglio grounds on the Golden Horn side, and forms part of the Museum buildings, and can best be reached by way of the Gate of the Cool Fountain, through the gates on the right, and straight up the slope. It then lies to the left and faces east. Continuing to the right, you reach the First Court of the Seraglio near the stump of the famous janissary tree. The best pictures[3] and plans of the kiosk are to be found in Gurlitt's great work, *Die Baukunst Konstantinopels*. Plate 12a gives a section and

---

[1] See White, *Three Years in Constantinople*, vol. i, p. 289.

[2] *Three Years in Constantinople*, vol. iii, p. 314.

[3] H. G. Dwight gives a good photograph of a beautiful wall fountain in *Constantinople Old and New* (New York, 1915), p. 357.

plan, while 12*b*, 12*c*, and 12*d* give views both inside and outside. It will be seen after inspecting 12*a* that the plan of the kiosk is a Greek cross, and that the re-entering angles carry a dome with pendentives. In each of the re-entering angles there is a room surmounted by a dome, and the north arm ends with a hexagonal apse. Outside runs a fine portico the entire length of the building, supported by fourteen columns, and surmounted by a tiled architrave, having a stone cornice above with stelliform piercings. The front, or eastern, façade presents a single story, but the portico is some eight feet from the ground, being reached by a double central flight of steps. There are storerooms under the portico, entrance to which is gained directly from the front. At the back there are two stories, each with a double tier of windows.

The whole kiosk can be regarded as a unique exhibition of Turkish tiles of the first period, and, quite apart from its exhibits as a museum of ceramics, glass, etc., should be examined from that point of view before any other.

The Director of the Seraglio, Tahsin Chukru, made a special study of Turkish tiles, and referred me, in one of my conversations with him on the subject, to his article in the *Transactions of the Oriental Ceramic Society*.[1] I shall have occasion later to refer to it again when discussing certain rooms in the *harēm* and *selāmlik*, but here I shall confine my extract and remarks to the tiles in their bearing on the Chinili Kiosk.

The Turkish tile industry originated in the fifteenth century, reached its height of perfection during the sixteenth century, and died out in the first half of the eighteenth century. Constantinople and Brusa can illustrate the complete history from beginning to end, and a study and comparison of their mosques, *türbehs*, *madrasehs*, and kiosks is as interesting and instructive as it is pleasing and easy to accomplish. Turkish tiles can conveniently be divided into three periods, the first stretching from the beginning of the fifteenth century to the first half of the sixteenth century. The second period ends early in the eighteenth century, when it began to decline. After this the industry died out. An effort was made in 1725 to revive it, and the painted tiles produced at a new factory established

---

[1] 1934, pp. 48–61.

at Tekfur Serai constitute the third period. They cannot compare with those of the preceding period.

The Chinili Kiosk tiles belong to the first period, the forms of tiles and decoration originating in Brusa at the famous Green Mosque *Yeşil Cami* and neighbouring Green Türbeh of Muhammad I. The colours are green, turquoise, and dark blue; the shapes are square, rectangular, hexagonal, and triangular. The tile inscriptions are of two kinds: those in tile mosaic and those in square tiles. The lettering in both kinds is generally in white or yellow on a dark blue ground, and the ornamental designs in the intervals of the inscriptions are turquoise blue, golden yellow, and green, while the borders also introduce white, black, and dark blue. Tiles were used for both exterior and interior of buildings, and just as glass mosaic was used as an incrustation in stone, so earthenware tiles were set among stonework. Panels were also made of tiles combined with pottery.

Every variety of first-period tile is to be found in the Chinili Kiosk. Tahsin Chukru thus describes them:

> First we come to the tilework inscription placed above the doorway of the year A.H. 877 (A.D. 1473); the tile panel bearing the date is in mosaic. On the two sides of the archway of the door the legend "Tévekkeltu-alallah" ("Thy reliance on Allah") is expressed by a geometrical design formed of square tiles in turquoise light blue and white. There are star designs amongst the dark and light blue and white tiles decorating the surfaces above the doorway and the inscription. The word 'Allah' is found also amongst the flowers of the tilework mosaic border obliquely enclosing the arcade. On either side of the façade there are similar decorations. The rooms of the kiosk are likewise decorated with the most delightful ornamentation, consisting of hexagonal, square, triangular, and rectangular tiles in dark and light blue and white. The other faces of the building are also decorated with tiles.

Further examples of the first period of Turkish tiling may be seen at the Chekirge mosque at Brusa (near the baths to be described in a later chapter), the Chinili mosque at Isnik, and the mosque of the Conqueror, the *türbeh* of Mehemed Pasha, the mosque of Selim and its *türbehs*, the *madraseh* of Hasseky, and the *türbeh* of Prince Mehemed, son of Suleiman, at Constantinople.

Tiles of the second period will be referred to in the *Ḥarēm* and

Selāmlik chapters. To conclude this present chapter there remains but to speak of the Gülhane Kiosk, situated on the Marmora side of the Seraglio, outside the southern corner of the wall of the Second Court near the kitchens. It has, or rather had (since it has now been pulled down), no pretensions to beauty, and is famous only on account of its being the scene of the *Hatti Sherif*, the great scheme of national reform issued in 1839 by Abd ul-Mejid. The document declared that the decline of the Empire during the preceding 150 years was due to disregard of justice and law; that hence, relying on the assistance of the Almighty and the intercessions of the Prophet, the Sultan sought by new institutions to bestow upon his provinces the benefits of a good administration. It guaranteed security of life, honour, and property to all, a uniform and just system of taxation, and uniformity in conscription and military service. It is to be regretted that national inertia and prejudice prevented full advantage being taken of such a noble and honest effort to resurrect the glorious days of Suleiman the Magnificent.[1]

The name of the kiosk (*gül* means rose) was due to the fact that in former days rose sweetmeats were prepared here, under the personal supervision of the Chief Confectioner, for use in the *harēm*.

---

[1] For further details I may refer readers to Grosvenor, *Constantinople*, pp. 712–713, from whose pages the above account has been taken, to White, *Three Years in Constantinople*, vol. i, pp. 110–113, and Sir H. Luke, *The Making of Modern Turkey* (London, 1936), p. 49 *et seq.*

CHAPTER IV

THE FIRST COURT

On the summit of Seraglio Hill, in the centre of the land-wall, stands the Imperial Gate, *Bab-i-Humayun*, giving direct access to the First Court, often known to Europeans as the Court of the Janissaries. The Imperial Gate is a massive triumphal arch of gleaming white marble, having its outer and inner gates some fifteen yards apart. Originally it was a two-storied structure with two rows of windows stretching across the complete façade; to-day there is but a parapet of pierced marble, exactly similar to that built round the pool in the Fourth Court and the courtyard of the Princes' *Kafes*, or Cage. In Grelot's time the upper story was surmounted by "Four little round Towers which are like so many small round Chimneys; they are only for Ornament, and to show that such a Gate gives entrance into a Royal Pallace."[1] In the following century the number was reduced to two,[2] while in Fossati's drawing (to which I shall refer again) they have entirely disappeared.

On each side of the double-arched portal are mitred niches, where the heads of important officials were exposed. Over the inner arch are the builder's seal and a gilded inscription attributed to Muhammad II, "God shall make eternal the glory of its builder; God shall strengthen his work; God shall support his foundations."

A guard of *kapici*, or gatekeepers, some fifty strong, was on duty during the day, being reinforced at night by janissaries, "in little movable wooden houses on wheels, who are watchmen and notice everything so that they can awaken those who are within and give any warning that may be needed."[3]

The First Court was of a semi-public nature, and entry was refused to nobody, whatever his rank or creed. Owing possibly to the contour of the hill and the great church of St Irene, the shape of the

[1] *Relation nouvelle*, p. 80 of the English edition.
[2] See d'Ohsson's engraving.
[3] Bon, p. 60.

court is irregular, and after passing through the Imperial Gate one bears considerably to the left in order to reach the centre of the court.

To the right were the infirmary, the Imperial bakery, and the waterworks; to the left the great wood-yard, the church of St Irene,[1] the Imperial mint, the Privy Treasury, the Palace storehouse, and two pavilions for members of the Outer Service. In the middle, to the left, stood a horse fountain and the famous janissary tree, while near the *Ortakapi* were two 'example stones,' on which the heads of the decapitated were sometimes exposed, and the Fountain of Execution, in which the Chief Executioner and his assistant washed their bloodstained hands.

One rule strongly enforced was that of silence. Nearly all travellers have remarked on the extraordinary silence that was maintained in the different courts with increasing degrees of intensity, until in the Third Court it was like 'the silence of the tomb.' Writing in 1551, Nicolay says:

> And notwithstanding the number of the people coming together from all partes is very great, yet suche silence is kept, that yee could scarce say that the standers by did either spit or cough.[2]

And about 1700 we read in Tournefort:

> Anybody may enter the first Court of the Seraglio ... but everything is so still, the Motion of a Fly might be heard in a manner: and if any one should presume to raise his voice ever so little, or shew the least want of Respect to the Mansion-place of their Emperor he would instantly have the Bastinado by the Officers that go the rounds; nay, the very Horses seem to know where they are, and no doubt they are taught to tread softer than in the streets.[3]

The famous plane-tree under which the janissaries so often overturned their 'kettles' as a sign of revolt, and from the branches of which so many have hung, is now reduced to a mere stump—in reality part of the great hollow trunk that stood here only a few years ago—resting

---

[1] For a detailed and comprehensive account of this most interesting church (which has never been converted into a mosque) see van Millingen, *Byzantine Churches in Constantinople* (London, 1912), chapter iv.

[2] *Quatre premiers livres*, p. 51 *verso* of the English and p. 66 of the French edition.

[3] *Voyage into the Levant* (London, 1741), vol. ii, p. 183.

on a stone support. In 1895 it was a fine tree with enormous spreading branches, as the photograph in Grosvenor's *Constantinople*[1] will show.

The court was unpaved save for cobbled paths leading to the various gates and entrances of the different buildings. Important people, such as ambassadors and certain members of the Inner Service, could enter the court on horseback, but all had to dismount outside the *Ortakapi*.

Before describing Melling's drawing I might quote once again from Bon (1604-7):

> What makes this Seraglio dignified and sedate is the order of its arrangement—a fact that cannot be passed over in silence. In the first place there is the entrance by a most spacious and noble gate with a very roomy colonnade underneath, having a guard of about 50 men provided with their proper arms—namely, arquebuses, bows and arrows, and a good supply of scimitars. Having passed through this gate, by which the Pashas and other persons of consequence may enter on horseback, one reaches a large piazza where the courtyard is a quarter of an Italian mile in length and about the same in width, with a single colonnade on the left hand made to protect the horses and servants in wet weather. On the right of the entrance to this great courtyard is the hospital, or infirmary which serves the whole Seraglio, being provided with all essentials; it is in charge of a eunuch, with various officials all allotted to the service of the patients. Opposite, on the left side, is a very large place where timber, carts, and other articles of manual labour are kept for the use and service of the Seraglio. Above it is a great hall where there is a store of ancient arms such as helmets, coats-of-mail, *zacchi* [gauntlets (?)], arquebuses, and javelins, which are used in arming the janissaries, the corporation of the arsenal, and other residents for meeting the King or Pasha-general [Grand Vizir] when they make their solemn entry into the city of Constantinople.[2]

Now in Melling's drawing of the First Court, reproduced opposite p. 86, we are right *inside* the court, and consequently see neither the Imperial Gate, nor the infirmary, nor the wood-yard. They all appear, however, in Fossati's painting[3] (in two sheets) made about 1852, and reproduced by Dr Miller in her *Beyond the Sublime Porte*,[4]

[1] P. 716.   [2] P. 61.
[3] G. Fossati, *Aya Sofia* (Constantinople, 1852), oblong folio. Some editions are coloured.
[4] P. 166.

where an excellent account of the various buildings will be found together with a reconstructed plan.[1]

Melling gives us a picture of the everyday life of the court, and has introduced figures in such a way as to illustrate the different services, customs, and costumes connected with the Seraglio. For instance, several groups of servants attending some important personages on horseback will be noticed. It is, then, the hour when Ministers of State are received in audience, the degree of their rank being shown by the number of their retinue. On reaching the *Ortakapi* they dismount, and the servants tend the horse and keep it perfectly quiet while their master proceeds to the Divan to transact his business. In the centre foreground is a sick man in a litter being taken to the infirmary, to which the men are proceeding in a direct line. Thévenot (1687) says the sick are borne "in a little close Chariot, drawn by two men; when they see that Chariot, every one steps aside to make way for it, even the *Grand Signior*, if he happen'd to meet it would do so."[2] The infirmary was under the jurisdiction of the Chief White Eunuch, and all the porters, orderlies, litter-bearers, etc., were also white eunuchs. It was used exclusively by the pages of the Palace School, the hospital on the Marmora being for the members of the Outer Service.

The organization and general running of the infirmary appear to have been excellent, and J.-B. Tavernier tells us how the pages try to get in on some pretext or other:

> They continue there for the space of ten or twelve daies, and are diverted, according to their mode, with a wretched kind of vocal and instrumental Musick, which begins betimes in the morning, and holds on till night. The permission they have there to drink wine, which they never have elsewhere, is a greater inducement for their coming in thither, than the Musick.[3]

But apart from this the smuggling in of skins of wine was carried on to a large extent, and was a means of making the eunuchs lax in their duties, so that certain vicious practices, impossible in the Seraglio proper, could here be indulged in with impunity.

[1] Facing p. 160. [2] *Travels into the Levant*, pp. 23–24.
[3] *A New Relation of the Inner-Part of the Grand Seignor's Seraglio* (London, 1677), p. 22.

Looking again at Melling's drawing, we see two janissaries coming from the direction of the infirmary bearing on their shoulders a pole from which is suspended the 'kettle,' to which I shall return later. In front of them walks a non-commissioned officer carrying the ladle.

Various Seraglio servants will be noticed: one walking by the wall of the Imperial bakery with a tray of covered dishes (presumably hot rolls for the infirmary) on his head, while others wearing conical felt hats are engaged in more menial tasks.

As we have already seen in chapter iii (p. 66), the Imperial mill and bakery was situated on the Marmora near the *Değirmen Kapi*, or Mill Gate, and was in active use until in 1616 Ahmed I built a new bakery in the First Court. So high a standard of bread was required that even in times of shortage no excuse was taken if the pure whiteness of the Royal bread was affected in the smallest degree. Bon tells us that the bread was of several kinds: very white for the King, the Sultanas, the Pashas, and other grandees, moderately good for the middle folk, and black for the *ajem-oghlans*. "For the Royal taste," he continues,

and that of the Sultanas Brusa flour is used, extracted from corn grown in the Province of Bithynia in the patrimonial territory of the Ottoman Empire. The annual production is from seven to eight thousand *clilò* [kilos], which is possibly about three thousand Venetian *stara*, the corn yielding splendid flour by the mills that are in that city of perfect quality. As for the others, all the corn comes from Greece, where are the patrimonial estates of the said Emperor, the grain of which is always consumed by the army, biscuits being made from it at Negroponte, and some is also sold to the Ragusans, who come to lade it furnished with the necessary bills [*comandamento in mano*]. Of this corn thirty-six to forty thousand *clilò*, about fifteen thousand *stara*, comes to Constantinople every year and is used by the Seraglio. No surprise is shown at the Porte's consuming such a large quantity, for apart from the ordinary service, all the married Sultanas, all the Pashas, all the grandees, and many more besides have their daily allowance of bread from the *Chilier*, which is the store, or else from the King's supply—thus the Sultanas would receive twenty, the Pashas ten, the *mufti* eight, and so on, proportionally down to one per head as determined at the will of the Grand Vizir, each apportioned share being left with the head of the store. Each loaf is as big as a good cake, tender and spongy.[1]

[1] P. 96.

Overleaf:
THE FIRST COURT OF THE SERAGLIO
From an engraving by A.-I. Melling, *Voyage Pittoresque de Constantinople* (Paris, 1819)

THE FIRST COURT OF THE SERAGLIO, SHOWING THE CHURCH OF ST IRENE ON THE LEFT AND THE ORTAKAPI
IN THE MIDDLE DISTANCE

On the opposite side of the court are the cupolas of the mint, which (apart from St Irene, not shown in the reproduction opposite p. 86) is the only building of the First Court still standing. It was transferred from its earlier site on the Third Hill some time prior to 1695. The mint included the Pavilion of Goldsmiths and Gem-setters, in which all the elaborate ornamentation used in the decoration of the rooms in the *ḥarēm* and the *selāmlik* was made, as well as the *kadins'* jewellery. Among the archives of the Seraglio Tahsin Chukru, the Director, recently discovered a book containing a list of the craftsmen employed in 1536, together with their rates of pay. They number 580 in all, and include the following:

58 goldsmiths	3 workers in amber
4 makers of silver thread	14 carvers
9 engravers	18 swordsmiths
5 gold chasers	18 cutlers
8 shield-makers	19 coppersmiths
22 makers of damascened sabres	16 armourers
4 silk weavers	11 makers of musical
16 seamsters	instruments
12 potters or tile-makers	15 upholsterers
22 relief decorators	3 glovers

Specimens of their work can be seen not only in the Seraglio Museum, but in the incrustation and inlay work in the passages, walls, cupboards, sofas, ceilings, and the floors of rooms in both the *ḥarēm* and the *selāmlik*.

There still remain the Palace waterworks to be discussed. They are situated in the far right-hand corner of the court, hidden away behind a high wall. Access is gained from the Second Court through a small door near the corner where the kitchen buildings commence. The door leads to a slope under the main wall, at the bottom of which are two wells, one round and the other oblong. Both are connected with the main well, which lies some fifty paces farther on. The work is that of the great Sinan, and so apparently was built at the same time as the kitchens. The well is still in active use, being supplemented by a dynamo, the whole now enclosed by a new brick building. One passes through the power-house, and in a chamber beyond is the well itself, having a diameter of some twelve or fourteen feet.

It is a solidly constructed well. A narrow iron bridge runs across the surface, and electric lights placed at intervals on the walls enable one to get a good view of this interesting specimen of sixteenth-century domestic architecture.

As mentioned at the beginning of this chapter, the First Court was often known as the Court of the Janissaries, and not without good reason, for throughout its bloody history this corps had been inseparably linked with the Seraglio.

It is advisable, then, to get some idea of the origin and development of this first Turkish standing army, especially when most of the long-accepted traditions have been found to crumple up and wither before the light of recent research. But so attractive is the old picturesque legend to account for both the origin, and the name, and the dress of the corps that it may well be related here before we discard it for good.

According to the traditional story Orkhan (1326–59), having selected a number of Christian youths from those taken captive, sent them to be blessed by Haji Bektash, the celebrated dervish, whom they found living near Amasia. Standing in front of their ranks, he stretched the sleeve of his gown over the head of the foremost soldier, and delivered his blessing in these words:

"Let them be called janissaries [*yeni cheri*, or new soldiers]! May their countenances be ever bright, their hand ever victorious, their sword keen! May their spears always hang over the heads of their enemies! And wheresoever they go may they return with a *white face*!"

And as the holy man raised his hand in blessing the thick sleeve of his robe hung down in a double fold, and in commemoration of the benediction a cloth flap modelled on the sleeve was henceforth attached to the hat of the janissaries. Whatever may have been its true origin, the headdress is certainly curious, as a glance at the plate opposite p. 94 shows.

Now there are several points about this legend which should be noted. Firstly, it dates from only the second half of the sixteenth century—that is to say, two centuries later than the event related. Secondly, it was quite arbitrary to which Sultan to attribute the event. Although Orkhan is the favourite, Osman I, before him, and Murad I and Murad II, after him, have also been credited with the institution of the janissaries. It is only natural to conclude that the corps took considerable time to become properly organized, and that each succeeding Sultan improved or re-formed it as he thought fit.

The question has, however, been fully dealt with by the late F. W. Hasluck,[1] who shows that, so far from dating back to Orkhan or even Murad II, the organization of the system must be referred to a date subsequent to 1472.

Briefly the evidence leading to this conclusion is as follows. The distinctive feature of the janissary system is the recruitment of the corps from a levy of the Christian children of the Empire, who were forcibly converted and specially trained for their profession. Now, although seventeenth-century writers, such as Evliyá, refer to it, there is no mention whatever of this systematic collecting of Christian children in the fourteenth- and fifteenth-century accounts of the janissaries by such noted and observant travellers as Ibn Batuta, Schiltberger, and Bertrandon de la Brocquière. It would appear, therefore, that, following the Muhammadan law by which royalty had the right to one fifth of the prisoners and booty captured in battle, the earlier Sultans maintained a kind of bodyguard or *corps d'élite* formed of bought or captured slaves, who would naturally be mainly Christians.

This force was reorganized after Orkhan's time, and the prisoners who composed it were induced to become Muhammadans and undergo a thorough military training. The members of this corps are called by Chalcondyles and Ducas, the Byzantine historians of the fifteenth century, πόρτα or θύρα, inferring that they stood at the Sultan's gate.[2] Later they were known as Slaves of the Gate. That the levy of Christian children was not yet (fifteenth century) systematized seems obvious, or surely the Greek historians would have mentioned it; and as late as 1472 another historian, Cippico, still describes the janissaries as recruited largely from the Sultan's fifth of the prisoners of war. Turning to the connexion of Haji Bektash with the janissaries, we gather that he was originally only a tribal saint subsequently

---

[1] *Christianity and Islam under the Sultans* (Oxford, 1929), vol. ii, pp. 483–493.
[2] Hasluck suggests that this association with the gate, through *janua*, aided in the formation of the Western word 'janissary.'

'captured' and adopted by the Hurufi sect, who foisted their own doctrines as those of Haji Bektash on the latter's disciples. As the sect grew in power this ex-tribal saint became more and more respected, and numerous legends began to attach themselves to him. The sect was soon in a position to 'father' the entire janissary organization, and Haji Bektash was adopted as their patron, the connexion being officially recognized from 1591 onward. It was just prior to this that the story of the saint's blessing of the corps first made its appearance. Not only is it not universally accepted, but it is emphatically denied by contemporary historians, one of whom was from Bektash's own country. In view of the evidence, then, we must regard the canonized legend of Haji Bektash, Orkhan, and the first janissaries as purely fictitious. At the same time that in no way interferes with the subsequent history of the corps, its customs and general organization.

The recruits were obtained from all conquered countries, but mainly from Albania, Bosnia, and Bulgaria. Their education and training followed immediately, the majority becoming *ajem-oghlans* and doing hard manual labour to fit them for every type of physical endurance that might be necessary later on. The selected few were attached to the Palace School, and went through a complete system of education. Subsequently they would be put in command of some frontier garrison, and moved about from province to province as occasion demanded.

The laws were at first most strict, enforcing implicit obedience, absolute concord among the corps, abstinence from all forms of luxury, forbidding marriage or domestic ties of any kind, and demanding observance of all religious laws of Haji Bektash. Members of the corps were not to trade in any way, were to observe certain rules as to their toilet and dress, were not to leave their barracks, were to have no pay in peace-time, and were to receive arms only in time of war. Their rations were quite inadequate, and soon led to the breaking of some of the regulations. As time went on all kinds of abuses occurred, as we shall shortly see. In 1551 Nicolay describes the janissary as being armed with a "scymitar, and a dagger with a little hatchet hanging at his girdle, using also long harquebusses which they can handle very well." Janissaries were not allowed to wear beards, but "to the intent they should seem the more cruel and furious in the aspect of their faces they let their mustachioes grow very long gross and thick." Their dress consisted of a dark blue cloth coat, while among the older members the Bektash headdress was enriched by an enormous plume of bird-of-paradise feathers, which fell in a curve down the back nearly to the knees. Nicolay gives a good drawing of this, as well as of the *Agha* (or Chief Commander) of Janissaries, with his embroidered under-coat, long hanging sleeves, and big turban. The colour of the boots at once proclaimed the rank of the wearer—red, yellow, and black in descending order being the colours worn.

The names of the officers were all connected with the culinary art. Thus the *Agha* was known as the *Chorbaji-bashi*, or Head Soup-distributor; then came the *Asçi-bashi*, or Head Cook, followed by the *Sakka-bashi*, or Head Water-carrier. Their standard was emblazoned with a huge *kazan* ('kettle' or cauldron), which merits some detailed consideration. It is hard to say exactly when these 'kettles' began to play such an important part in the history of the corps. It seems clear, however, that it was not until some considerable time after its foundation. At first the connexion was simply one of reverence; it was only later on when the corps began to get out of hand that the 'kettles' became an object of terror and the sign of rebellion and bloodshed. In actual fact the 'kettles' were mess cauldrons covered with a lid used for the distribution of the food.

According to tradition the first 'kettles' issued were modelled on those in daily use by the Bektashi dervishes, and were presented by Muhammad II to the different *odas*[1] previous to the attack on Constantinople (1453). Before that time each man had to provide his own rations, but henceforth each *oda* was to have its own mess officer to procure supplies of bread, salt, rice, and suet as daily rations. Hence the oath of fidelity with bread and salt. Each *oda* had a large regimental copper, while the ordinary-sized 'kettles' were distributed in the proportion of one to every twenty janissaries. Although, as seen

[1] The word *oda* literally means 'room' or 'chamber,' and by extension 'lodging,' 'house' (in the way the word is used in English public schools). Thus in the Seraglio it denoted a chamber of pages or *ḥarēm* recruits, while in a military sense it became the barracks, and finally the unit of a corps (*ocak*, formerly *ojaq*, 'hearth'). Closely allied is the word *orta*, 'centre,' 'middle,' and so a battalion of an *ocak*.

in Melling's drawing (p. 86), the large spoon was carried separately by a non-commissioned officer, each man wore his own spoon for the ordinary 'kettles' in a brass socket sewn into the front of his cap.

And so the 'kettles' came by degrees to be symbols of military pride, and, like our drums, were piled in the front of the tent of the *Agha* when the janissaries were in camp. On the march the 'kettles' were carried by recruits in relays, and their loss during a battle was a lasting disgrace to the *oda* of the *ocak*. The large regimental copper was borne by older men, and its loss was considered so grave that only some exploit of great daring could efface the stain. In times of peace the janissaries assembled in the Second Court after midday prayer every Friday to receive their due allowance of *pilaf*. The Sultan waited in the kiosk between the Divan and the Gate of Felicity, and watched the proceedings with considerable anxiety. If the 'kettle'-bearers fetched the rice from the kitchens at the accustomed signal all was well, but if they stayed in the ranks and turned the 'kettles' upside-down it was a symbol of dissatisfaction and possibly revolution. The immediate action of the Sultan depended upon the justness of the complaints and the personal ability of the particular Sultan to check insubordination and revolt. The results were often terrible and swift; the *bostanji* would be summoned, the ringleaders and 'kettle'-bearers seized, and a pile of heads would soon appear outside the *Ortakapi*.

On the other hand, from the seventeenth century onward the power of the janissaries became tremendous, and not less than six Sultans were either dethroned or murdered through their agency. But let us trace briefly how this state of affairs was brought about. The original corps, being composed of Christian captives, soon realized that the Sultan was their new father, and that everything they had, were, or could ever become was entirely in his hands. So long, therefore, as he led them into battle and retained the warlike spirit of the early Sultans the military *moral* was maintained and the corps became the finest standing army in Europe. But when the Sultans exchanged the battlefield for the *ḥarēm* regulations became lax, the original spirit of the corps was neglected, and all kinds of abuses soon turned this fine body of men into the scourge and bane of the Ottoman Empire. Until the time of Murad III (1574) the number never exceeded 20,000 all told, but irregularities started in the middle of his reign, and by the end of the century the janissaries totalled over 48,000. This was due to several factors, all detrimental to the corps. No longer were the *odas* recruited only by the Christians, but by true Ottomans who had personal ties with the people, and no more did they look upon the Sultan as their father. Long intervals of peace had stained the celibate janissaries with all kinds of vices and evil practices, and as soon as they felt their power growing they began to marry, and so became more independent than ever. If money or food was short a fire could easily be started, when wholesale looting would naturally follow. It is estimated that during the reign of Ahmed III (1703–30) no less than 140 such fires occurred. The married janissaries were allowed to live out of barracks, and soon not only their children, but friends and relations, became enrolled as members of the corps. Thus in time the percentage of utterly useless men and downright scoundrels was very considerable, and early in the nineteenth century the number on the pay-roll had reached the enormous figure of over 130,000. The efforts of Selim III to organize a new force ended in failure, and although Bairakdar Pasha was more successful in 1806 the new troops were again suppressed. It remained for Mahmud II (1808–39) to crush the corps once and for all. His was no sudden and unpremeditated step, but was the culmination of no less than sixteen years' careful and studied preparation.

Mahmud had already witnessed the appalling horrors of a janissary revolt, he had seen the city covered with a sheet of fire, he had heard the cries of women and children and the groans of the dying. This experience did not stop the Sultan from planning innovations, as the janissaries hoped and believed; on the contrary, it engendered in his soul the firm determination to eradicate the entire corps for ever, preparing the way by every means possible. Honours and bribes were bestowed in certain quarters, while others who proved troublesome soon found their way to the Bosphorus never to appear again. The power of distant Pashas was undermined, and the janissaries were thus deprived of the help of discontented provincial allies. The new corps of regular soldiers, *eshkenji*, was increasing all the time, and many of the janissary officers had been gained over: thus mutual distrust arose in the ranks of the *odas*. By 1826 Mahmud was ready. The rising had been carefully provoked by the Government, and the janissaries marched to the Et-meidan Square and reversed their 'kettles' in the usual manner to signify a revolt. Finding that their *Agha* had deserted to the Government, they attacked his Palace and abused what remained of his *ḥarēm*. Thence they went to the Porte, and burned the archives and destroyed everything they could lay hands on. But their end was in sight. The seashore was guarded, the Seraglio was full of armed *bostanji*, and the new army was pouring into the city.

The Prophet's sacred Standard was unfurled, and a curse and sentence of eternal dissolution on the janissaries was pronounced. A *fetva* was obtained from the Sheikh-ul-Islām, giving a spiritual sanction to the proceedings, and the attack commenced. The work of the new army was made easy by the corps' returning to the Et-meidan Square, and every avenue leading to it was soon occupied by the enemy. After a moment of uncertainty the guns did their work, and the grapeshot played terrible havoc in the crowded, narrow streets. Those who escaped the artillery and the sword were burned in their barracks. But even then Mahmud was not satisfied, and men who had hidden in their homes or escaped out of the city were hunted down and drowned in the Bosphorus. Altogether it is estimated that over 25,000 men perished, and the janissaries were no more.

Before we leave the First Court behind us let us examine in detail the engraving by Melling which is reproduced opposite. This engraving shows a portion of the great procession making its way, on the feast of *Baïrām*, from the First Court of the Seraglio towards one of the outside mosques—Sancta Sophia or Ahmed. It is represented as just issuing from the *Bab-i-Humayun*, or Imperial Gate, and continuing past the beautiful fountain of Ahmed III towards the square of Et-meidan, whence entrance to either of the two above-mentioned mosques would be obtained.

The Imperial Gate is shown before the removal of its upper story, and although the perspective tends to minimize the size of the main entrance, a general idea of Imperial solidity and consequence is undoubtedly conveyed.

To the right the wall stretches away towards the Marmora, where it meets the sea-walls near the *Akhor Kapi*, or Gate of the Stables. The conical tops on two of the towers have long disappeared, but otherwise the wall remains the same to-day, as does also the fountain of Ahmed III opposite.

On inspection of the main subject of the engraving it will be noticed that the artist has cleverly taken several representative figures out of the procession and placed them in the foreground in order that their costumes can be more easily studied.

Beginning on the extreme left under the tree, we notice a Pasha on horseback accompanied by his servants, some of whom clear the way in front, while the rest follow closely behind.

In front of his horse, in the foreground, is an officer of the janissaries of the rank of *Segban-bashi*, next below that of *Agha*. His ceremonial dress includes a jacket with upturned epaulettes of a curious pointed design. To his right is a prancing horse on which fine trappings and shovel stirrups can be seen. It is being restrained by a *baltajiler*, or halberdier of the Outer Service, a unit to be discussed in the chapter on the Second Court.

The curious pendant hat will be noticed, and enables members of the corps to be picked out in different parts of the procession. They acted as a bodyguard, among their other duties, and walked by the side of the horses or carriages of those they were guarding. They usually carried halberds, but in the present engraving this particular weapon is seen in the hands of the *peiks*, whose duty it was to run in front of the Sultan and go on missions whenever necessary. These *peiks* formed a branch of the halberdiers, and their costume is especially interesting as it was taken over *in toto* from the Byzantine Court.

Melling has placed one almost in the middle foreground of his picture. His tall truncated conical hat surmounted by a triple plume differs considerably from the pointed hat worn by the man standing next him on his immediate right. This latter is also a *baltajiler*, but belongs to that section known as *Zülüfli*.

To the right of the couple stand two janissaries, so arranged that the curious headdress, already discussed, can be closely studied. It will be noticed that these janissaries line the route of the procession.

To the right of the two janissaries stands a *kapici*, wearing an enormous headdress of white feathers. Besides being doorkeepers the *kapici* accompanied the Sultan in times of war and acted as guards of his tent.

In the main body of the procession Selim III will be noticed surrounded by a white feathery mass, which is merely the headdress of numerous *kapici*.

In front of the Sultan rides the Grand Vizir, who is preceded by other important officials. Immediately behind is the Sword-bearer, or *Silihdar*, and behind him again is the Chief Black Eunuch, or *Kislar Agha*.

Other pages of high rank, such as the *Chokadar*, or Bearer of the Royal Robes, and the *Sharabdar*, or Cupbearer, do not appear in the engraving, but would be somewhere behind in the First Court.

For purposes of comparison mention might be made of two coloured engravings of "le Cortège du Sultan" by Melling, to be found in J. M. Tancoigne, *Voyage à Smyrne, dans l'archipel et l'île de Candie en 1811–14.*[1]

[1] Paris, 1817.

CHAPTER V

THE SECOND COURT, OR COURT OF
THE DIVAN

So far all we have seen has been of a semi-public nature, because of the rigid enforcement of certain rules to which attention was drawn in the last chapter. By the officials of the Inner Service the First Court was never regarded as part of the Palace proper, and consequently with them the numbering of the courts began at the gate which led into the Court of the Divan, and not at the Imperial Gate. But, as we shall shortly see, there were many other much more important rules and regulations made to leave no shadow of doubt in the minds of all concerned that the *Ortakapi* was the threshold of sovereign majesty, and as such must be approached with due reverence and humility.

The Court of the Divan is separated from the Outer Palace by a strongly built wall known as the Inner Wall, in the middle of which stands the *Ortakapi*, or Central Gate. This gate at once attracts attention by its curiously medieval appearance, and kindles a persistent desire to know more of its history and significance.

Although it is impossible to say for certain when it was built, there is good reason to believe that it represents one of the few portions of the original palace as built by Muhammad II. For if we look at the woodcut at p. cclvii of Hartmann Schedel's *Nuremberg Chronicle*[1] we can at once recognize the *Ortakapi* as it is to-day. Certainly renovations have occurred from time to time. One of the present iron doors is dated A.H. 931—*i.e.*, A.D. 1524-25—but in structure and design, as well as in position, the two are identical. Two stoutly built octagonal towers pierced with loopholes and capped with conical tops like candle-snuffers flank a gatehouse surmounted by a battlement. The merlons have sloping tops decorated with a small ornament at each end, and conceal a walk, reached by a flight of

[1] 1493.

stone steps behind each tower, broad enough to hold cannon in time of need. There was a strong guard of fifty gatekeepers (*kapici*), who were constantly on duty within and without the gate. If we can rely on the evidence of travellers and historians, this number remained unchanged for at least three centuries. Part of the duties of the guards was to see that absolute silence was maintained, and that the horses of those seeking audience were properly attended by the equerries or servants while their masters were within. For, as mentioned in the last chapter, even the few high functionaries of the Inner Service and visiting ambassadors who alone were allowed to ride into the First Court past the Imperial Gate had now to dismount and proceed on foot. The knowledge of the lengthy Court ceremonial that began as soon as a foot had crossed the threshold did not tend to mollify the air of mystery that already surrounded the *Ortakapi*, while the not infrequent sight of severed heads being carried out of the gate must have filled many with great concern, if not with abject terror.

But the gate was still a place of reception, and for this reason was formerly called *Bab-el-Selām*, or Gate of Salutation. So let us go in and inspect it for ourselves. As we pass under the outer porch, with seated recesses either side, we reach a double iron door heavily embossed, above which is the *tuğra*, or Imperial seal, while above that again and covering the full breadth of the door is the Islamic creed "La ilaha illa-llahu, Muḥammad rasūl allahi."[1] We at once find ourselves in a vestibule some fifteen feet long by twenty feet broad, the walls of which are adorned with arms of no particular value or interest.[2]

To-day the vestibule is merely used for the sale of postcards and as a depository for cameras and other forbidden tourist impedimenta. Dark and narrow passages lead off either side, communicating in both cases with various small rooms. Those to the right are twice as large as those to the left, which accounts for the fact that the canopy over the inner door, through which we shall soon emerge to the Court of the Divan, has its columns unequally divided, there being five on one side and only three on the other.

---

[1] "There is no God but God [Allah], Muhammad is the apostle of God."

[2] I understand that the rarer specimens that were here once are now in the arms museum housed in the church of St Irene, in the First Court.

The larger rooms to the right were used by the foreign ambassadors and other important visitors while awaiting audience. We are told that in order that they should be duly impressed with the might of the Sultan and his Court they were often kept waiting hours or even days on end. By the end of the eighteenth century, however, more respect was shown to envoys of foreign Powers, and (as we shall see later) an ambassador was conducted straight to the *Ortakapi*, where he was offered a seat in the vestibule, while the *Chaush-bashi* (Grand Master of Petitions) proceeded to the Divan to announce his arrival. At the same time the existence of a small wash-room and lavatory contributed to make a temporary residence here quite possible.

To the left are the guard-rooms and the *Cellât Odasi*, or Room of the Executioner. They are all very small, being, in fact, divisions of a single room. Below all these rooms are the dungeons into which the unfortunate people were thrust who had displeased the Sultan. From the small cells in one of the towers, where they were usually put in the first instance, they were removed to the dungeons, then into the cistern below, and finally to the Room of the Executioner.

If they were officials of high rank their heads were placed on a row of iron spikes which formerly extended above the outer gateway, slowly to blacken in the sun. If their rank was below that of Pasha the several heads were carried to the *Bab-i-Humayun*, or Imperial Gate, where, as we saw in the last chapter, they were exposed to the public gaze in the niches on either side of the main entrance. In either case a *yafta*, or conical-shaped scroll, was affixed on the adjoining wall stating in bold characters the name of the offender and the nature of his crime, "to be a warning to those who would be warned." There the *yafta* would remain, competing with the head to see which would stand up longer against the vicissitudes of the climate, unless a bereaved relative bribed the Chief Gatekeeper to remove it.

From this grim portal we pass on towards the Court of the Divan, and find ourselves standing under a canopy supported by ten pillars, eight in front and one either side. They are all of marble except one, which is of granite, and form the central part of a colonnade running practically round all four sides of the entire court. In describing the canopy about 1550 Pierre Gilles says, "the roof of it proudly glitters with gold, and is beautify'd with the most rich and lively colours of

Persian work."[1] Apparently it was kept in excellent order and continually repaired, for just a hundred years ago we find Miss Julia Pardoe still extolling its beauty:

> The roof itself is pointed, and crowned by a flashing crescent of gold; while underneath it is divided into a lattice work of gilt bars, traversing a ground of brightest blue, and looking like a sheet of turquoise. The elaborately tessellated pavement beneath, apparently intended to represent the reflection of the roof, is composed of curious stones, cemented together with some preparation, which, in its present state, appears as though liquid gold had been used to connect the different portions.[2]

But sad changes have been wrought since then, and to-day it presents a very effete appearance, and modern horrors of Turkish mural paintings disfigure the walls.

From our feet radiate four paths lined with box-hedges, cypresses, and plane-trees, stretching away to various parts of the court, which we shall soon inspect in detail. An air of quiet and repose pervades the court, and, judging by the early descriptions that have come down to us, the general aspect has changed but little during the centuries.

"One enters another courtyard," says Ottaviano Bon,

> a little smaller than the first but much more beautiful, owing to its variety of elegant fountains, avenues flanked by very tall cypresses, and the presence of certain stretches of lawn where the growing grass provides pasture for a number of gazelles which breed and are regarded with pleasure.[3]

The fountains have gone, save for a single ruin (No. 2 in the plan), and the gazelles have strayed, but the charm of the court remains, and the memories of the past still people it with a thousand ghosts hardly more silent than the members of the Inner Service themselves in the days of the mighty Suleiman.

The court, according to the most recent estimates,[4] measures about 459 feet in length and 361 feet in width at its widest point. As the name by which it was most usually known (the Court of the Divan) implies, the chief unit was the Hall of the Divan, where the Council of State met four times a week to dispense justice and give audience,

---

[1] *Antiquities of Constantinople*, p. 39.
[2] *The Beauties of the Bosphorus* (London, 1839), pp. 70–71.   [3] P. 61.
[4] Dr Miller, *Beyond the Sublime Porte*, p. 176.

and generally to attend to matters both civil and religious. Thus it united the two great divisions of the Government, the Ruling Institution and the Muslim Institution. We shall return to the Divan later in order to describe the building in more detail, and give some account of the ceremonies which took place in it.

Although the whole of the right-hand side of the court was taken up with the kitchens it was, above all else, a court of ceremonial, and throughout its long history has been the scene of great spectacular events—military, civil, and religious. The commencement of a war, the accession of a Sultan, the circumcision of a Prince, the marriage of a Princess, the feasts of *Baïrām*, the reception of a foreign ambassador—all provided an excuse for an elaborate and impressive 'show,' continuing in some cases for weeks on end.

Here, and here alone in the Seraglio, the Government had ascendancy over the *ḥarēm*—at any rate on the surface—and the pageantry of Court ceremonial, the brilliancy and variety of costumes, the flashing of jewels from turban and scimitar, the waving ostrich plumes and extravagant headdresses, the silent and almost grim background afforded by the double lines of janissaries, all contributed to attest the power of the Sultan and to impress the foreigner with the might and majesty of the Ottoman Empire.

As far as can be ascertained, both the site and the general architectural features of the Divan building have remained the same since the founding of the Palace. Situated on the left-hand side of the court and breaking the long colonnade by forming a large projecting right angle, the building consisted of a rectangular room divided by an arched partition into two nearly square chambers of equal size, each surmounted by a dome. That to the left, on the outside, was the Hall of the Divan (*Kubbealti*), while the other chamber was the registry (*Defterhane*), used mainly for the preparation, inspection, and storing of all Council documents. A third room, of slightly smaller dimensions, led off to the right, and was employed chiefly as a private office for the Grand Vizir. It was domed like the other two, and had its own exit to the portico outside. According to early descriptions the decoration of the rooms was truly magnificent, the use of gold and jewels being on a lavish scale.

In 1574 a fire did great damage to the Divan, and although the rebuilding by Murad III and subsequent repairs by Selim III and Mahmud II did much to restore it to its former condition, we can safely say that the decoration and richness of the hangings were not on the same scale as they had been in the time of Suleiman the Magnificent. So also has the Divan Tower, which raises its familiar pointed spire immediately behind the Divan itself, suffered by fire and been rebuilt and repaired several times. But here again its general shape, form, and position have been so well preserved that in the Nuremberg engraving of 1493 we can recognize it at once. A covered portico with a richly ornate roof and enclosed by handsome wrought-iron gates and railings lends a sense of importance and dignity to the whole.

To-day the interior decoration of the rooms is attractive by its simplicity—ordinary panelling with baroque ornamentation of Louis XV style at once proclaiming its date as about 1725-30. Sofas run round the rooms at the bottom of the panelling, which ceases at the commencement of the vaulting.

Signs of mural decoration still show on the pendentives. The principal point of interest in the Divan room, however, is the little grilled window opposite the door, and built high up above the Grand Vizir's seat. Although formerly flush with the wall, and consequently less noticeable, it now projects like an oriel window, and is decorated in the Louis XV style in accordance with the rest of the room.

It was the unfailing practice of the early Sultans to attend the Divan personally, but Suleiman discontinued it and built this little window, into which he could creep unobserved without the Council's knowing if he were there or not. In this way a certain check was kept on the proceedings, which always had to take place as if in the actual presence of the Sultan. At the same time the breaking of the old tradition was a mistake, and historians have traced the beginning of the decline of the Ottoman power to this very act. That the efficiency of the grilled window still holds I can personally guarantee, for it so chanced that as I sat in it one day looking down on the room below a guide entered with several tourists and immediately began to explain to them its history and purport. And as their eyes were all turned towards it they little guessed that it was occupied as of old, and at that very moment playing the part for which it was originally designed.

It is impossible to get a proper idea of the Divan unless we know what went on while the Council was in session. As we have noted, it met regularly four times a week, on Saturday, Sunday, Monday, and Tuesday, but from early in the eighteenth century only on Tuesdays. The reception of ambassadors was usually confined to Sundays or Tuesdays, on which occasions the ordinary business of the Court was reduced to a minimum. Moreover, a day was generally chosen to coincide with the janissaries' pay-day, an extra ceremony thus being provided to impress the foreigner.

Many accounts have come down to us,[1] and the sessions appear to have increased in length and ceremonial as time went on. In order to enable us to make comparison let us take the early seventeenth-century account of an ordinary session as given by the Venetian *Bailo* Ottaviano Bon, and contrast it with Melling's description of the reception of a foreign ambassador at the end of the eighteenth century, just before the Divan finally closed.

In reading these accounts, especially that of Melling, it should be remembered that the Public Divan was held in the building (No. 23) under—or, rather, closely adjoining—the Divan Tower (No. 22), while the audiences to which ambassadors were invited were held in the *Arzodasi*, usually called the Throne Room, or Chamber of Presentation (No. 96), in the Third Court, just behind the Gate of Felicity, or *Bab-i-Sa'adet*. But as some of the preliminary ceremonies preceding an audience took place in the Public Divan and then others in front of the Gate of Felicity in the Second Court, it will be

---

[1] The most detailed accounts are those of von Hammer, *Staatsverwaltung* (Vienna, 1815), pp. 412–436; d'Ohsson, *Tableau général*, vol. ii, pp. 211–232; and Melling, *Voyage pittoresque*, No. 9 in the volume of text, No. 13 in the volume of plates; while for the sixteenth century only we can turn to J. W. Zinkeisen, *Geschichte des osmanischen Reiches in Europa* (Hamburg and Gotha, 1840–63), vol. iii, pp. 117–125. Many of the Venetian *Bailos* have left interesting accounts. See, for example, B. Navagero (1553), Trevisano (1554), and C. Garzoni (1573)—all in E. Alberi, *Relazione*, third series (3 vols.), Florence, 1840–63. Among many other contemporary accounts are G. A. Menavino, *Trattato* (Florence, 1584), p. 169; G. Postel, *De la Republique des Turcs* (Poitiers, 1560), p. 122; and Tavernier, *New Relation*, pp. 29–34. In English we have R. Knolles, *Generall Historie*, (London, 1603), p. 833; E. Barton, in Rosedale, *Queen Elizabeth and the Levant Company*, pp. 12–16; Bon, in Withers, *Grand Signor's Seraglio*, pp. 18–36; and Evliyá Efendí, *Narrative of Travels*, I, pp. 105–106.

understood that the whole ceremony involves both courts. For many years the Sultan never appeared in the Public Divan, only occasionally hiding himself in the oriel window, into which he crept to see how things were going, and to have a look at the ambassador without being seen himself.

A description of the Gate of Felicity and the quarters of the white eunuchs on either side will be given later in this chapter.

Both Bon's description and Melling's are important as being in all probability given from first-hand knowledge.

That part of Bon's account dealing with the Public Divan is as follows:

> The chamber called the Public Divan is an apartment built not many years ago, and is a square room about eight paces each side with a serving room leading off, and with another room situated in a corner on the right of the entrance, merely separated from the Divan by the *antæ* which give ingress to it. Not far from this door are two small wooden houses for the residence of the ministers, besides another a little farther off intended for business transactions. In this Divan, named, as already stated, Public because all kinds of people may congregate there publicly and indiscriminately to demand justice for the settlement of actions and lawsuits of whatever sort and kind, they assemble four days of their week, which finishes on Friday, that being their festival day: the assembly days are Saturday, Sunday, Monday, and Tuesday.
>
> [The members of the Divan are as follows:] the Grand Vizir and the other Pasha Vizirs; the two *cadì leschieri* [*Kaziaskers*] of Greece and Natolia, who are the heads of all the *cadì* of these two provinces (the *cadì* being men who profess the law and who govern by special grant as rulers in all the places and cities of the Emperor); the three *Defterdari*, who resemble the Roman quæstors, whose duty it is to collect the Royal rents and pay out all the money to the militia and other salaried people of the Porte; the *Nisangì*, who is the Grand Chancellor, and seals the orders and letters with the Royal seal; the secretaries of all the Pashas and other grandees, together with a vast number of notaries who always assist at the door of the Divan; the *Chiaus* Pasha, who is the Chief of the Ushers, not to say commanders, with a good number of the said *chiausi* under his command. This man carries a silver staff in his hand, and the others are used to summon and lead the deputations, as captains, as guards, and, in short, for any similar duties. Everybody assembles at daybreak.
>
> As soon as the Pashas have entered the chamber of the Divan they

seat themselves one after the other on a bench attached to the wall to the right facing the entrance, such places being below that of the Grand Vizir.

To the left on the same bench sit the two *cadì leschieri*—first that of Greece as being the most noble and esteemed province, and then that of Natolia. At the entrance to the right are seated the three *Defterdari*, who have behind them in the room mentioned above all the notaries, who sit on the ground, paper and pencil in hand, ready to write down what happens and whatever may be bidden them. Opposite these *Defterdari*—that is to say, in the other part of the room—upon a bench is seated the *Nisangì* Pasha, pen in hand, surrounded by his assistants, while in a body in the middle of the room stand those who are seeking audience.

Seated in this fashion, they start straight away with the assembled claimants, who being all without advocates and accustomed to handle their own cases personally, present themselves before the Grand Vizir, who, if he so wishes, can dispatch them all, because none of the other Pashas may speak, but wait to be interrogated by him or to be elected judges. This latter often happens, because after the Grand Vizir has grasped the essential part of the case he dissociates himself from it further; thus if it be a case of civil law he refers it to the *cadì leschieri*, if it be one connected with accounts to the *Defterdari*, if it be calumny, as often happens, to the *Nisangì*, and if it be commercial business about difficulties of probation to one of the other Pashas. In this way he frees himself of the cases one by one, reserving for himself exclusively only those which are of high and international importance.

Everybody is occupied with these matters till midday, when the hour for dining arrives, at which time one of the stewards appointed for this service receives orders from the Grand Vizir to serve the food. Whereupon all the people are immediately dismissed from the room, in which, when all is clear, the tables are arranged in the following order: one is set in front of the Grand Vizir and one, or possibly two, other Pashas; a similar arrangement is made for the other Pashas, who eat all together, and so also with the *cadì leschieri*, the *Defterdari*, and the *Nisangì*. Some of the servants then spread napkins over each person's knee to preserve his garments, and then bring them the meats, having handed to everybody a trencher [*mezolere*] with bread of all kinds— fresh and good in every case. The meats are brought in one by one and set down in the middle of the trencher in a large roomy dish, which they call a *tapsi*; and when one is finished they remove it and bring in another—the usual fare being mutton, guinea-fowl, pigeons, goose, lamb, chickens, soup made of rice, and vegetables prepared in various ways, and an assortment of pastries as dessert, the whole being eaten with great alacrity. All the other ministers of the Divan dine in front of this table, and anything they may need is brought in from the kitchen. The Pashas and other grandees are only given something to drink once, and that is sherbet served in large porcelain bowls placed on plates of the same material or of leather decorated with gold. The others either do not drink at all, or if they are thirsty have water brought them from the fountains near by. At the same time that the Divan is dining all the other ministers and officers also take their meal; they number usually not less than five hundred mouths, and are only given bread and *sorbà*—that is to say, soup. The repast being over, the Grand Vizir attends to public business, consulting with the other Pashas on what seems to him fit and proper, giving judgment on the whole, and preparing it to be delivered to the King, the usual custom being that out of the four days' Divan he goes in on two of them—Sundays and Tuesdays—to submit to his Majesty the report on all affairs dealt with, for which purpose the King grants audience.

He too, having dined, passes from his apartments into the Audience Chamber [*i.e.*, the *Arzodasi*, literally Chamber of Presentation] within. After taking his seat he orders to be summoned in turn, by the *Capigiler Chiaiasi* [*i.e.*, *Kapijilar-Kiayasi*, or Grand Chamberlain], who carries in his hand a long silver staff, first the *cadì leschieri*, who rise, and after bowing to the Grand Vizir advance—accompanied by the above-mentioned *Capigiler* and the *Chiaus* Pasha, who precede them with silver staffs in their hands—into the presence of the King, and render him an account of their offices to the extent required.

After dismissal they depart and return straight to their homes. Next the *Defterdari* are summoned, and, observing the same ceremony, inform the King what business they have carried out and take their leave, making way for the Pashas, who come last in file one after the other. On reaching the King's presence in the Chamber, with their hands crossed and heads bent, all looking alike, the Grand Vizir alone speaks and renders accounts as he sees fit, showing the petitions one by one; then, replacing them in a crimson satin valise, he lays it with great deference beside the King. In the event of no questioning (the other Pashas keeping silent) they depart and mount their horses outside the Second Gate previously mentioned, accompanied by their own followers and the rest, the most important first—and so they go to their own Serragli. And thus the Divan is concluded for that day, which might be about the hour of vespers.[1]

Bon then continues with a description of what happens "when ambassadors from crowned heads go to kiss the Emperor's robe" and

[1] Pp. 64–67.

THE ORTAKAPI, OR ENTRANCE TO THE SECOND COURT OF THE SERAGLIO

THE SECOND COURT OF THE SERAGLIO
From an engraving by A.-I. Melling, *Voyage Pittoresque de
Constantinople* (Paris, 1819)

THE HALL OF THE DIVAN, OR KUBBEALTI, SHOWING THE SULTAN'S GRILLED WINDOW

VIEW FROM THE HEAD NURSE'S BALCONY

[See p. 156]

the courtyard is crowded with Spahis, janissaries, and other troops, all richly attired, and forming a magnificent spectacle with their fine turbans, coloured plumes, and sparkling jewels.

But by way of contrast let us see how Melling describes the scene at the beginning of the nineteenth century. After telling us how the Ambassador is conducted with due ceremony to the *Ortakapi*, or Central Gate, in the Second Court of the Seraglio, and explaining the significance of the janissaries' meal of *pilaf*, he gives a short account of the preliminary ceremonies.

As soon as the Ambassador's presence is reported to the Grand Vizir the written request for an audience is conveyed to the Sultan with much ceremony. When the reply is received by the Grand Vizir he puts it to his mouth and forehead, breaks the seal, reads the reply, and puts the document in his breast. The Ambassador then dines in state.

Melling thus describes the reception which follows:

> The Ambassador, accompanied by the chief interpreter and ushers of the Porte, and followed by his *cortège*, is then led in the court under a gallery built between the Chamber of the Divan and the Gate of the Throne, Bab-el-Saadet. There the Grand Master of Ceremonies clothes him in a sable robe. The chief members of the *cortège* are given robes lined with ermine, of *kereke* and *caffetan*, being garments of the second order. Meanwhile the Grand Vizir has moved from the Chamber of the Divan to the Throne Room. Soon after the Ambassador is led to it with twelve or fifteen of the chief members of the Embassy; each person is assisted by two *Capidgi-Bachi*, chamberlains. Pages and white eunuchs are drawn up in ranks on both sides of the gallery which leads to the Throne Room. The grandeur of this room far from equals the importance of the ceremonies that are enacted in it; nevertheless it is sufficient, seeing that etiquette only allows very few people to approach his Highness's throne. It is placed along one side of the room: Oriental luxury has exhausted all its arts to make this throne more magnificent.
>
> It looks like a bed of antique design; gold and fine pearls enhance the splendour of the rich drapery with which it is covered; its columns are silver gilt. The Grand Seigneur takes his position there clad in a ceremonial robe that recalls the ancient costume of the Tartars; his turban is surmounted by an egret enriched with diamonds; he wears yellow boots, his feet being supported on a step. The Grand Vizir and Admiral-in-Chief occupy a position to the right of the throne; to the

left are the Chief Black Eunuch and Chief White Eunuch. All remain
standing, including the Ambassador, who approaching the throne
makes his address to his Highness. His words are repeated in the
Turkish language by the Chief Interpreter of the Porte, after which the
Grand Vizir, in the name of the Grand Seigneur, makes a reply which
the Interpreter translates to the Ambassador. He then takes the
credentials from his secretary's hands; he gives them to the *Mir-Alem*
(Chief of the Standard, Commander of the Chamberlains), who passes
them on to the High Admiral. This officer presents them to the Grand
Vizir, who places them on the throne. The audience immediately
comes to an end and the Ambassador retires with his suite. On regain-
ing the First Court he mounts his horse, as does also his *cortège*; and,
lined up on one of the sides, they watch the janissaries and the
entire Ottoman Court march off. Immediately after the Ambassador
begins his march back to his palace in Pera in the same order that he
came.

Looking at Melling's drawing, we notice that the banquet in the
Divan is being furnished not from the main kitchens on the right
side of the court, but from the Sultan's private kitchen, or from one
specially built for the Divan, on the left. Although the main kitchens
were more than sufficient to provide enormous meals, many of the
Sultans preferred to have their own private kitchens near at hand.
Consequently it is not surprising to find others in different parts of
the Seraglio. There is one near the main door of the *ḥarēm* (next
No. 40 in the plan), and this one on the left of the Second Court was
probably built at a Sultan's whim. This kitchen, however, occupied
only a small part of the long building on the left, the greater portion
being used as a dwelling-place by officers attached to the high State
dignitaries.

Immediately adjoining the Divan is the *Içhazine*, or Inner Treasury,
now the *Silâh Müzesi*, or Arms Museum. It is one of the oldest
portions of the whole Seraglio, and is said to have been built by
Muhammad II. Its eight domes, resting on three large square central
pillars, and typical late fifteenth- or early sixteenth-century vaulting,
at once proclaim it to be original work. Certain slight alterations
have occurred since it housed the arms, particularly in the far corner
by the chief entrance to the *ḥarēm*, but apart from this there has probably been little change. Here was stored the money needed for use
in the Hall of the Divan, including that paid out to the janissaries. It

was the provincial revenue, delivered in sacks and stored in the vaults beneath. According to Bon the Royal wardrobe was also stored somewhere here. He describes it and the Treasury as if they were side by side:

> They are two most noble buildings, which have separate rooms on the ground floor and in the vaults, large enough for the many commodities they contain, and exceedingly safe, with very thick walls. They have small windows that are all barred, and only one door to each made of the strongest iron, which is always kept bolted, that of the Casnà [Treasury] being also sealed with the Royal seal.[1]

Before we discuss the kitchens on the right-hand side of the court there still remain several buildings on the left between the Inner Wall and the Divan.

Immediately to the left of the *Ortakapi* in the far corner is a small unpretentious gate now blocked up. It is the *Meyyit Kapi*, or Gate of the Dead, through which all bodies of the Palace *personnel* made their final exit—except, of course, those which found a less dignified end in the Marmora or the Bosphorus. A similar connecting gate pierced the other wall, and thus the bodies were conducted outside the Seraglio walls. Quite close to here is all that remains of a mosque and bath built by Beşir Ağa, one of the most famous Chief Eunuchs, who died in 1746. There are several other buildings in Istanbul erected by him. The remainder of this large area which occupies the lower slope of the hill is devoted to the stables and the quarters of the halberdiers.

The stables are now in a state of ruin, but were once fine buildings, with rooms on the first floor containing a collection of valuable trappings. They were, however, only the Privy Stables, in which some twenty-five or thirty horses were kept for the Sultan's personal use.

The Great Stables were outside the Seraglio buildings near the seashore, as we have already seen in an earlier chapter. Bon inspected the Privy Stables personally, and tells us that the caparisons are extraordinarily rich and handsome,

> since there are saddles, bridles, pectorals, and cruppers set with jewels of every kind with much taste and cunning and in large numbers;

[1] P. 60.

and they amaze every one who sees them because they surpass the bounds of imagination.[1]

Tavernier is equally enthusiastic in his description.[2]

We now come to the quarters of the halberdiers, built after the fire of 1574, and consisting of a unit complete in itself, with courtyard, mosque, dormitory, coffee-room, baths, etc.

The halberdiers formed a corps of servants of the Outer Service of the Seraglio, but their duties brought them into close contact with both the *selāmlik* and the *ḥarēm*, since they were responsible for much of the manual labour of the Palace, such as wood-cutting and general portage. They also served as a kind of bodyguard to members of the *ḥarēm* when changing quarters, etc., and on these occasions were armed with halberds; hence their name. A large number of these weapons can be seen in the Arms Museum, mentioned above. Their Turkish name was *baltajiler*, and the corps was divided into two sections: those who served the *selāmlik* and those whose duties were confined to the *ḥarēm*. The former *baltajilers* were called *yakali* ('possessing collars') and *yakasiz* ('without collars'), according to which sub-section they belonged. Those connected with the *ḥarēm* bore the curious name of *Zülüfli Baltajilers*, from *zülüf*, a curl or tress, because two false curls hung down from their tall hats, in order to hinder them from viewing the women when taking the monthly supply of wood into the *ḥarēm*. Similar 'chastity curls' were worn by the Sword-bearer (*Kiliçdar* or *Silihdar*), and the Chief Musician, and several other members of the Seraglio. If von Hammer is correct, at one time the *Zülüfli Baltajilers* were white eunuchs, but if so the curls would seem to be an unnecessary appendage.[3]

The quarters of the halberdiers are entered by a small gate only a few paces away from the door next to the Divan Tower leading to the black eunuchs' courtyard. A long flight of steps runs down to the lower terrace on which the entire quarters are built. They lead directly to a narrow courtyard, known as the Court of the Fountain. To the right is a square room originally used as a mosque, while farther down are the baths and latrines. To the left are seven square

[1] P. 62.　　　　　　　　[2] *New Relation*, pp. 28–29.
[3] For a further account see d'Ohsson, *Tableau général*, vol. iii, p. 294, with the engraving No. 152.

narrow wooden pillars supporting the bedrooms or sitting-rooms of the officers of the corps. Parallel to these pillars, but more to the left, lies a large dormitory with a gallery, running completely round the room and supported by nine wooden pillars at the sides and three each end, counting the corner pillars twice. The side of the ground floor nearest the court is tiled; the colouring is still bright, and the designs are charming. To reach the gallery above it is necessary to go outside and ascend the staircase to a point where an archway leads to other stairs to the left. The gallery is most interesting, the wood-work being brightly painted in red, and many of the lockers for bedding still *in situ*. A huge dark ball hangs from the centre of the roof.

As we return to the Court of the Fountain a small room will be noticed at the end on the left. It apparently served as the coffee-room, and is lined with low divans. Immediately beyond are a few steps leading to the general mess-room of the halberdiers. It is a square, lofty apartment, surrounded on three sides by low wooden sofas composed of lockers, while on the wall opposite the door are some thirty long narrow lockers in which, I suggest, the halberds were stored. Dr Miller thinks they were used for the *nargilehs*, or Persian water-pipes. But the lockers are quite three times too long for such a use, besides which I doubt very much if servants of the standing of the halberdiers would own such an expensive variety of pipe. Anyway, they could easily fit in the lower lockers. In the centre of the room is a large rectangular brazier with an inner ledge used for coffee-pots. Owing to the small windows and the trees outside there was little light in the room although the sun was shining brightly. I was therefore unable to take a good photograph, but as I understand this curious little room has never been 'taken' before I have ventured to reproduce my effort (opposite p. 112).

Returning once again to the courtyard and walking to the extreme end, one notices a staircase which leads to two rooms over the baths. As far as I could ascertain, they belonged to the captains of the corps. They are in such a bad state of repair that it is dangerous to venture inside.

A broad terrace supporting an abundance of shrubs and trees, among which the fig-tree is especially noticeable, abuts on to the end of the dormitory nearest the main stairway. It forms the upper part of what was once the courtyard of the stables.

There remain only the kitchens to be described. As can be seen from the plan, they occupy the entire right-hand side of the Second Court. They therefore form by far the largest separate unit in the whole of the Seraglio. Rebuilt with thick massive walls by Sinan after the great fire of 1574, they occupy the same site as in the original palace of Muhammad II. Certain minor alterations have been made in the course of the centuries, and many of the dependent buildings are in ruins; but the kitchens themselves have been saved by the solidity of the walls—just as in other parts of Istanbul it was the thick walls of the baths that withstood fires and earthquakes—and must be one of the most remarkable specimens of sixteenth-century domestic architecture in existence.

The whole quarters not only consist of ten large double kitchens arranged in line one after the other overlooking the Marmora, but include suites of rooms for the chief kitchen functionaries, two mosques, baths, and storerooms, offices, and pantries, and quarters for the cooks, food porters, confectioners, scullions, wood-cutters, ice-collectors, water-carriers, etc. There are also the remains of a school of cookery, musicians' rooms, a tinning shop, ablution fountains, and dormitories. Many smaller rooms, the use of which has been forgotten, were very possibly used as divans or coffee-rooms for the various sections of the kitchen community, which, according to several old writers, were all separate and distinct. Thus each section would have its own coffee-room—purveyors of meat never sitting down with, say, the tinners or confectioners. The arrangement of all these rooms, however, was quite simple owing to the presence of a long corridor running the entire length of the buildings parallel to the columns in the courtyard, to which access was gained by three separate entrances.

The side nearest the courtyard was occupied by all the suites and offices of the several sections of the kitchen staff, while the Marmora side, being over twice as broad, supported the massive kitchens, the two mosques, and also the quarters of the food porters in the extreme corner near the waterworks.

It is difficult—and really of little importance—to state with any

ENTRANCES TO THE QUARTERS OF THE HALBERDIERS (ON LEFT) AND TO THOSE
OF THE BLACK EUNUCHS (ON RIGHT)

MESS-ROOM OF THE HALBERDIERS, SHOWING THE TWO STYLES OF LOCKERS AND
THE BRAZIER IN THE CENTRE OF THE ROOM

degree of accuracy how the kitchens were allocated at different times. This is due to the fact that as soon as one author makes a list all subsequent writers copy it, either because they have no opportunity of checking it, or because of the sense of authoritative confidence that such a list seems to inspire. Thus it is accepted without question. Who made the original list I cannot say, but our old friend Bon certainly seems to be a likely recipient for the honour. His list (1604–7) was copied exactly, not only by Baudier and Withers, but by Louis Des Hayes,[1] and by Tournefort[2] in about 1700, and appears unaltered in Grosvenor,[3] and subsequently in Murray's *Handbook*.

The allocation given in these lists is as follows:

(1) The Sultan.
(2) The Sultan Validé, sometimes called the Queen.
(3) The Sultanas, meaning the *kadins*.
(4) The *Kapi Agha*.
(5) Members of the Divan.
(6) The *Iç-oghlans*, or Sultan's pages.
(7) Humbler members of the Seraglio.
(8) The other women.
(9) The less important members of the Divan.

Nobody seemed certain about the tenth kitchen; it was quite possibly used for the kitchen staff itself; but at a later period it was allocated to the confectioners. Occasionally we do get variants in the lists in those rare cases of original inquiry.

Thus Tavernier, while noting the nine kitchens, tells us that now (c. 1664) the number in actual use has been reduced to seven. The change of allocation or reduction of the number in use was merely due to special circumstances, such as the wish of the Sultan or *kadins* to have their kitchens nearer the *harēm*, or to the fact that there was no Sultan Validé alive at the time. An unusual and temporary effort to economize might cause the closing of some of the kitchens. Alterations have doubtless been made from time to time in the construction of the roofs, chimneys, and cupolas. To-day each kitchen is divided into two parts, the inner of which contained the fire on a low stone

[1] *Voiage de Levant* (Paris, 1624).
[2] *Voyage into the Levant*, vol. ii, p. 184.   [3] *Constantinople*.

hearth in the centre of the room, the smoke passing up to a dome pierced by a long chimney. The outer part, or that nearest the kitchen corridor, is surmounted by a polygonal dome with a pierced centre, which can also serve as a chimney, but there is no chimney-stack. Hence, when viewing the Seraglio from the Marmora we see only a single line of ten tall chimneys. It appears that alterations have been made in the chimneys and domes, and it is not at all clear if both varieties of chimney were always used as such, or whether possibly one served as a means of ventilation. In 1700 Tournefort writes:

> The Offices and Kitchens are on the right, embellish'd with Domes, but without Chimneys; they kindle a Fire in the middle, and the Smoke goes out through the Holes made in the Domes.[1]

In Melling's engraving there is clearly only a single line of chimneys in the form of round domes, while in that of d'Ohsson, published only a dozen years earlier, there is a double line of chimneys polygonal in shape, and at one point there are three rows. As both men were reliable observers it would seem clear that alterations were continually being made. Writing in 1551, Nicolay says there are 150 cooks, of which those who dress the Sultan's food are the most important:

> those of the privy kitchens have their furnaces apart, to dress and make ready the meat without smell of smoke, which, being sodden and dressed, they lay in platters of porcelain, and so deliver it unto the *Cecigners*, whom we do call carvers, to serve the same unto the great lord, the taste being made in his presence.

Several years earlier (1534) Ramberti gives the following list of the kitchen *personnel*:

> The Ashji-bashi, or chief cook, with fifty cooks under him. He has forty aspers per day, the cooks under him four, six, or eight aspers each.
> The Helvaji-bashi, or chief confectioner, with forty aspers, and he has thirty companions with five to six aspers per day each.
> The Chasnijir-bashi [the Chief Taster], chief of the cupboards, with eighty aspers: morning and evening he brings with his own hand the dish of the Signor, and he has under him a hundred *Chasnijirs* with from three to seventy [seven (?)] aspers each.
> The Mutbakh-emini [Steward of the Kitchen] with forty aspers. He has a secretary with twenty aspers a day.

[1] *Voyage into the Levant*, vol. ii, p. 184.

A hundred *Ajem-oghlans*, who transport on carts the wood of the palace. They have three to five aspers, and are provided with clothing. Ten *Sakkas*, who carry water on horse-back in leather sacks, with three to five aspers each.[1]

Bon gives much interesting information about the food supplies in general:

From Egypt come large quantities of dates, plums, and prunes, all of which are placed in the care of the servers and cooks, being in the cooking—both roast and boiled. The honeys which are consumed by the Porte in enormous amounts, because they are used in all food as well as in the sherbets for the poorer folk, come from Walachia, Transylvania, and Moldavia [Rumania and part of Hungary]; as well as presents made to the King by the *Vaivodes* [Moldavian Dukes]. But for the King's kitchen a stock is laid in from Candia which is of greater purity and delicacy. The oil, of which they use a large amount, comes from Corone and Modone[2] in Greece, the Sanjak Bey being obliged to provide as much as is required by the Seraglio; but for the King's kitchen that from Candia is supplied, being odourless.

The butter, of which a lot is consumed, comes by way of the Black Sea from Moldavia, and from Tana and Caffa [near the Sea of Azov], and is sent packed in enormous ox-hides. It is stored in warehouses, and when there is an abundant supply it is sold in the city to the great advantage of the Porte; little fresh butter is eaten, because the Turks do not care for dairy produce.

As regards meat, each year in the autumn the Grand Pasha orders the Pastromani [meat beaten out flat] for the Royal kitchens, and it must be from cows in calf, because their flesh is more savoury and salted. It is kept dried, made into sausages and hash, and preserved in barrels for the whole year, being used not only in the Seraglio, but in every house. However, the Pasha controls these operations, for which as a rule four hundred cows are used.

The remainder of the meat consumed daily in the Seraglio is:

Young mutton	200
Lambs or kids when in season . . .	100
Veal for the eunuchs	4
Young geese (pairs)	30
Guinea-fowl (pairs)	100
Poultry (pairs)	100
Pigeons (pairs)	100

[1] Lybyer, *Government of the Ottoman Empire in the Time of Suleiman the Magnificent*, pp. 245–246.

[2] Both in the province of Messenia, in the Peloponnesus. They were annexed to Turkey by Bayezid II in 1502.

Fish is not usually eaten, but if the *Agalari* want it every kind is available, since these seas are well stocked, and fishing can be easily done from the private houses.

Fruits are not lacking for the King and all in the Seraglio, because they receive great quantities as presents, and the Royal gardens, of which there are many in the vicinity, provide every day large baskets of the best and finest that can be gathered, the *Bustangibassi* [*Bostanjibashi*, Head Gardener] being obliged to take what is left over for sale in a place apart where only the King's fruit is sold, the profits from the sale being delivered weekly to the King's *Bustangibassi*, who then hands them to his Majesty. This is known as his pocket money, and he gives it away without counting it to his mutes and buffoons.

The kitchen utensils are a sight to see, because the pots, cauldrons, and other necessary things are so huge and nearly all of copper that of things of this kind it would be impossible to see any more beautiful or better kept. The service of dishes is of copper tinned over, and kept in such continual good repair and so spotless that it is an amazing sight to behold. There is an enormous quantity of them, and they are a very considerable expense to the Porte, and especially because the kitchens provide food for so many both within and without, particularly on the four days of the Public Divan,[1] so that the number stolen is a thing to marvel at.

The *Defterdars* wanted to have them made of silver so as to hand them over to the Treasurer, but owing to the great cost the idea came to nothing. The wood consumed in the kitchens amounts to countless *pesi* (so it is sold in Constantinople), and a *peso* is 40 pounds gross weight. I will but say that thirty large *caramussali* [Turkish merchantmen] in the service of the Porte sail the Greater [Black] Sea to the King's forests to procure it. And this they do at little cost to the Treasury, because those who cut down and load the wood are slaves.[2]

There is no lack of material dealing with the preparation and serving of Turkish food—with the making of *pilaf* and similar national dishes, the different varieties of sherbets, the innumerable sugary confections so dear to the Ottoman palate—but, after all, this is not a gastronomical work, so I will merely refer readers to Tavernier, who has much to say on the subject, and to White's *Three Years in Constantinople*,[3] for more modern recipes.

Evliyá Efendí[4] gives a most interesting account of how the

[1] On Divan days an extra four or five thousand would be fed, in addition to the usual thousand or more.　　　　[2] Pp. 97–98.　　　　[3] Vol. iii, pp. 81–97.
[4] *Narrative of Travels* (London, 1834), vol. ii, pp. 156–157.

Seraglio is supplied with the enormous quantities of ice required. He tells us of the great ice-pits where snow is stored, and how on days of procession the snowmen wear turbans made entirely of frozen snow, and drag on wagons loads of snow of the size of a cupola, and that there are also from seventy to eighty files of mules loaded with the purest snow from Mount Olympus. He also speaks of the fish-cooks, sugar-bakers, confectioners, and divers conserves of almonds, pistachios, ginger, hazel-nuts, orange-peel, aloes, coffee, etc.

The only Turkish sweetmeat, however, known throughout the world is, of course, Turkish delight. No less than some 750 tons are exported annually. It consists of the pulp of white grapes or mulberries, semolina flour, honey, rose-water, and apricot kernels. It rejoices in the attractive Turkish name of *Rahat Lokum* ('giving rest to the throat').

As we have already seen, the entrance from the Second into the Third Court is through the Gate of Felicity, or *Bab-i-Sa'adet*, behind and to the right and left of which are the quarters of the white eunuchs, formerly occupied by the Great and Little Halls of the Palace School.

I shall discuss the Gate of Felicity first. It has other names, derived either from the proximity of the eunuchs' quarters or from the fact that the gate led into the private apartments of the Sultan. Thus it is known as *Akağalar Kapisi*, the Gate of the White Eunuchs; while Bon (1604–7) knew of it as the King's Gate and the Royal Gate.

The date of its erection is unknown, but in spite of its thorough restoration in 1774–75 there is every sign of its being early sixteenth century at the latest, with the general style—a double gate surmounted by a heavily ornamented canopy and flanked by marble columns on each side—preserved throughout. Flachat[1] (1740–55) describes the gate as having a fine portico flanked by sixteen columns of porphyry or *verd-antique*, the vaulted roof of the canopy which supports it being gilded at the base and decorated with leaves and flowers in relief. The façade of the gate itself was enriched by large panels of polished marbles matching the pillars, but these have unfortunately been replaced with modern mural paintings just as bad

---

[1] *Observations sur le commerce*, vol. ii, p. 174.

as those on the inner side of the *Ortakapi*. The portico is supported by six columns, of which only the front four are free. Six more columns support the colonnade each side, making a total of eighteen. So far this was the most private and respected part of the Seraglio. It was here that the personal part of the Palace began; at this gate each new Sultan was announced; its threshold was kissed by any-one entering. Through its gates the bodies of the highest officials have been thrown to the surging mass of angry janissaries who have thundered at its closed portals. The bodies of dead Sultans have been borne hence in times of sedition and revolution. But without giving details of the grim scenes in which the Gate of Felicity has played a leading part it will suffice to say that it was always regarded as the closed gate, sacred to majesty, beyond which nothing was officially known. That it led directly to the *Arzodasi*, or Throne Room, was the limit of public knowledge. Thus Bon tells us in his account that it gives entry into that part of the Seraglio reserved solely for the Royal household and the slaves who serve it. "And nobody may enter," he continues,

> by this gate save at the pleasure of the Emperor (speaking of persons of consequence), but other members of the service, such as doctors or those who look after the pantry and kitchen, may enter there by permission of the *Kapi Aga*, who is the chief major-domo to whom the supervision of these people is entrusted. He is always at hand, since his rooms are close by with his *Aga* eunuchs like himself. And everything is secret to this extent, that whatever is intimated of what goes on beyond this gate is for the most part mere inference, because either nothing can be seen at all or, if any trifling thing *can* be seen, it is on those occasions when the King is absent, and one is introduced by some favourite through the Sea Gates.[1]

According to Bassano da Zara the guard consisted of thirty eunuchs, while other sixteenth-century accounts state that this was the number only on Divan days, while ordinarily it was twenty or twenty-five. The quarters of the white eunuchs were situated in such a position as to command a view of both the Second and Third Courts. The suite of the *Kapi Agha* (*Kapiağasi Dairesi*), Chief of the White Eunuchs, lay to the right, while the quarters of the rest lay to the left. To-day

---

[1] P. 63.

it is difficult to form any idea of the suite to the right, as the rooms have now been turned into electrical and fitting workshops. All that I can say is that after passing through a small courtyard one reaches a long passage with three rooms to the left. There is a fountain and washing-room at the far end on the right, close to the confectioners' mosque. All rooms are necessarily oblong in shape; all signs of decorations have long since disappeared.

With the general quarters to the left of the gate I was much more lucky, for not only were they in good condition, but they were fully occupied by some of the present museum staff, who at the time of my first visit were sleeping, studying, making coffee, etc.—in fact, behaving exactly as the white eunuchs did. On passing through the small courtyard, corresponding to that in the Chief Eunuch's suite, I encountered a very irate dwarf, who rushed out at me wildly, gesticulating and shouting, doing all in his power to prevent me from entering. My credentials, however, were too strong for him, and he sulkily went away, leaving me in possession. I passed first of all into a large room resembling somewhat that of the halberdiers, only smaller. A broad balcony runs round the room, and served as a dormitory for the guards. Mats were spread out or rolled neatly away in all parts of it, several of the former being occupied by men fast asleep. On the ground floor several partitions have been made, while in the far right-hand corner is a raised chamber, used apparently by the eunuchs of higher rank.

Passing on, one comes to the general dining-room, and at the time of my visit food was being cooked in a large brazier that occupied the centre of the room. On the far left-hand side several men were squatting before ablution fountains which extended in a line against the wall on the Second Court side. There is also a small third room which was used as a storeroom.

The duties of the white eunuchs in the Seraglio were chiefly concerned with the five chambers of pages, which formed such an important part of the Inner Service of the Palace. Just as it was the duty of the black eunuchs to control all matters connected with the ḥarēm, so it was the duty of the white eunuchs to look after the selāmlik and its numerous activities. Since ordinary servants were not allowed past the Gate of Felicity the duties of the white eunuchs and

Royal pages were really divided between education in the Palace School and personal service to the Sultan as members of the Royal household.

In the sixteenth and seventeenth centuries there appear to have been four head eunuchs, while a fifth was added subsequently.

These were the *Kapi Agha*, the *Hazinedar-bashi*, the *Kilerji-bashi*, and the *Serai Agha*, the fifth being the *Has Oda-bashi*.[1] The position of the Chief White Eunuch (*Kapi Agha*) was of the highest, and until the rise of the black eunuchs he reigned supreme. But even then he ranked equally with the *Kislar Agha*, although some of his privileges had been transferred to his black rival.

First and foremost, the *Kapi Agha* was head of the Inner Service, which naturally meant that he was the personal confidant of the Sultan and the head of the Palace School. He was also Gatekeeper-in-Chief, head of the infirmary, and general master of ceremonies of the Seraglio. In former days he controlled all messages, petitions, and State documents addressed to the Sultan, and alone was allowed to speak to the King in person. Many of these privileges were largely transferred to the Chief Black Eunuch, as we shall see in a later chapter. The dress of the *Kapi Agha* consisted of a loosely fitting pelisse of brocade or velvet edged with rich furs, with long hanging sleeves. Underneath was a shorter garment of the same material. A belt, yellow shoes, linen or silk drawers, and a white sugar-loaf turban completed the costume.

The next in command, the *Hazinedar-bashi*, had charge of the Treasury, and was head of the corps of pages attached to the *Hazine Oda*, or Chamber of the Treasury, which formed the second chamber of the pages. He was responsible for all the Royal treasures, and made all the Inner Service payments, and kept detailed accounts of everything paid out.

The third officer, the *Kilerji-bashi*, supervised the Sultan's food and controlled the whole of the kitchen staff.

On the fourth, the *Serai Agha*, devolved charge of the Seraglio in the Sultan's absence. He was also assistant director of

[1] See vol. iii, pp. 176 *et seq.*, of the *Turkey* volumes of Shoberl's *World in Miniature* (London, 1822). It is translated from the French edition of Castellan. The coloured plates are charming.

the Palace School and head of the *Seferli Oda*, or Chamber of Campaign.

In direct personal touch with the Sultan were the selected members of the *Has Oda*, or Inner Chamber. In Suleiman's time the head of this chamber was the chief page, but as the position grew in importance and duties increased it was entrusted to a white eunuch, known as the *Has Oda-bashi*. Apart from his duties to the Sultan's personal wants, he was the depositary of one of the three Imperial seals set in a ring, with which he used to seal the most precious objects kept in the Royal apartments, such as the phials of sacred water into which the corner of the Prophet's robe had been dipped. He also had charge of the robes of honour given to foreign ambassadors and other people of distinction.

The rest of the white eunuchs acted as assistants to the above officers in one capacity or another. The infirmary was entirely run by them, and they acted as litter-bearers, as well as managing the arrangements of the wards and the Commissariat.

As regards the supply of white eunuchs, plenty of opportunities offered themselves when the Ottoman power was at its height, and Hungarian, Slavonian, and German prisoners of both sexes were pouring into the capital. The number of white eunuchs made at this time, however, seems to have been very small, more care being taken to recruit the Turkish legions with men capable of bearing arms. Owing to the fact that castration was forbidden in the *Korān*, it is usually stated that the operation was performed outside Constantinople, and the newly made *castrato* was then sent into the Seraglio to be taught his duties.

From the early seventeenth-century description by Bon it would seem that in some cases the operation was performed in the Seraglio itself. Thus we read:

> All are castrated and cut clean, and they choose some of the renegade boys, who are given as presents to the King, as I have said, but are rarely castrated against their will, because the Master of Ceremonies says that they would incur great danger of death. Although aware of this, the youths are tempted by the certainty of becoming in time men of great consequence if they live; and, castrated as they are, they are educated with the rest, and are taken away in due course from the

fourth *oda* into the King's service, as happens to the others who are not castrated.[1]

Another supply of slaves was procured from Armenia, Georgia, and Circassia—first by right of conquest, and subsequently by peaceful negotiations, particularly in the case of Circassia, a traffic which had been quite unknown in the case of the transportation of negroes. The cargoes were mixed, and it was not long before the beauty of the Georgian women became proverbial, and a thriving trade soon sprang into being, the merchandise being shipped in boats across the treacherous Black Sea. When the Georgian supply was temporarily checked by the Russian advance that from Caucasia increased, and small boats packed with men and women for the markets of the Levant made their way to Trebizond, which now became the *entrepôt*.

As far as the Circassian women were concerned, they often went entirely of their own free will, being anxious to exchange a peasant life for the gamble of becoming a Pasha's wife, or maybe even the concubine of the Sultan himself. But as regards the men, the number that became eunuchs was still small, the reason being that whereas any amount of black eunuchs could be used to look after the *ḥarēm* the number required to keep the Court pages in order was limited.

After the Circassian slave-dealers had been driven from their country in 1864 they merely carried their nefarious trade nearer Constantinople, in Rumelia, and on the Asiatic coast at Brusa. When a white eunuch was required he would be found and duly delivered, but by far the greater trade was in women, not only to supply the slave markets, but to provide material for enthusiastic amateurs, who after carefully training the girls would sell them later to advantage.

In spite of all efforts to stop the slave trade, and the actual passing of a decree by the Turkish Government itself abolishing slavery among the Circassians, the trade continued unabated as before, only not quite so openly. It was only some terrific national upheaval, coupled with lessening of the demand, that could end a system that was part and parcel of the social and religious life of the community. Such an upheaval has occurred, and to-day a curious Turkey presents itself to us, a Turkey that is looking West perhaps, but a Turkey that

[1] P. 89.

has lost so much of its old charm and beauty. Unless the visitor to Constantinople of to-day is blessed with the all too rare faculty of seeing the half-hidden glories of what is perhaps the most marvellous city in the world he will merely be disgusted with the pathetic attempts to turn Pera into a modern city by a vulgar display of tawdry and garish Americanism that makes any thinking man or woman weep.

Before passing on to a consideration of the black eunuchs I shall conclude this chapter with a brief architectural discussion dealing with the numerous styles of capitals to be found on pillars in different parts of the Seraglio, especially one in this Second Court, which I would call the lotus capital. It occurs not only here, but in many other places in the Seraglio—namely, the corridor of the black eunuchs, the courtyard and bedrooms of the *ḥarēm* slaves, the courtyard of the Sultan Validé, the veranda of the Baghdad Kiosk, and elsewhere.

It is at once recognized by the lotus-leaf *motif* which it displays in strong relief. The capital itself is clearly based on an early Byzantine pattern, and resembles somewhat those in the *Bin Bir Direk*, or Cistern of 1001 Columns, although here they assume a slightly convex shape by having their base angles rounded. In Sancta Sophia straight-edged capitals are found in the Western Gynæceum (sometimes called the Visitors' Gallery), with branch chandeliers surmounting them.[1] This shape must have appealed to the Turkish architect, for we find it copied to support the Tribune of the Sultan (*Maṣil-i-Humayun*) and the *masbata* arcades which were built alongside the piers of the great dome on the northern flank.

But apart from Byzantine buildings, this lotus capital is to be found in several mosques in different parts of Constantinople—*e.g.*, Mirimah and Rustem Pasha, both built by the famous Sinan about 1550. So too it occurs in mosques in Pera and Scutari.[2]

Another form of capital in the Seraglio is stalactitic or honeycomb in form, resembling some found in various parts of the Alhambra, at Granada. Examples will be found in the veranda surrounding the

---

[1] See the illustration at p. 515 of Grosvenor's *Constantinople*.
[2] See Gurlitt, *Die Baukunst Konstantinopels*, text p. 63, abb. 125, and Plates G. 29*b*, G. 28*d*, G. 26*c*, and G. 24*b*.

Arzodasi, or Audience Chamber, in the Third Court and also in the Sultan's bathroom. Several mosques, such as that of Rustem Pasha, can also show examples of this type of capital.

A third, and somewhat modified, type can be seen in the portico of the Third Court. Except for the unnecessarily heavy echinus it reminds us again of similar work at the Alhambra.

But are we entitled to call these capitals Turkish? As in so many other matters, the Turks copied the architecture of the countries they conquered. Thus in order to discover genuine Turkish art among so many borrowings it is necessary to go very warily. The Byzantine architects had both Corinthian and Ionic capitals as models before their eyes. But with the abandoning of the architrave an entirely new group of capitals had to be invented to support arched brick construction in such a way as to present a perfect harmonious whole with the column, capital, and arch. A visit to the ever-glorious Sancta Sophia will show how they have succeeded.

At first no such thing as Turkish art existed, and both designs and material for building were taken from ruined Byzantine churches, private houses, baths, etc. Thus we find beautiful columns of porphyry, syenite, *verd-antique*, granite, and other stones in the most unlikely places surmounted with capitals that never belonged to them. The modified Byzantine capital and arch became to a large extent the Turkish capital and arch—but not quite, because in the sixteenth century Sinan created a real national art. He not only was a builder of numerous mosques, hospitals, libraries, and baths, but produced a great amount of humbler domestic work, such as wells, kitchens, cisterns, etc. Still, his art was but a hybrid, produced by a fusion of Syrian and Armenian designs brought to a definite existence by his own genius as Turkish art. Much of this we can see in the Seraglio, and still more in Constantinople, Adrianople, and Brusa.

This is not the place, nor do I possess the knowledge, to discourse in any detail on the position Turkish art occupies when considered in relation to its forerunners both East and West. That it has a separate existence cannot be doubted, but it is no easy matter to gauge the debt to men like Anthemius and Isidorus, the architects of Sancta Sophia, and yet give full credit to an art that was sprung from Anatolian and Syrian soil.

CHAPTER VI

THE BLACK EUNUCHS

1. Their Quarters and their Duties

As can be seen from a glance at the plan, the quarters of the black eunuchs (Nos. 32–37) lay behind the left-hand northern corner of the Second Court, having the Divan and the Treasury on one side and the apartments of the *harēm* girls on the other. The Golden Road, emerging from the heart of the *selāmlik*, ended at the main *harēm* door (No. 41), which led into the eunuchs' courtyard (No. 34). Another door (No. 40) communicated at this point directly with the Third Court, while at the opposite end (No. 30) access was gained to the Second Court by passing under the Divan Tower.

It will thus be seen that these quarters occupied a central and commanding position, at once signifying the great responsibility vested in the *Kislar Agha* and the subordinate eunuchs.

The entrance from the Second Court is by a small, unpretentious door (shown in the plate opposite p. 112) similar to that on the left leading to the quarters of the halberdiers. It is known as the Carriage Gate (*Araba Kapisi*), because it was at this point that the ladies of the *harēm* entered the vehicles (*araba*) that were to take them for excursions up the Bosphorus or visits to the Old Seraglio, etc. As this little gate gave direct entrance to the courtyard through which the women passed on their way to the Second Court it was always heavily guarded. It leads immediately into a square, high, vaulted room, known to-day as *Dolapli Kubbe*—Domed Anteroom with Cupboards (No. 31), as it is fitted with wall cupboards enclosed by large painted wooden doors. It has doubtless had many uses at different periods, but seems to have served the double purpose of anteroom and guard-room with sleeping accommodation, which was folded up in the cupboards during the day. The ladies would doubtless assemble in this room before being conducted into their waiting carriages outside.

A door the same size as the Carriage Gate leads into an oblong chamber (No. 32) nearly double the size of the *Dolapli Kubbe*. It is beautifully tiled in the form of floral panels surrounded by a deep frieze of Cufic writing. The room is really a kind of hall or anteroom, having no particular use in itself, but serving many purposes and giving access into many important places, as I shall show presently. It is divided into two parts, the first of which is vaulted and very high, allowing a second Cufic frieze, parallel to the other one, to stretch some eighteen or twenty feet up across the complete breadth of the room. To the left is an ancient panelled wooden gate, with a large window above it, leading to a long, narrow alleyway that separates the *ḥarēm* from the quarters of the halberdiers, and ultimately leads into the garden surrounding the outer walls of the Seraglio through the Shawl Gate (No. 62).

Immediately next this gate is another door leading into the eunuchs' mosque (No. 33), built after the great fire of 1665 and containing much fine faïence work with interesting marble tablets recording gifts of various eunuchs towards the upkeep and beautifying of the rooms. There is a small anteroom to the mosque, and another door leads into the courtyard, which is, however, best entered from room No. 32, to which we now return. The second part of it is not vaulted, but has a flat ceiling tastefully decorated in faïence and stucco. On the mosque side is a large marble mounting-block with steps either side. It was used by Sultans riding out to the sacred mosque at Eyyūb. Near by is a marble octagonal fountain. On the opposite side is a double door leading to the staircase that gives entrance to the *loge* or window overlooking the Hall of the Divan. The stairs continue through the several floors into which the interior of the Divan Tower is divided.

Next comes the open courtyard (No. 34), with a row of ten marble pillars on the left side. A wooden canopy, supported by slanting poles, stretches down the entire length of this side, protecting the windows and tiling from the extremes of the weather. Of the ten columns, which all display the lotus-*motif* capital (see p. 123), the first six are free, and form a colonnade flanking the black eunuchs' dormitories, to which access is gained between the sixth and seventh columns. On entering this most interesting little enclosed corridor

THE COURTYARD OF THE BLACK EUNUCHS

(No. 35), with its three stories of small rooms facing each other about eight feet only apart, one is at once impressed by the solidity of the building and the atmosphere of monasterial austerity that pervades the place. If it suffered in the 1665 fire one imagines that restoration would have been easy and the damage comparatively trifling. Although this part of the eunuchs' quarters is usually described as the dormitories it included the living rooms as well. As far as I was able to ascertain, the ground-floor rooms were used as bed-sitting rooms by the elder eunuchs, except for a 'common room' on the left, double the size of the others, and a coffee-making room on the extreme right. There are six rooms on the right and five on the left. At the end of the corridor is a typical Turkish fireplace surmounted by a pointed canopy of decorative tiles, while the wall behind was also completely tiled, but in this case with plain coloured tiles.

Visitors are still shown the bastinado boards to which the feet were tied, and the noose into which the hands were put for similar chastisement. The first floor resembles an open balcony, and supports the second floor by short, stumpy octagonal pillars surmounted by the lotus *motif* as in the courtyard. The only actual windows on this floor are close to the fireplace. Here, apparently, the senior eunuchs slept, but whether the ground-floor rooms were additional or not used to sleep in at all I cannot say, as information on the point is uncertain and conflicting. The second floor has no balcony, and the small rooms were used by the young eunuchs. Although several would share a room the accommodation seems hardly sufficient for such a large number of eunuchs as were employed here. At the same time it must be remembered that the great majority would be on duty in different parts of the Palace, and as soon as any came back they would immediately be relieved. Another factor possibly worth mentioning is the surprising number of people that sleep in the same room in Turkey without any apparent discomfort, or that crowd round a small brazier sipping coffee and puffing at their *nargilehs* in the happy state of *keyf*, or *dolce far niente*. On one of my rambles in the dirty Jewish quarter of Istanbul, known as Balata, I entered a doss-house overlooking the Golden Horn. Curiosity took me upstairs, the only entrance being up a ladder through a trapdoor. There lying on the floor fast asleep were nearly a dozen men, their thin rugs (you could hardly call them mattresses) nearly touching each other; and yet there was plenty of room where men had left and rolled their rugs up in neat bundles. The point to be remembered is that there is no furniture whatever, and thus in a room about twelve feet square as many as eight men can sleep at the same time.

Returning again to the courtyard, we notice that the next three pillars are engaged in a finely tiled wall. This is the Princes' School, where the early education of the Royal male children was carried on until they were eight or ten years old. The entrance is through a small fore-court by the last pillar, whence access is also gained to the suite of the Chief Eunuch, or *Kislar Agha*. These two sets of apartments, the Princes' School and the Chief Eunuch's suite, are closely related both architecturally and scholastically, for the chief rooms in the school extend over the Eunuch's suite on the upper floor, and it was the Chief Eunuch whose duty it was to superintend the education of the Princes, as well as that of the girls.

According to Ottaviano Bon (1604-7), the boys live in the women's quarters until they are eleven years old. From the fifth year to the eleventh they have their *kogia*, or tutor, chosen by the King and assigned to them as master. He enters the *ḥarēm* every day, and is led to a room in the black eunuchs' quarters without even seeing the women. In this room the boys are accompanied by two old black slaves. The tutor teaches them for as many hours as he is permitted to stay, and then goes outside again. When the heir to the throne has finished his early schooling and has been circumcized, or whenever the Sultan sees fit not to keep him any longer in his company, he organizes a household for him complete in every respect, and gives him one of the chief eunuchs as controller, who is called the *Lala Pasha*, assigns him his master, and gradually provides him with servants either from the Seraglio or from outside, in proportion as the claims of his position demand, allotting to him and all the others whatever allowance seems appropriate.

The school consists of several rooms all decorated in a highly rococo style, displaying French influence that proclaims a later date than, for instance, one finds in the simpler tiled rooms which often serve as anterooms. One of these contains an elaborate map of

Mecca, entirely in tiles, dating from about 1665. Good specimens of Cufic inscriptions over the doors, and interlaced wooden door panelling, reminiscent of similar work in the Alhambra, at Granada, will be noticed.

The suite of the *Kislar Agha* (No. 37) is small and compact. It includes several rooms, chief among them being a delightful coffeeroom, a bedroom, a smoking-room, and a lavatory. All the rooms are now open to the public and well repay a visit.

The right side of the courtyard is taken up with the apartments of the Treasurer and the Chamberlain (Nos. 38 and 39). As already mentioned, the courtyard leads directly to the door of the *harēm* itself (No. 41). Through this door access is gained to the courtyard of the Sultan Validé (No. 64), on the left, and to the Golden Road, straight ahead through a small door in the right-hand corner of the *harēm* anteroom, or guard-room (No. 42).

We now turn to the number of black eunuchs employed and their several duties. At first the status of the white eunuchs had been much more important than that of the black, but so great had been the depredations and embezzlements perpetrated that they gradually began to lose power, which was transferred to the black eunuchs, who were really, to a certain extent, their rivals. It was Murad III who, in 1591, dispossessed the white *Aghas* of so much of their power. As far as the Chief Eunuch was concerned, the loss was very considerable, for it included not only the high position of Chief of the Girls, but also the lucrative post of *nazir*, or inspector of the *vakfs*, or religious endowments of the Imperial mosques, as well as those of the holy cities of Mecca and Medina. From that time onward the powers of the *Kislar Agha* continued to grow. He became commander of the corps of *baltaji*, or halberdiers, held the rank of Pasha with three tails, was confidential messenger between the Sultan and the Grand Vizir, was alone entitled to have both eunuchs and girls as slaves, was allotted as many as 300 horses for his personal use, could alone approach the Sultan at all times of the day and night, was described as "the most illustrious of the officers who approach his August Person, and worthy of the confidence of monarchs and of sovereigns," was the most feared, and consequently the most bribed, official in the whole of the Ottoman Empire. Naturally he was a member of the Privy Council, and, in consultation with the Sultan Valide, made appointments to vacant posts, not only in the Seraglio but also outside. Anybody wishing to gain a favour from the Sultan by means of the Sultan Valide would only be able to do it through the Kislar Agha. As already mentioned, many of the honours and offices originally under the authority of the white changed to black eunuchs. In certain reigns some of these were again restored to the white eunuchs. This, therefore, explains the contradictory accounts we sometimes read. In the time of d'Ohsson four officials of the Outside Service are given as being subordinate to the Kislar Agha:

1. The chief official in charge of the tents and pavilions of the Sultan (Chadir-Mihter-bashi). He was in command of a corps of 800 men, divided into four companies of 200 men each. Forty of the chief among them constituted the Veznedars, or weighers of the money received by the Sultan. They were immediately under the Veznedar-bashi, Inspector of the Public Treasury, which was situated in the First Court. The corps also furnished executioners, who awaited orders near the Ortakapi.

2. The Superintendent of the Outer Treasury (Hazinedar-bashi). With twenty men under him as assistants, this officer had charge of the Depository of Archives of Finance, the store of robes of honour, the satin purses and golden cloths used in the dispatching of orders by the Ministry.

3. The Purveyor (Bazerkian-bashi) of cloths, linens, muslins, and similar goods needed in the Sultan's household.

4. The Keeper of the Presents (Peshkeshji-bashi), who looked after all gifts offered the Sultan both by his own subjects and by ambassadors on behalf of their Governments.

In the time of Suleiman the Magnificent all these officials were under the orders of the Kapi Agha, or Chief White Eunuch.

The costume of the Kislar Agha consisted of an under-robe of flowered silk with a broad sash wound round the waist. Over this, and usually almost entirely concealing it, was a pelisse of green, blue, or red material with long sleeves nearly reaching to the ground. It was trimmed with sable or other rare furs. The hat was a huge white sugar-loaf affair, worn at a slant on the back of the head.[1]

[1] See E. J. W. Gibb, History of Ottoman Poetry (London, 1900-9), vol. iii, p. 295 n. 2.

THE KISLAR AGHA, OR CHIEF BLACK EUNUCH

Mention might here be made of the collection of figures now on view in the galleries of the church of St Irene, in the First Court of the Seraglio. This interesting collection shows the costumes of the various officials of the Turkish Empire, and was made by Abd ul-Mejid (1839–61). In his time the figures were in all probability dressed with every detail historically correct. But since those days the collection has made many journeys, and when finally it returned again to St Irene in 1914 many of the figures had been broken, costumes mixed up or torn beyond repair, and most of the labels hopelessly misplaced. The *Kislar Agha* himself has been entirely, and incorrectly, re-dressed. I possess a drawing of the *tableau* in which he originally appeared, and there his dress corresponds exactly to the description given above, save for the fact that the sleeves are not trailing.[1] In his 1924 guide-book Dr Mamboury describes the thirty-one groups into which the figures are divided, but any attempt to trace them all or find them in their correct groups is doomed to failure. They well deserve proper restoring and re-dressing by experts, since, to quote Murray's *Handbook*, "in no other place can the visitor obtain such a vivid impression of that strange old Turkish life which passed away for ever when Mahmud II introduced his reforms."[2]

As is only to be imagined, the *Kislar Agha* was an enormously rich man, and rarely relinquished his post of his own accord. But such occasions have arisen, and in all cases he is sent to Egypt. In fact, several of them purchase property in Egypt solely with a view to retiring there later and spending their last days in Oriental splendour. No objection is made by the Sultan to these acquisitions, since he himself is the heir of the *Kislar Agha*, and knows that everything will come back to the Crown in time. A handsome pension is given on retirement.

The *baltaji*, and also the negro and other women doing paid work in the Palace, receive their wages from a secretary of the *Kislar Agha*,

---

[1] In addition to the drawing of the *Kislar Agha* reproduced opposite p. 130, see *Recueil de cent estampes* of M. de Ferriol (Paris, 1714–15), Plate 4. Compare with this Fig. 5 in Plate II of Arif Pacha, *Anciens costumes de l'empire ottoman*; and especially Fig. 21 of Preziosi, *Stamboul* (Paris, 1858), where the "Eunuque de Sérail" is represented as a huge and ugly creature on horseback with a gross and cruel face and blubber lips. He carries a whip of hippopotamus hide in his hand, and an attendant is walking by his side.

[2] P. 74.

who also keeps an account of the mosque revenues and other moneys
that help to swell his master's income. Yet with all this dignity and
importance the Chief Black Eunuch was a crude, ignorant, and cor-
rupted man, and the thrusting of such power into his hands played
a large part in the decline and fall of the Ottoman Empire.

Next in importance to the *Kislar Agha* came the *Hazinedar Agha*,
or Grand Treasurer, who often succeeded him in office. To his care
was entrusted the financial side of the *ḥarēm* as well as that of the
baltaji. He rendered his accounts quarterly, when they were passed
on to the treasurer of the *oda*. He held the rank of Pasha with three
tails. His deputy was known as the *Hazine-Vekil*.

Next was the *Bash-Mussahib*, who acted as *liaison* officer between
the Sultan and the *Kislar Agha*. He had eight or ten officers under
him, called *Mussahibs*, who were on duty in pairs throughout the
day to carry orders from the Sultan to the Mistress of the *ḥarēm*.

Other officers were the *Oda-Lala*, Master of the Chamber, the
Bash-Kapi-Oghlan, Chief Gatekeeper of the Apartments, and the
Yaïlak-Bash-Kapi-Oghlan, his assistant. In addition to these, further
officers would be appointed if there was a Sultan Validé in the
Seraglio. In this case she would have her own Chief Eunuch, her
treasurer, *imām*, children's tutor, Keeper of the Sherbets, and other
black eunuchs in minor offices, all with numerous assistants ready for
any eventuality. It will thus be seen that the total number of black
eunuchs employed in the *ḥarēm* at the height of its power could not
have been much less than 600 to 800. Early estimates of the number
employed were very small. About 1517 Menavino suggests forty,
while in 1537 Junis Bey reduces the figure to twenty. But we must
remember that it was not until after the time of Suleiman that the
ḥarēm began to grow to any appreciable extent. The number of
women in the *ḥarēm* in his time was only 300, while under Murad III
it had risen to about 1200, and the number of black eunuchs increased
accordingly. At the beginning of the seventeenth century Bon
tells us that some thirty of them guarded the Sultana's gate alone.
D'Ohsson gives a conservative estimate of "some two hundred," and
subsequent figures vary between 300 and 500. It is only quite recently
that, with the greater knowledge of the *personnel* of the Seraglio and
of the actual construction of the rooms and passages of the *ḥarēm*,

we have been able to realize how large a number could be employed, if as many as thirty were detailed to guard a single gate. That the number fluctuated largely is certain, but more than this is mere guess-work. The work entrusted to the ordinary black eunuchs was chiefly that of guards, not only of the outside and inside doors, but of passages, courtyards, and storerooms. The more personal offices were given either to the very young or to the old and experienced men. It should be realized that the negro eunuch went through a long and careful training just as the *ajem-oghlans* did. Once again we can turn to Bon, who gives us a clear account of their apprenticeship:

> The boys are watched and disciplined by the other youths of the Seraglio, till at a certain age they are ready for service. They are then removed thence and sent to the women and placed under others in the service of the Sultana, being under the command of their chief, the *Kislar Agha*, or Head of the Virgins. They have a considerable allowance, of 60 to 100 *aspri* a day, two robes of finest silk, clothes, and other things for their needs throughout the year, besides what is plentifully bestowed on them from other quarters. They bear names of flowers, such as Hyacinth, Narcissus, Rose, and Carnation; since as they are in the service of women they have names suitable to virginity, whiteness, and fragrance.[1]

The eunuchs are also entrusted with taking and receiving messages between the Sultan and the Sultanas, transacting business, visiting the men's apartments, carrying notes to the *Kapi Agha* for him to deliver to the Sultan, and many other similar duties. But from the moment they enter it they must never leave the Seraglio without special permission from the Sultana, even though bidden to do something by one of the lesser wives. No white eunuchs are allowed to visit their black brethren in any circumstances whatever. Even the Chief Physician passes in between a double file of black eunuchs without seeing the sign of a woman, and the extended hand of the patient is the most he is permitted to inspect.

The offices and duties of the white eunuchs have already been discussed when their quarters were being dealt with, which occupy a position between the Second and Third Courts (see pp. 119–121).

---

[1] P. 90.

2. The Use of Eunuchs by the Turks and the Origin of the Custom

Although the use of eunuchs to guard women had been customary for centuries both in the Middle and in the Far East, the practice was unknown and unnecessary among the Turks until they had established their capital in Europe and had begun to adopt so many of the customs of the Byzantine Greeks. The practice was not new to Constantinople, and although the employment of eunuchs had been forbidden by Domitian in the first century of the Christian era we find constant mention of them in Byzantine times.

The early Sultans knew nothing of eunuchs, just as they knew nothing of the *ḥarēm*, royal seclusion, elaborate Court ceremonial, or the almost exclusive employment of Christians to form a slave government.

At the earliest it was not until the middle of the fifteenth century that the use of eunuchs began to be adopted. Adrianople had become the capital in 1361, and gradually assumed the true nature of a capital: the city was fortified, public buildings were erected, mosques were built, and a royal palace was set up. As time went on the Byzantine custom of the seclusion of majesty began to impress itself on the conquerors, and the methods previously employed to protect that majesty were also adopted, and so gradually the *ḥarēm* and the employment of eunuchs came into being. The two things went together as they always had done. Despotism and polygamy had created the necessity for eunuchs, and the injunctions of the *Korān* were overlooked with surprising rapidity and casualness. It was, of course, the swift development of the Turkish Empire that forced the pace. The continual victories in different parts of Bulgaria, Croatia, and Greece as well as in Asia Minor, Syria, Egypt, and Persia produced a rich booty in slaves. Presents of slaves, both male and female, from conquered Emirs or princes wishing to gain the Sultan's favour and protection, would often include eunuchs, and once the innovation had proved a success the demand could easily be supplied. Turkish historians date the introduction of the employment of eunuchs in the first quarter of the fifteenth century under Muhammad I and Murad II.

This apparently refers only to white eunuchs. The black variety, however, were in use about 1475, while by the time of Suleiman the Magnificent Roxelana's personal guard consisted of both white and black eunuchs. With the moving of the Royal *ḥarēm* from the *Eski Serai* to the new palace on Seraglio Hill about 1541 the institution became firmly established. As the power of the Ottoman Empire grew and the State coffers became full, so also the numbers in the Seraglio increased, and Court ceremony became even more elaborate than before. If formerly two eunuchs were sufficient to guard a door, now it was ten. And so the true Oriental love of pomp and display was given full rein, and the Greco-Byzantine splendour was revived once more.

But the reign of the eunuchs was a long one, and even in this twentieth century, in the time of Abd ul-Hamid II, their power was as great as ever.

It would be hard to find a eunuch more cruel and vile than was Djevher Agha, a huge, swollen, balloon-like creature of extraordinary stature who ended his wretched life at the rope's end on Galata Bridge. In Nadir Agha, the second eunuch of this period, a man bought at the age of ten from an Egyptian slave merchant for 150 francs, we see an example of the girlish, slim variety. The revolution of 1908 was the death-blow to a system that was rotten to the core.

It may be of interest to trace, as briefly as possible, the origin of the use of eunuchs, the route by which the custom came to Europe, and whence in later years the Turkish supply was obtained.

The original home of the eunuch appears to have been Mesopotamia, the cradle of so many institutions to be transplanted westward. The contention of Ammianus Marcellinus[1] that the first person to castrate men was Semiramis may perhaps be not so far from the truth after all. But we must no longer regard her as the Ishtar-like goddess of Greek myth, but identify her with Sammuramat, who ruled Assyria as queen-mother from 811 to 808 B.C. It is proved from extant texts that eunuchs were employed in Assyria, and their constant mention in the Old Testament (whatever meaning *sārīs* may have in each particular reference) only tends to support this

---

[1] xiv, 6, 17.

assertion. With the eunuch priest of Ephesian Artemis, Atargatis, and the Cybele-Attis cult we are not concerned, nor does our brief inquiry touch religious sodomy, widely spread not only in Africa, but also among the ancient Semites and American aborigines. The mention of the existence of such strange cults is made to show how the ' religious ' eunuch was gradually moving westward—from Mesopotamia to Syria, from Syria to Asia Minor, and from Asia Minor to Europe.

But this was not the end of the unholy wedlock between religion and eunuchs, and the unnatural development of asceticism in the early Christian Church was as virulent as it was amazing. " The Kingdom of Heaven is thrown open to eunuchs," declared Tertullian, while Origen was only one of many who castrated himself. The patristic code of morality, as evidenced by the writings of men like Athanasius, Clement of Alexandria, St Jerome, St Ambrose, and Gregory of Nyssa, advocated the absolute necessity for chastity *at any cost*, and woman was regarded as the obstacle to that chastity. The doctrine was dangerous in the extreme, and much appalling unhappiness must have resulted. To the Church, too, must be laid the guilt of countenancing the vile practice of castrating boys to preserve their voices for the Papal choir in the Sistine Chapel. Although condemned by Benedict XIV the custom continued until the accession of Leo XIII in 1878. Closely connected was the use of eunuch singers on the Italian operatic stage, where in the eighteenth century these *castrati* were extremely popular, and male sopranos —Nicolini, Grimaldi, Senesino, Farinelli, and many others—became famous throughout Europe.

The only other ' religious ' eunuchs of which mention should be made are the Skoptsi (*skopets,* ' eunuch '), first discovered in 1772 in villages around Orjól, in the districts of Belev and Aléxin. This secret Russian sect, from a mere sixty, numbers some 100,000 to-day, although many of its members have not submitted to the rite of castration. One of their curious beliefs is that Adam and Eve were created sexless, and that after the Fall the halves of the forbidden fruit were grafted upon them as testicles and breasts. Hence it is their duty to restore the disfigured image of God, by aid of the Knife, to its original form. The sect has a strange attraction for

Finns, who appear to be temperamentally disposed to religious fanaticism.

But to return to the 'lay' eunuch, used to guard ḥarēms, we soon find the practice spreading from Assyria to Persia, and the Persians are probably the first people we know for certain to have castrated prisoners for the express purpose of employing them to guard the ḥarēm. When Cyrus captured Babylon in 538 B.C. he decided that as eunuchs had no families they were in the unique position of having nobody to love and serve other than him who employed them.

According to Xenophon his argument was as follows:

. . . he observed that as eunuchs were not susceptible to any [family] affections, he thought that they would esteem most highly those who were in the best position to make them rich and to stand by them, if ever they were wronged, and to place them in offices of honour; and no one, he thought, could surpass him in bestowing favours of that kind. Besides, inasmuch as eunuchs are objects of contempt to the rest of mankind, for this reason, if for no other, they need a master who will be their patron; for there is no man who would not think that he had a right to take advantage of a eunuch at every opportunity unless there were some higher power to prevent his doing so; but there is no reason why even a eunuch should not be superior to all others in fidelity to his master. But he did not admit what many might very easily be inclined to suppose, that eunuchs are weaklings; and he drew this conclusion also from the case of other animals: for instance, vicious horses, when gelded, stop biting and prancing about, to be sure, but are none the less fit for service in war; and bulls, when castrated, lose somewhat of their high spirit and unruliness but are not deprived of their strength or capacity for work. And in the same way dogs, when castrated, stop running away from their masters, but are no less useful for watching or hunting. And men, too, in the same way, become gentler when deprived of this desire, but not less careful of that which is entrusted to them; they are not made any less efficient horsemen, or any less skilful lancers, or less ambitious men. On the contrary, they showed both in times of war and in hunting that they still preserved in their souls a spirit of rivalry; and of their fidelity they gave the best proof upon the fall of their masters, for no one ever performed acts of greater fidelity in his master's misfortunes than eunuchs do. And if it is thought with some justice that they are inferior in bodily strength, yet on the field of battle steel makes the weak equal to the strong. Recognizing these facts, he selected eunuchs for every post of personal service to him, from the door-keepers up.[1]

Although in a few exceptional cases the judgment of Cyrus has proved correct, yet as a general rule the power of eunuchs has brought in its trail nothing but cruelty, intrigue, corruption, and disaster.

Herodotus[2] tells us how the Persians castrated the Ionians and carried them off, together with the most beautiful virgins, to their king. Thus the custom became only too well known in Greece at an early date. In the opposite direction, castration was already well established in China, and flourished there until the fall of the great Palace of Pekin.

But in the West the contagion of Asiatic luxury introduced the eunuch to Rome as well as Greece, and Gibbon has much to tell us of the reign of the eunuchs over the Roman world:

> Restrained by the severe edicts of Domitian and Nerva, cherished by the pride of Diocletian, reduced to an humble station by the prudence of Constantine, they multiplied in the palaces of his degenerate sons, and insensibly acquired the knowledge, and at length the direction, of the secret councils of Constantius.[3]

But there were those who feared not to attack this cancer that was rotting the heart of the Empire, and Claudian, the last of the classic poets, devotes an entire poem to an attack on Eutropius, the eunuch who dominated Arcadius (378–408) so utterly. With pen dipped in vitriol he finds it hard to express his loathing and contempt for the eunuch and the depth to which the state has sunk to allow such vermin to govern. " Up hastens the Armenian," he cries,

> skilled by operating with unerring knife to make males womanish and to increase their loathly value by such loss. He drains the body's life-giving fluid from its double source and with one blow deprives his victim of a father's function and the name of husband.[4]

But in spite of everything the custom lingered in the Levant, and when the Turks first began to seclude their women the Byzantines

---

[1] *Cyropædia*, vii, v, 60–65, translated by W. Miller, vol. ii (1914), the Loeb Classical Library.   [2] vi, 32.

[3] See further *Decline and Fall*, chapter xix.

[4] Translated by M. Platnauer, 47–51, vol. i (1920), the Loeb Classical Library.

were able to supply the necessary eunuchs for a time. But soon they began to look farther afield. White eunuchs were obtainable from many of the conquered areas, but they often proved delicate, and the mortality was great. The negro was tried, and proved both cheap and successful. Thus a demand for them was created, and the slave-dealers soon taught the African chiefs that a living prisoner was much more valuable than a dead one. This is not the place to discuss the growth of the slave traffic, but a word might well be said on the locality from which these negroes were drawn and the routes by which they reached their destination. Although the supply of negroes went entirely to Muhammadan countries, it was in all probability only geographical considerations that kept them from ever reaching the other great palace which employed such enormous quantities of eunuchs—that in the Forbidden City of Pekin. The great difference between the eunuchs in Turkey and those in Pekin was that whereas in China they were all Chinese, in Turkey they were anything but Turks. As far as the Levant was concerned, Egypt, Abyssinia, and Central Africa became a happy hunting-ground, and thus as time went on the Georgian and Circassian 'whites' were supplemented by the Abyssinian and Sudanese 'blacks.' According to Muhammadan law slaves captured in war became the absolute property of the victor, and, as any title to property could be transferred, the slave-dealer, having procured his slaves from an African chief or Arab kidnapper, could legally commit his right to any Muhammadan customer who cared to pay the price. Consequently a flourishing and lucrative trade was soon established. The chief locality from which the negroes were obtained was in the upper reaches of the White Nile, chiefly Kordofan, Darfur, and Dongola as well as the Bagirmi district to the south-east of Lake Chad. Others came from Abyssinia, whence they proceeded to the Red Sea ports of Massawa and Suakin to begin a weary journey to the chief emporiums, such as Smyrna, Beirut, Jeddah, Mecca, Medina, and Constantinople. For the most part the White Nile negroes would be taken up the Nile to Alexandria, crammed like sardines in tiny boats, or else they would be made to cross the Sahara partly on foot and partly on camel, finally to reach the coast at Tripoli, Tunis, or Morocco. The transportation of the human merchandise was naturally a tedious and risky

affair, and *entrepôts* had. to be established en route. On the Nile
route they were at Gondokoro and Khartoum, and at such places as
Kebabo and Marzuk, in the Fezzan district, on the Sahara route. It
was during the halts at these places that the castration of the negro
boys took place. The operation was dangerous, and, with only the
warm desert sand to use as a styptic, mortality was high, but the
slave-dealer had allowed for this, and such eunuch boys as *did* arrive
at their destination compensated for the losses by the large prices
they fetched. The caravan would also contain a large number of
negresses, to find a ready market in Cairo and Constantinople.
Eunuchs, being a luxury, were often privately sold, going to the
homes of the rich Pashas, if not to the Seraglio itself. The rest of the
stock would be taken to the slave market, which has only disappeared in recent years.

Some description of the methods of meeting the demand for white
eunuchs has already been given when we were dealing with their
quarters in the Seraglio (see pp. 121–122).

3. THE PHYSIOLOGICAL AND PSYCHOLOGICAL ASPECT

The inclusion of a short section on this side of the subject is due
not so much to the desire to make this chapter as complete as possible,
but rather to the fact that a better appreciation of the physical and
mental condition of eunuchs and their varieties will unquestionably
lead to the greater understanding of the *ḥarēm* system and to its
gradual decay and fall, so largely caused by the introduction and
increasing influence of this unproductive, sterile, unnatural, and
altogether unwholesome member of society—the eunuch.

From the earliest times a considerable interest has been shown in
regard to eunuchs. This is really only natural, for even freaks of
nature are sufficient to hold the interest of the curious, so much so that
no travelling circus is complete without its Siamese twins, bearded
lady, Tom Thumb, or some other example of the grim jokes of
nature.

But in the case of eunuchs everybody knows that the condition is
not natural, but is a terrible mutilation imposed by one male upon
another. The effect is seen—and heard—the reason is generally

appreciated; but the methods by which the mutilation is carried out and the different degrees to which this can be done appear to be hardly known at all. This general ignorance is certainly not due to lack of interest in the subject, but to several distinct factors—the scarcity of published information, the gradual discontinuance of the custom, the secrecy which has always surrounded the infamous trade of making eunuchs, and the consequential disinclination of those connected in any way with it to discuss the subject at all. Most of the writers on eunuchs wrote under *noms-de-plume*, while, with the single exception of the book by Millant (see p. 151), there appears to be no modern work on the subject whatsoever. As is often the case, the etymological history of the words connected with the subject affords a certain amount of information. There is, however, considerable difference of opinion among scholars about the derivation and meaning of the best-known word of all—'eunuch.' Several German philologists suggest that the Greek εὐνοῦχος is a loan word from the Semitic. I can, however, find no proof of this whatever, and inquiries from Assyrian and Hebrew scholars in Great Britain have yielded nothing in support of such a theory. It would seem, then, that the old derivation, from εὐνή, 'bed,' and οχ, the ablaut stem of ἔχειν, 'to keep'—the word thus meaning 'he who has charge of the bed'—should still be adhered to. The only Assyrian connexion appears to be through the Hebrew *sārīs*, 'eunuch,' which is a loan word from the Assyrian *ša rêsi*, meaning, as a passage in a medical text explains, *la alidi*, 'he who does not beget.' Thus these words are self-explanatory, whereas 'eunuch' tells us nothing of the physical condition. It should be noted, however, that the Hebrew *sārīs* had two distinct meanings—in fact, they were really two separate words —one being 'eunuch' and the other 'captain,' 'high official,' or 'chamberlain.' The latter occurs chiefly in the Old Testament (Deuteronomy, 2 Kings, Isaiah, Jeremiah, etc.), while in Matthew, Acts, and Romans the former is the meaning intended.[1] There are several other words connected with castration that are informative, as they show us that the condition was brought about by crushing, striking, cutting, and pulling.

[1] On this subject see further T. K. Cheyne and J. S. Black, *Encyclopædia Biblica*, vol. ii (1901).

The method of striking or crushing [1] is apparent in such words as the Latin *capo*, 'capon,' from the Greek κόπτω, 'strike,' the Greek θλᾰδίας, θλῐβίας, 'eunuch,' from θλάω, 'crush,' and the Sanskrit *vadhri*, 'eunuch,' from *vadh*, 'strike.' Cutting is shown in the Latin *castro*, 'castrate,' from root *kes*, in the Sanskrit *śas*, 'cut,' in the Greek τομίας, 'eunuch,' from τέμνω, 'cut,' and in the Sanskrit *niraṣṭa*, 'castrated,' from *aśri*, 'edge' or 'knife.' Finally, the operation of pulling or dragging appears to be implied in such words as the Greek σπάδων, 'eunuch,' from σπάω, 'drag.'

Thus it would seem that there are several kinds of eunuchs, quite apart from those born entirely impotent. The early Christians naturally followed Matthew, xix, 12, where we read:

> For there are eunuchs, which were so born from their mother's womb: and there are eunuchs, which were made eunuchs by men: and there are eunuchs, which made themselves eunuchs for the kingdom of heaven's sake.

Critics of this passage tell us that the word 'eunuch' is used symbolically, and the meaning is that those who have entirely devoted themselves to the interests of the kingdom of heaven cannot satisfy the claims of married life. However, Origen lived to repent his too literal rendering of the passage. It is interesting to note that Muhammad also uses the word in a symbolic sense when he condemns the making of eunuchs, and adds, "Castration in Islām may consist only in fasting."

In classical times the varieties of eunuchs were as follows:

(1) *Castrati*, clean-cut—both penis and testicles.
(2) *Spadones*, whose testicles only are removed by a process of dragging.
(3) *Thlibiæ*, whose testicles are bruised and crushed, the seminal glands being thus permanently injured—chiefly applied in the case of the very young.

The *thlasiæ* were almost identical with No. 3 above.

In the East, according to Burton,[2] there were also three kinds:

---

[1] Mentioned in the Sanskrit *Atharva-Veda*, VI, cxxxviii, 2.
[2] *Nights*, Supp. vol. i, pp. 71–72.

(1) *Sandali*, or clean-shaved. The parts are swept off by a single
cut of a razor, a tube (tin or wooden) is set in the urethra,
the wound is cauterized with boiling oil, and the patient
is planted in a fresh dung-hill. His diet is milk, and if
under puberty he often survives.

(2) The eunuch whose penis is removed. He retains all the
power of copulation and procreation without the where-
withal; and this, since the discovery of caòutchouc, has
often been supplied.

(3) The eunuch, or classical *thlibias* and *semivir*, who has been
rendered sexless by the removing of the testicles (as the
priests of Cybele were castrated with a stone knife), or
by their being bruised (the Greek θλᾰσίας), twisted,
seared, or bandaged.

Methods seem to have been similar in all countries, the only differences being in the local means employed to stop hæmorrhage and to
prevent the passages from swelling. Stent gives a detailed description
of the method adopted with Chinese eunuchs:

The operation is performed in this manner:—white ligatures or
bandages are bound tightly round the lower part of the belly and the
upper parts of the thighs, to prevent too much hemorrhage. The
parts about to be operated on are then bathed three times with hot
pepper-water, the intended eunuch being in a reclining position.
When the parts have been sufficiently bathed, the *whole*—both testicles
and penis—are cut off as closely as possible with a small carved knife,
something in the shape of a sickle. The emasculation being effected, a
pewter needle or spigot is carefully thrust into the main orifice at the
root of the penis; the wound is then covered with paper saturated in
cold water and is carefully bound up. After the wound is dressed the
patient is made to walk about the room, supported by two 'knifers,'
for two or three hours, when he is allowed to lie down. The patient
is not allowed to drink anything for three days, during which time he
often suffers great agony, not only from thirst, but from intense pain,
and from the impossibility of relieving nature during that period. At
the end of three days the bandage is taken off, the spigot is pulled out,
and the sufferer obtains relief in the copious flow of urine which
spurts out like a fountain. If this takes place satisfactorily, the patient
is considered out of danger and congratulated on it; but if the unfortunate wretch cannot make water he is doomed to a death of

agony, for the passages have become swollen and nothing can save him.[1]

The mortality is not great, although exaggerated figures have been given. It is obvious, however, that the number of fatal cases among young negroes at the mercy of unskilled 'knifers' would be considerable. In fact, a large discount for 'losses *en route*' was always allowed. In speaking of eunuchs in the Seraglio Sandys and Rycaut mention the fact that they carried quills of silver hidden in their turbans, through which to make water.

The physical and mental effects of castration naturally vary according to the age at which the operation is performed. If the subject is a child not yet arrived at the age of puberty and if proper precautions are taken the operation is not dangerous. But after puberty both physical and mental effects become a very important factor. The mind has begun to realize the promptings of nature even if actual intercourse has not taken place, and consequently the full realization of the irreparable loss brings an agony of mind that is hard for us to realize. But even if sexual thoughts or desires were absent it would often happen that when constant attendance upon women had created a knowledge, all too late, of what pleasures awaited the normal man, a feeling of terrible resentment would be experienced, coupled with a mingled feeling of revenge and despair. No wonder, then, that eunuchs have been described as ill-tempered, morose, childish, petulant, revengeful, cruel, and arrogant; and on the other hand as simple, credulous, harmless, fawning, fond of pleasure, and very generous in their dealings. This apparent contradiction of characteristics would seem to arise from the widely varying effects the operation has on different subjects. It is not only the age of the victim that has to be considered in the forming of his mental make-up, but the circumstances that led to his castration. A boy captured in a raid and sold later would never bear the terrible grudge against humanity in general, and his parents in particular, as a boy would who had been sold by his parents for the mere lust of gain. The physical effects of castration are well known—complete lack of bodily hair, the feminine 'cracked' voice (deeper, however, in the black races), the gradual flabbiness of the body, often accompanied by

[1] *Journal of the Royal Asiatic Society*, North China branch (1877), p. 171.

obesity and ugly wrinkling of the skin in later life. Among other effects of castration may be mentioned a weak bladder, loss of memory, insomnia, and bad eyesight. Eunuchs have no liking for alcohol, of which the smallest amount is sufficient to make them incapable. They prefer cakes and sweetmeats to meat. Their favourite colour is red. They like music, especially the rhythmic beat of the drum or tambourine and all Central African instruments. They are neat in their habits, but are miserly and fond of accumulating wealth. They unite the small brain of the negro with the childish imagination of the ignorant Oriental. Consequently they believe the wildest stories, and once an idea has entered their minds nothing can change it. A terrible story about a Chinese eunuch, related later, goes to illustrate this point. They adore what we call 'fairy stories,' and can listen to recitations of the *Thousand Nights and a Night* and similar collections for an indefinite period. They love children and animals, including chickens, sheep, cows, and monkeys—but most of all cats, which they keep as pets and treat with the utmost care and attention.

As regards sexual feelings, it is quite incorrect to imagine that a castrated male loses all desires immediately. Not only is he often attracted strongly to women, but, strange as it may seem, evokes affection in return, and in the history of the *ḥarēm* many marriages of eunuchs have taken place. In such cases, however, the eunuch 'lives out,' and is usually drafted to one of the lesser palaces in the town. Such venereal promptings are naturally regulated by the state of the prostate, which in the case of eunuchs castrated before puberty is entirely atrophied.[1]

In a manuscript[2] dated 1699–1700, in the British Museum, by J. Richards, one of the Richards brothers, of Solsborough, County Wexford, is an interesting reference to marriages of eunuchs:

> There is a 3ᵈ Sort of Marriage if it may be so called between an Eunuch and a Woman and I hear meane those who are cut close, notwithstanding wʰ it is credibly reported that they have commerce in a manner unknown to us, and it is no great matter, nay eaven the

[1] See further Hikmet and Regnault, two Constantinople doctors, in "Les Eunuques de Constantinople" (*Bulletin et mémoires de la société d'anthropologie de Paris*, tome ii, Série V, Paris, 1901, pp. 234–240).

[2] Stowe MSS., 462, ff. 47*b*–48.

Women amongst themselves have ways of Suplying the Deffect of Men & it is not to be wondered att that these miserable Creatures who have no other knowledge of themselves than that [they] are made for the use of Man, nor that faith w^h teaches a future reward and punishment for Vertue & Vice, it is not to be admired [wondered (?)] att y^t they should give themselves up to all mañer of Lusts & Sensuality in w^h they say y^t they excell all other Women.

The sentiments that Montesquieu puts into the mouth of the Chief Eunuch in his 9th and 64th Letters may well express the true feelings of a man castrated after puberty. Montesquieu, we know, relied chiefly on Tavernier and Chardin for his knowledge of the Seraglio and its customs, but his knowledge of women was first-hand. In the 9th Letter, speaking of his disillusionment about the peace and quiet of mind that would be his after castration, when he found to his horror that women still attracted him, the eunuch continues:

. . . far from being relieved, I found myself surrounded by objects which continually whetted my desires. When I entered the Seraglio, where everything filled me with regret for what I had lost, my agitation increased every moment; a thousand natural charms seemed to unfold themselves to my sight only to tantalize me; . . . I never led a woman to my master's bed without feeling wild rage in my heart, and despair unutterable in my soul. . . . I remember one day, as I attended a lady at the bath, I was so carried away that I lost command of myself, and dared to lay my hand where I should not. My first thought was that my last day had come. I was, however, fortunate enough to escape a dreadful death; but the fair one, whom I had made the witness of my weakness, extorted a heavy price for her silence: I entirely lost command of her, and she forced me, each time at the risk of my life, to comply with a thousand caprices.

At length the fire of his youth died out, and in its place arose a desire to pay back for all the misery he had endured by harsh treatment:

The Seraglio is my Empire; and my ambition, the only passion left me, finds no small gratification. I mark with pleasure that my presence is required at all times; I willingly incur the hatred of all these women, because that establishes me more firmly in my post. And they do not hate me for nothing, I can tell you: I interfere with their most innocent pleasures; I am always in the way, an insurmountablé obstacle; before they know where they are they find their schemes frustrated; I am armed with refusals, I bristle with scruples; not a word is heard from me but duty, virtue, chastity, modesty. . . . Do not suppose that in my turn I have not to suffer endless unpleasantness. Every day these women seek occasions to repay me with interest and their reprisals are often terrible.

And the unhappy man tells of the thousand and one tricks they play on him, arousing his suspicion, anger, sympathy, and doubt just to make mock of him; and how all his efforts may be undone when their false tears, sighs, and embraces melt their master's heart. "It is their time of triumph," he concludes, "their charms are arrayed against me . . . and nothing can plead for me with a master who is no longer himself."

That eunuchs often nurse their grievances for years, and take their revenge if opportunity offers, is well known from the history of Hermotimus the Pedasian, the most favoured of all the eunuchs of Xerxes. According to Herodotus[1] he was taken by an enemy and sold, being purchased by one Panionius, a Chian, who gained a livelihood by most infamous practices. For whenever he purchased boys remarkable for their beauty, having castrated them, he used to take and sell them at Sardis and Ephesus for large sums. Hermotimus had been one of these unfortunate boys. Chance brought him in touch with Panionius once more, and he persuaded him to move to Sardis with his wife and children. Having thus got his old enemy into his power, Hermotimus upbraided him for his terrible livelihood and forced him to castrate his own four sons. Not being yet satisfied, he then made the sons castrate their father. "Thus the vengeance of Hermotimus overtook Panionius."

The knowledge that coitus was possible for quite a long time after partial castration led the 'fast' women of degenerate Rome to take full advantage of the situation. Thus Martial's bitter epigram demands:

> Do you ask, Pannychus, why your Cælia only consorts with eunuchs? Cælia wants the flowers of marriage—not the fruit.[2]

And again, referring to Domitian's law forbidding castration, Martial says:

---

[1] viii, 105, 106.   [2] vi, 67.

It used to be a sport to violate the sacred ties of marriage; a sport to mutilate innocent males. Both you forbid, Cæsar, and so help the generations yet to come, as you order that births are to be free from guilt. Thus while you are ruler no man will be eunuch or adulterer; but formerly (what morals!) even a eunuch was an adulterer.[1]

Juvenal gives us more detail on the same subject:

Some women always delight in soft eunuchs and tender kisses, and in the absence of beard and the fact that the use of abortives is unnecessary. The height of their enjoyment, however, is when the lads have been led to the doctor in the heat and first flush of youth with a bush of dark hairs already visible; and the testicles they have waited for and encouraged to grow in the early stages, as soon as they reach a couple of pounds, the surgeon, Heliodorus, seizes and scores just that much over the barber. Made a eunuch by his mistress, conspicuous from afar, he enters the bath the cynosure of all eyes, and vies with [Priapus] the guardian of our vines and gardens. Let him lie with his mistress, but, Postumus, trust not your Bromius, already grown to manhood, to him.[2]

Indeed, the fact that the eunuch who has lost only his testicles can have erections for a considerable time and enjoy sexual intercourse was fully recognized whenever such people were employed. In fact, the *motif* (if so it can be called) forms the main theme of the "Tale of the First Eunuch, Bukhayt," in the *Nights*.[3] A negro youth seduces a girl and suffers castration as a punishment. He is then made her *Agha*, but continues to have connexion with her until she dies. In a typical note on the tale Burton tells us that his *erectio et distentio penis* would last as long as his heart and circulation kept sound. Hence the eunuch who preserves his penis is much prized in the zenana, where some women prefer him to the entire man, on account of his long performance of the deed of kind; but chiefly, I may add with Juvenal, because *abortio non est opus*.

It was impossible to stop every form of sexual indulgence in the Seraglio, and a eunuch in touch with the outside world could easily smuggle artificial *phalli* and similar erotic *succedania* into the ḥarēm and to a certain extent play the part of Lesbian, which by its very novelty and perversion might help to satisfy the cravings of a bored and neglected woman. Even a married eunuch, then, was not

[1] vi, 2. [2] vi, 366-378. [3] Burton, vol. ii, pp. 49-50.

entirely deprived of all sexual enjoyment. Burton gained the confidence of a eunuch's wife, who told him that her husband practised the manifold *plaisirs de la petite oie* (masturbation, tribadism, irrumation, *tête-bêche, feuille-de-rose*, etc.) till they induced the venereal orgasm (the secretion of the prostate gland?). At the critical moment she held up a little pillow for her husband to bite, who otherwise would have torn her cheeks or breasts. There is ample evidence to show that eunuchs often had a deep and genuine affection for some of their charges, entirely free from any question of subsequent gain. It is more difficult to appreciate the technique employed by the woman to induce orgasm in the eunuchs, and no satisfactory accounts appear to exist. The procedure probably centres about the region immediately surrounding the opening of the urethra, as eunuchs sometimes report erotic sensations in that area. Anal massage would also play its part, while the knowledge and use of aphrodisiacs would assist.

It will thus be realized that after adopting the Byzantine custom of employing eunuchs to guard their *ḥarēms* the Turks were very careful to use only those who were fully emasculated. White eunuchs—Georgians and Circassians—were given jobs that would never bring them into close touch with the women, as in most cases their castration was incomplete. But as regards the negroes, the highest prices were paid for those who, besides being entirely *rasé*, possessed the ugliest and most revolting faces, it being imagined (correctly or not) that this was a further guard against any profligacy on the part of the women. The Seraglio doctors not only inspected the eunuchs on admission, but examined them every few years just to see that everything was in order and that nothing had grown again! A curious tale is told of an arrogant Chinese chief eunuch who flourished in Chien-lung's reign (1736–96). One day he insulted the omnipotent President Liu, telling him that his power was unable to extend to eunuchs. The next day Liu informed the Emperor that many of the eunuchs had grown to such an extent as to render recastration necessary, and that licentiousness and disorder were rife between them and the women. An immediate inspection was ordered, with the result that under the fresh operation many eunuchs died and appalling suffering was endured afresh. The arrogance of the eunuchs was thus forcibly checked for a time. Superstition and ignorance was capable of anything, and Stent tells us of another eunuch named Wei-chung-hsien who secretly kept a concubine and tried every known medicine to regain his powers of procreation. A doctor told him that if he extracted the brains of seven men and ate them his genitals would return to their original state. He therefore procured seven criminals, had their heads split open, the brains extracted from them, and devoured the revolting mess. Tradition does not inform us whether this horrible remedy produced the desired effect or not.

But the days of the eunuch are over. With the passing of the *ḥarēm* in the Muhammadan world (save in Mecca itself) the necessity for the eunuch has disappeared, and despite all my efforts in Turkey I met only two, or possibly three, of these strange beings. I was told that these were the last of them. They had been a necessary evil where despotism and polygamy held sway, but now they are a thing of the past—and already have returned in our minds to the pages of the *Arabian Nights*, where alone they seem rightly to belong.

4. BIBLIOGRAPHY

Bibliographically the eunuch will not detain us long, as there appear to be only three or four works entirely devoted to him. I have already given a list of articles and references to the eunuch,[1] but at that time could only discover one actual book: that by Ancillon published in 1707. I can now add two or three more. But first of all I might mention that 'Ancillon' was the *nom-de-plume*—or, rather, anagram—of Comte d'Ollincan, and his work was translated into English by Robert Samber (anonymously) in 1718.[2] Of the other books I have come across the earliest is one by Joannes Heribertus, which is a *nom-de-plume* of Teofilo Raynaud, the Italian Jesuit theologian and conversationalist.[3] The title is as follows: *Eunuchi nati, facti, mystici ex sacra et humana litteratura illustrati.*[4] The British

---

[1] *Ocean of Story* (London, 1925), vol. iii, pp. 328–329, "Indian Eunuchs."
[2] Under the title of *Eunuchism displayed, describing all the Different Sorts of Eunuchs . . . with Several Observations on Modern Eunuchs*, written by a Person of Honour (London).
[3] He wrote many curious works, for some description of which see Brunet, *Manuel du libraire*, under "Raynaud."   [4] Divione, 1655.

Museum library contains three copies of it. The next book is by Hieronymus Delphinus, *Eunuchi conjugium; hoc est, scripta varia de conjugio inter eunuchum et virginem juvenculam anno 1666 contracto.*[1]

At the time of writing the latest work on the subject appears to be *Les Eunuques à travers les âges*, by Le Dr Richard Millant.[2] It is as yet the most comprehensive work extant. My attention was drawn to it by Dr E. D. Cumming, of New York, who is busy on a history of castration.

There remains only to mention the work of H. R. M. Chamberlain, *The Eunuch in Society*, which was finished several years ago and, I believe, still awaits a publisher.

[1] Ienae, 1685. The British Museum library possesses two copies of this edition, and others of 1697, 1730, and 1737. Brunet knew only of the last two. Pisanus Fraxi (H. S. Ashbee) gives some description of the 1697 edition in his *Catena librorum tacendorum*, pp. 15–20.

[2] Published in Paris, 1908, as vol. xiii of the *Bibliothèque des perversions sexuelles.*

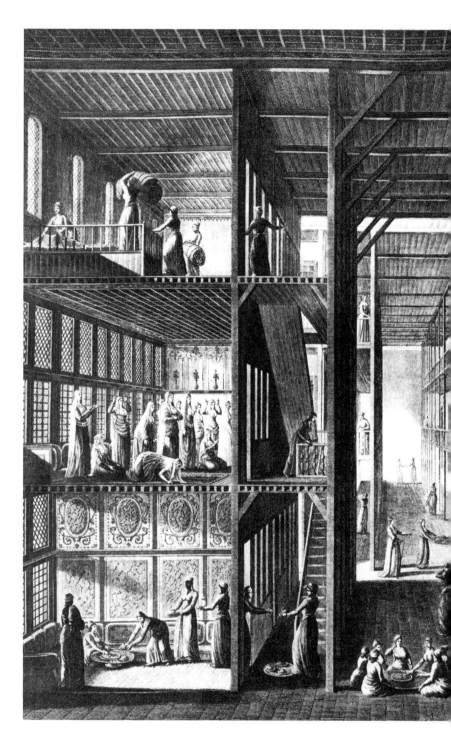

The Royal Harēm

CHAPTER VII

THE ḤARĒM—I

Bᴇғᴏʀᴇ we discuss the working arrangement of the *ḥarēm* system when it was at its height, and consider some details of the various ceremonies and activities carried on within its walls, readers will probably want to know how much remains to-day, and just what they would see if they visited the Seraglio to-morrow. I shall therefore give most of this chapter to a description of the *ḥarēm* buildings, both outside and inside, so far as I know them. I make this reservation purposely, because at the present moment it is impossible for anybody to examine every part of every room and corridor of the *ḥarēm*, even if he is armed with special permission issued by Kemal Atatürk himself. The reason for this is that the fragile state of many of the floors renders them dangerous to walk on; while several rooms and passages are entirely blocked up either by general *débris* or else by piles of packing-cases, trunks, enormous chandeliers, derelict sofas, etc. I consider myself very lucky in having been able to obtain the photograph of the courtyard of the *ḥarēm* girls (opposite p. 156), especially as even the official photographer has never been accorded such a privilege. For the full appreciation of this curious mass of little buildings which constitutes the *ḥarēm* it should be realized at once that its component parts were continually changing. Each Sultan would satisfy his whims and fancies by the erection of a new suite for a favourite *kadin*; a new courtyard would be built in one reign, only to be destroyed to make room for a kiosk in the next. As a rule private suites of past favourites were not repaired and handed over to a new occupier. On the contrary, when the ex-wives had been moved to the Old Seraglio (*Eski Serai*) on a Sultan's death, the rooms were usually left empty and allowed to fall into gradual decay. In more recent times many structural alterations and redecorations were made, especially when the French styles (Louis XIV and Louis XV) began to be popular at the Porte. We have already noticed the influence in the Hall of the Divan and certain rooms in the black eunuchs' quarters, and we shall notice it still more in the Fourth Court, where every conceivable kind of European decoration and furniture found its way to the Kiosk of Abd ul-Mejid.

Of considerable interest is Melling's drawing of the *harēm*, which I shall discuss in detail later on. At the moment I would merely refer to it in order to make clear that the *harēm* was never like that at all. The picture merely represents what Melling would have built had he been entrusted with the complete remodelling of the Seraglio, as doubtless he hoped he would be. He had already made a good beginning in being appointed architect to Hatijeh Sultan, the favourite sister of Selim III, and from what we know of his work up the Bosphorus and in the Summer Palace, we should be thankful that political events prevented him from achieving his object, and robbing one of the most interesting and unique spots in the world of what is left of its past history as evidenced by the buildings themselves, not to mention the atmosphere of romance and mystery that still pervades these tiny rooms, narrow corridors, rickety staircases, broken marble baths, musty store-cupboards, empty courtyards, heavily barred windows, and creaky, iron-studded wooden doors.

If you go there try and get rid of your guide and sit and muse alone as I did. Your powers of imagination must be poor indeed if the atmosphere of the place remains silent and tells you nothing. Naturally you should read up as much as possible before the visit; you will be rewarded a thousandfold.

Interesting as the *harēm* rooms open to the public are,[1] only half the story is told until the closed ones have been inspected as well. But most interesting of all, I think, are the rooms of the upper stories. Here the personal atmosphere reigns supreme, and when we actually stand in the boudoirs and bedrooms of members of the *harēm*, and realize that we are in the most secret and forbidden spot of a people whose name was once a terror to Europe, our perspective begins to change and we feel like intruders, and a sense of reverence mingled with what almost amounts to fear takes hold of us.

But we are anticipating.

[1] In 1935–36 they were, apart from the black eunuchs' quarters and the Princes' School, the suite and courtyard of the Sultan Valide, the Corridor of the Bath, the Sultan's bathroom, and the rooms used by Selim III and Abd ul-Hamid I.

It is not easy to say exactly where the *ḥarēm* begins and where it ends, or how distinct it was in the early days from the *selāmlik*. That the two approached each other very closely architecturally is obvious from an inspection of the buildings as they are to-day. Roughly speaking, the 'general' portion lay directly north-west of the black eunuchs' quarters, while the various suites were in the vicinity of the courtyard of the Sultan Validé, or Queen-Mother, along the south-eastern side of which ran the Golden Road, connecting the *selāmlik* with the courtyard of the black eunuchs and the Hall of the Divan. If the wall between the two Royal bathrooms (Nos. 79 and 80) was prolonged in both directions it would mark roughly the dividing line between *ḥarēm* and *selāmlik*.

There were two outer gates connecting with the main door of the *ḥarēm*. The first of these (No. 30) has already been mentioned as that near the Divan Tower, known as the Carriage Gate, since it was here that the ladies entered their carriages on those rather rare occasions when they went out for an airing. The second outer gate (No. 40), known usually as the *Kuşhane Kapisi*, or Gate of the Aviary, led from the western corner of the Third Court, and acted chiefly as a service gate. A narrow passage leads round to the main door (*Cümlekapisi*) which gives immediate access to the *Nöbetyeri*, or Guard-room (No. 42). As can be seen from the plan, this room occupies a very important point strategically, as it is necessary to pass through it in order to reach every part of the *ḥarēm*. In one corner is the entrance to the Golden Road, while from the opposite side the courtyard of the Sultan Validé and the courtyard and rooms of the *ḥarēm* slaves are reached.

The quarters of the *ḥarēm* slaves can be discussed first. They are divided into two separate sections, the first being next to the *Nöbet-yeri*, and the other right round the corner to the left. It should be pointed out that whereas this first building (No. 43) is described by the Director of the Seraglio as "the apartments of the women slaves," it is impossible to say if this was always so, and I am of the opinion that although some members of the *ḥarēm* occupied all three floors, they were not always of the lowest class, but, owing to the very position of the building, were in all probability *kadins*, and each floor would constitute a suite. In later years it is quite likely that changes occurred, but the majority of the rooms of the *ḥarēm* slaves were clustered round the courtyard to the left (No. 44), and by their communal nature are much more fitted to the housing of a large body of women than is the first building. Immediately behind is a square reservoir, supplying the neighbouring fountains and baths.

As we turn to the left the courtyard of the *ḥarēm* slaves appears, and it was at the entrance to it that I took the photograph reproduced in the plate opposite p. 156.

An arcade of nine arches, supported by as many pillars with lotus capitals, lines the whole of the left side and farther end (No. 44). The ground floor on this side is occupied by the kitchen, baths, and stairway leading to the bedrooms on the first floor, which extend all round the far end of the courtyard and, as we shall see later, communicate by a well with others on the ground floor. The kitchen is a small room immediately to the left opposite the second and third pillars, and needs no description, as it is entirely dismantled and used as a storeroom. Next this is the *hamam*, consisting of two rooms of unequal size, both originally lined with white marble, as shown by sections which still remain *in situ* at odd places. The basins are in a good state of preservation. There is a small window let into the wall between the two rooms used as a lamp niche. At the back of the smaller room is a lavatory of the usual type, consisting merely of marble foot-pieces and a sunken receptacle behind. Farther down the court are the rooms of the *ḥarēm* commissary and the coffee-maker.

On the opposite side of the court, not shown in the photograph, are three long, narrow rooms, occupied by the Head Nurse, the Mistress of the *ḥarēm*, and the Chief Laundress, and another large room apparently shared by other members of the *ḥarēm* staff. I cannot guarantee the allocation of these rooms, as the information given me in the Seraglio was not at all clear and may only refer to comparatively recent times.

The most interesting of the rooms is that of the Head Nurse, which is divided by a small toilet and large cupboard into two almost equal parts. The first of these has some fine tiling on the walls. The second contains six painted wall cupboards and two windows leading on to a balcony. I was informed that the cradles of the Sultan's numerous progeny were put out here for an airing. It is certainly a most delightful spot, looking straight out on to the gardens, with the Bosphorus ahead and the Marmora to the right. A most beautiful golden cradle encrusted with precious stones (*Murassa altin beşik*) is to be seen in the Seraglio Museum.

It would appear that certain alterations have occurred, because in an old picture each of these three rooms had a separate balcony, and to-day there is only one long balcony, as the photograph reproduced opposite p. 107 shows. Adjoining the Head Nurse's room is a double doorway opening on to a flight of stone steps which lead under the building to the gardens below. Farther along past the room of the Mistress of the *ḥarēm* is another double door, through which access is gained to the *ḥarēm* hospital, but I shall return to that below.

As already mentioned, the staircase on the left of the courtyard leads up to the girls' bedrooms. Beyond a small lavatory on a half-landing a narrow passage is soon reached at the top of the stairs, off which lead several small rooms, apparently the suite of the Mistress on night duty. The main room at the end of the passage is interesting from several points of view. Its walls are extremely thick, with three double windows heavily barred and three mattress cupboards on the garden side, three more windows on the courtyard side closer together, and three more mattress cupboards on the connecting side to the right. Eight short pillars with lotus capitals, too heavy for the room, support the ceiling, and enclose a parapet protecting a large rectangular opening through which nearly the whole of the ground-floor room can be seen. This lower room is also a large bedroom, lined with mattress cupboards, and here some of the original mattresses can still be seen in a sad state of repair. A small lavatory and water-tap complete the fittings of the upstairs room. The girls' mattresses would be laid out in a row right round the wall opening, and the Mistress would find it easy to control the occupants of both floors by this simple arrangement. Mention might be made of a small parasol box or cupboard at the angle of the passage just outside the door of the first room at the top of the stairs.

Returning to the courtyard and crossing over to the other side, we come to the double doors leading to a long flight of fifty-three stone steps, broken at intervals to form small landings giving access to rooms on both sides connected with the so-called *ḥarēm* hospital,

THE COURTYARD OF THE ḤARĒM SLAVES

AN ACCOUCHEMENT IN THE ḤARĒM

to which they ultimately lead. On reaching the bottom one finds oneself in a charming courtyard full of trees, surrounded by an arched colonnade supported on eight square columns each side, but none at either end. It would be hard to imagine a more sequestered or unexpected spot. Hidden away on the lower side of the hill, reached only by a secret staircase under the other buildings, and visible only from the Head Nurse's balcony, this little courtyard and its surrounding rooms are as romantic as they are fascinating, even if they did constitute a hospital, which I am inclined to doubt. The rooms themselves vary in depth and size, mainly owing to the slope of the outside wall. They occupy two floors, the entrance to the second floor being gained from the first landing up the steps again. The present condition of the rooms is deplorable, and as many of them are entirely without windows, or have them blocked up or shuttered, it is difficult to inspect them in any detail—especially as the masses of *débris* hinder progress, besides which some of the floors and ceilings have holes in them, and the danger of falling slats, plaster, and masonry is by no means negligible. However, the general impression is favourable as far as the facilities provided for the running of quarters of this size are concerned. On the ground floor there is a series of deep dark rooms to the right, now devoid of all decoration. Following the rooms round the courtyard from right to left, one comes to a large *hamam* of considerable artistic interest. Several beautiful marble fountains are to be seen, some still *in situ*. The amount of broken masonry and rubbish is, however, so great that it is practically impossible to state the exact extent and condition of the marble flooring and panelling.

Continuing round the far corner, we observe that two floors of rooms occupy this shorter side, and appear to be the kitchen quarters —the coffee-room and bedrooms of the kitchen staff. The kitchen itself lies to the left, a large high room on the ground floor, capable of providing for fifty people at the least. Remains of ovens and serving-tables can still be recognized among the *débris*. Next the kitchen is a large toilet-room containing five separate lavatories and a considerable space for washing and minor ablutions. The other rooms on this side closely resemble those opposite. They would appear, however, to be sitting-rooms rather than bedrooms.

The rooms on the first floor are for the most part small—obviously more bedrooms—except for another kitchen, and one of somewhat different proportions, which may possibly have been occupied by the matron. Most of the bedrooms are unsafe to walk in, and the visitor has to be content with standing at the threshold. From a small second landing a little yard can be seen connecting with some of the basement rooms, while on looking upward to the right we can distinguish the balcony of the Head Nurse's rooms. It is now realized how low down the hospital lies, for although this is the first floor, the Nurse's rooms far above us are on the ground floor of the main building.

Owing to the size, extent, and fittings of this so-called ḥarēm hospital, I cannot help wondering if it was always used as such, for it is much larger than the quarters of the ḥarēm girls, which hardly seems reasonable. The size of the baths, kitchens, and toilets suggests a busy crowded quarter continually in full working order rather than a hospital for which numbers would vary greatly, and which in itself hardly seems to agree with what little we know of the very secret way in which a Seraglio doctor was introduced to the room of a sick girl.

So much, then, for the entire quarters of the main body of the ḥarēm girls, or slaves as they are often called. Everybody was a slave of the Sultan, so that the term must not be taken too literally. The harder work was done almost entirely by negresses, whose lodgings were for the most part in the basements under the main building. The work allotted to the other girls varied according as to how far they had got in their training, which was an important part of the ḥarēm system, and to which I shall return in the next chapter. The remaining portions of the ḥarēm are devoted to the courtyard and suite of the Sultan Validé, the adjacent rooms connected with her retinue and the management of the ḥarēm, and the suites for specially favoured kadins. Such a suite would appear to have once existed in what is now described as the Sultanahmet Köşkü (No. 63 in our plan). The entrance lies almost exactly opposite the first row of columns in the girls' courtyard.

A steep flight of steps leads into a long and very high rectangular room now devoid of all decoration. Such a high room is quite out of keeping with the rest of the building, and at once suggests the collapse of at least one floor and subsequent partial renovation. High up in the corner is a small balcony, bright with coloured woodwork. Behind this is a landing with a few steps leading to a charming little painted room looking out over the suite of the Sultan Validé towards the Bosphorus. The style and decoration of the room, its pretty rounded shape, with its many windows and gaily coloured paintings of Italian gardens, proclaim it to be a kind of summer kiosk free to catch the breezes from the Bosphorus and Marmora and far removed from the inquisitive gaze of the less lucky members of the Imperial *ḥarēm*. The room is in bad repair, and merits immediate attention, as in its own quiet way it is a little gem.

From the square courtyard of the Sultan Validé access can be gained to her suite of four rooms. They consist of a small waiting-room to the right, a corridor room leading to the dining-room (*yemek odasi*), and a bedroom (*yatak odasi*) leading off to the left with a sofa lounge looking out towards the Bosphorus. All these rooms are open to the public, and so need little description here. They are for the most part beautifully tiled with large floral designs; painted and gilded ceilings and baroque gilded carvings show later additions. A few carpets remain, but little else. This, then, is the most important, if not the most intriguing, part of the *ḥarēm*. From here the whole Seraglio, and at times the whole Turkish Empire, was ruled. These tiny silent rooms could indeed a tale unfold, and we cannot help feeling privileged to see them at all, even in their altered, dismantled state. The courtyard has also undergone many changes, as the sudden discontinuance of the Turkish arches and pillars bearing the lotus capital clearly shows. A little tiling surrounding and lining a large niche to the right of the Sultan Validé's doorway is all that remains of what must have once extended much farther round the courtyard. The opposite side forms the inner wall of the Golden Road, while in the northern corner entrance is gained to the Vestibule of the Hearth (*Ocakli Sofa*) and the Vestibule of the Fountain (*Çeşmeli Sofa*). Here we are really outside the *ḥarēm*, but it is difficult to draw hard-and-fast rules, as considerable architectural changes occurred in this part towards the end of the seventeenth century. For instance, that part now occupied in the plan by Nos. 72 and 73 is described in the official guide-books as *Başkadin ve*

Kadinlar Dariesi (suite of the Chief Kadin and of the *kadins*). Thus this was obviously part of the *ḥarēm*, but in the seventeenth century it seems that a portion of it was separated off and used to form the Vestibule of the Hearth (No. 70) so as to connect the *Hünkâr Sofasi* (No. 77) with the courtyard of the Sultan Validé. The door leading from the courtyard (No. 69) was known as the Gate of the Throne (*Taht Kapisi*). The *Başkadin* room is now filled with *débris* of various kinds, but some of the original decoration is still visible.

The *Ocakli Sofa*, on the other hand, has been well preserved, and contains completely tiled walls surrounded by a Cufic cornice, a very fine brass chimney with conical canopy and pierced fire-guard. There is also a charming wall fountain, while the doors are of some dark wood—possibly ebony—inlaid with mother-of-pearl.

The neighbouring rooms all belong to the *selāmlik*, and will be discussed in a later chapter. The furnace-room and so-called bath of the Sultan, situated near the Sultan Validé's suite, will be described in the chapter on the baths (see pp. 205–206). The connecting link between the *selāmlik* and the *ḥarēm* was the Golden Road, a long corridor which displays on its walls some of the most lovely tile decoration in existence. At the end of the chapter on the walls and kiosks I mentioned how the Turkish tile industry originated in the fifteenth century, reached its height of perfection during the sixteenth, and died out in the first half of the eighteenth century. Three separate periods can be recognized, of which the Chinili Kiosk is the best example of the first, while in the second the finest work was produced, and no better examples can be found than those in the Golden Road of the Seraglio. The advance over the first-period work is very noticeable. The range of colours has increased, and the glaze has reached the utmost degree of brilliance. Yellow has disappeared, but its place is taken by a series of lovely reds, varying from a true scarlet to a coral- or tomato-red. These reds stand out in slight relief, and are an indication of tilework at its zenith. A lovely panel from the Golden Road (dated 1575) was reproduced as Plate XXIV in Tahsin Chukru's article already mentioned. "It is impossible," he writes,

> to examine these tiles without delight, for the ground is of the purest white, the glazes flawless, the draughtmanship is strong, the colours

do not merge with one another or run in the glaze, the pigments are perfect; they have been endowed by the fire with power of vivacity.

The great advance in the tile industry at this time was due to Sinan, whose architectural masterpieces prompted a parallel advance in decorative art.

Beginning at the Guard-room of the *ḥarēm*, the Golden Road runs along one side of the Sultan Validé's courtyard, and continues on between the suite of the *kadins* and the *ḥarēm* mosque, past the court-yard of the *Kafes*, or Cage, until it reaches the pillared hall near the Pavilion of the Holy Mantle.

This completes the survey of the *ḥarēm* rooms. Before discussing the administration and general customs of the *ḥarēm* I shall turn to the question of female costume.

In the chapter dealing with the black eunuchs, after briefly describing the costume of the *Kislar Agha*, I referred to the collection of figures now on view in the church of St Irene, in the First Court, and remarked that many of the costumes had become mixed up or been incorrectly repaired. To a considerable extent matters can be rectified (if nothing has been done officially since 1935) by a study of the many fine works on Turkish costume, and by photographs of the *tableaux* of the figures before they started on their wanderings (see p. 131)—photographs still to be obtained in Constantinople. It is interesting to note that among the 143 figures in the collection no woman is represented, even in outdoor dress, so that no idea of the *ḥarēm* costumes can be obtained at all. As compared with the magnificent costumes of the Turkish officials, it may be that the female dress is simple and uninteresting. Outdoors the women appeared to be little more than a hobbling bundle of rather drab-looking clothes, but the *ḥarēm* could tell a very different story, and so I will devote the rest of this chapter to a somewhat detailed consideration of the whole subject. But first of all a word of a general nature may be allowed.

In studying Turkish costume it should be remembered that several factors have played their part in producing such an unparalleled array of gorgeous clothes—from the gold and scarlet of the sailors to the brocade and sable robes of the nobles.

Among the early Sultans Orkhan devoted much time to the regulation of the cut and colours of the garments and the different forms of turbans, and costume became the distinguishing mark of rank among the ruling race, as well as the token of creed among the subject nations. As time went on the costumes grew still more elaborate, and with the expansion of the Ottoman Empire new posts were created and new uniforms became necessary. With the capture of Constantinople many Byzantine costumes were closely copied, and so the Turkish love of pomp and display found a fresh source from which to borrow.

By the time of Suleiman costume was no longer merely a matter of custom and tradition. It became law. In the *Kanuni Teshrifat*, or Law of Ceremonies, regulations concerning the colour, shape, materials, length, and breadth of robes and turbans were clearly laid down. The order of precedence and the observances proper to all occasions were also a matter of law.

The story of Constantinople has been described as a costume drama, and surely this is no exaggeration in a country where rules regarding costume and Court etiquette are not merely unwritten laws, but are given the rank and authority of Imperial laws. "All the classes of members of the Sultan's household," writes Lybyer,

all the high officers of government, and all the separate bodies of troops in the standing army were clearly distinguished from each other by costume or head-dress or by both. Each group, and every officer in each group, had his exact place in every ceremonial assembly and his exact rank in every procession.[1]

The ceremonies were as numerous as they were varied—whether it was the reception of a foreign ambassador, one of the feasts of *Baïrām*, the sailing of the fleet, the setting out of the army, or the circumcision of the Sultan's heir. Each would be the occasion for one of the most splendid exhibitions of costume the world had ever seen. Some very slight idea can be obtained from the Sultan's *Baïrām* procession to the mosque, as shown in the illustration opposite p. 94, but this was nothing to the more important and personal ceremonies, such as the circumcision of the heir to the throne. In all this pageantry

[1] *The Government of the Ottoman Empire in the Time of Suleiman the Magnificent*, p. 135.

of dress and ceremonial the part played by women was small indeed. A woman was not meant to be seen by any man except her husband, and that was the end of it! Yet time has proved that the very regulations of feminine costume greatly assisted the clandestine meetings of wives with their lovers. A husband would be quite unable to recognize his own wife in the street, and to touch or speak to a woman publicly would, of course, be unthinkable. Her veil and cloak were as sacred as the doors of the ḥarēm. And so even with women law was clearly established and recognized. In the Seraglio regulations regarding costume were followed as closely as those applying to the male officials in the town. Each season demanded an entire change of raiment, and the Sultan never saw any member of the ḥarēm twice in the same dress. The greatest care was naturally taken with the outdoor costume when trips up the Bosphorus were made, or shopping excursions indulged in during the reigns of the more lenient Sultans. It will be realized how difficult it was to obtain any account of the indoor costumes, and even in the Seraglio itself it was only the eunuchs who saw them. Thus travellers were dependent for their information on such descriptions as friendly eunuchs chanced to give, either direct or through other members of the Seraglio. For, after all, it was the woman and not the dress that was taboo. Another possible source of information would be through the clothes-dealers, both new and second-hand, and odd information and scandal would doubtless be obtained in the market-place from the Jewesses who sold trinkets, ribbons, and lace to the Seraglio.

As is the case in so many dealings with the Turks, we owe the first descriptions to Italians. The earliest I can find is that by Bassano da Zara (c. 1540), while the first drawings are those by Nicolas de Nicolay (1551). Bassano deals chiefly with the outdoor costume, as is only to be expected, but discusses at random such kindred subjects as 'make-up' and the depilatory. Some of the words in the text do not appear in dictionaries, but I have added notes where necessary:

> In Turkey the women, whether Christian, Turk, or Jewish, dress themselves very richly in silk. They wear cloaks [1] down to the ground lined just like those of the men. They wear closed-up boots, but fitting

---

[1] *Casacche*—i.e., *casacca*, a 'long cloak,' and also a 'jacket.' Similar words are *casaca cazeta*, meaning the same thing, while *casacchino* is a lady's cape.

tighter to the ankle and more arched than those of the men. All wear
trousers; the chemises are of very fine linen, some having them of
muslin, some white, and some dyed red, yellow, or blue. They are
fond of black hair, and if any woman by nature does not possess it she
acquires it by artificial means. If they are fair or grey through old age
they use a red dye like that with which horses tails are dyed. It is
called *Chnà*.[1] The same is used on their nails, sometimes the whole
hand, sometimes the foot following the shape of the shoe, and again
some dye the pubic region and four fingers' length above it. And for
this reason they remove the hairs, considering it a sin to have any in
the private parts. They decorate their hair with small bands of ribbon
and leave them spread out over their shoulders, and falling over their
dress. Covering their hair they have a coloured strip of thin silk (as
wide as a priest's stole) with a little fringe at the edges. On the head
they also have a small round cap, neat and close-fitting, embroidered
with satin, damask, or silk and coloured. Many of them wear one of
velvet or brocade, to which the above-mentioned stole is attached. I
have seen some women who fasten the stole to a little white cap, and
then put one of silk on the top of that. It is not more than half a palm
in height. They use cosmetics more than any other nation I have seen.
They paint their eyebrows with black stuff, very thick; and I have
noticed some of them make their two look like one by painting the
space between, a thing which (in my opinion) is very unsightly.[2]
They paint their lips red, which I think they learned from the Greek
women or from those of Pera, who devote much attention to this.
They have big breasts and crooked feet, and this comes from their
sitting on the ground cross-wise. For the most part they are fat
because they eat a lot of rice with bullock's meat and butter, much more
than the men do. They do not drink wine, but sugared water, or
Cervosa [herb-beer] made in their own manner. Christian women
who live in Turkish houses, for whatever reason, have to give up wine.
When they go out of doors over the cloak or *Dullimano*, which they
ordinarily wear, they put a chemise of the whitest linen. Just as with
the regular clerics among us, it is of such a nature that one can only

[1] *I.e.*, henna, the *khanna* of the Egyptians and *kena* of the modern Greeks (ancient
κύπρος, as it grew in Cyprus).

[2] Just as in the case of henna, which is a good preventive against perspiration, so certain forms of eye-black (*kohl, surmā, kājal, tutia,* etc.) give coolness to the eyes and help to
prevent ophthalmia, as well as being a guard against the evil eye. The meeting of the
eyebrows, while considered beautiful in Muhammadan countries, is not liked among the
Hindus, and in Iceland, Denmark, Germany, Greece, and Bohemia it is considered a sign
of a werewolf or vampire. See on the whole subject of 'make-up' my article in vol. i of
the *Ocean of Story*, Appendix II, "Collyrium and *Kohl*," pp. 211–218, and the note at
pp. 103–104 of vol. ii of the same work.

see half an arm's length of the cloak. The garment is like a surplice with tight sleeves long enough to cover the entire hand, so that one cannot even see the nails, and they do this because in Turkey neither man nor woman wears gloves whatever the weather may be. They wear a towel[1] round the neck and head, so that one can only see their eyes and mouth, and these they cover with a thin silk scarf a palm's width each way, through which they can see and not be seen by others. The scarf is fastened with three pins[2] to a suitable part of the head above the forehead, so that when they go through the streets and meet other women, they raise the scarf that hangs over their faces and kiss one another. These scarfs are of silk, as wide as towels, like those the men also wear, and are called *Chussech*. This then, that you have read, is their dress with which they are so covered that one cannot even see a finger-nail, and this is because the Turks are more jealous than any other nation.[3]

Before giving a detailed description of each article of clothing I will add one or two more accounts for the sake of comparison, and in order to cover a greater period of time and to introduce as many names as possible. First of all I will quote from Nicolas de Nicolay, who unfortunately gives no description in his text, but simply refers readers to the drawings. He visited Constantinople in 1551, and managed to get some of the dresses put on certain public women to enable him to make his "draughtes and protractes" correctly. After stating that only the Chief Eunuch could ever see the women he adds:

And therefore to finde the meanes to represent vnto you the maner of their apparrel I fel familiarly acquainted with an Eunuche of the late Barbarousse called zaferaga of nation a Ragusan, being a man of great discretion & a louer of vertue, which from his tender age had been brought vp within the Serail, who, so soone as he had perceiued that I was desirous to see the fashion of the attyre and apparrell of these women, to satisfie my mind, caused to be clothed two publique Turkish women, with very rich apparrell, which hee sent for [from] the Bezestan whereas there is too be solde of all sortes, by the which I made the draughtes and protractes heere represented vnto you.[4]

[1] *Sciugatoio*—i.e., *asciugatoio*, meaning a 'bath towel,' 'napkin,' or 'antimacassar.' Here it is apparently a cloth or woollen under-scarf.
[2] *Acucchie*. I cannot find this word, but it would seem to be connected with *acuire*, 'to sharpen.'
[3] *I Costumi et i modi particolari de la vita de Turchi* (Roma, 1545), pp. 6–7.
[4] P. 53 *verso* of the English and p. 67 of the French edition.

The elaborate embroideries and incrustation of jewels in which most of the girls became adept can only be imagined, although a good idea of the work can be obtained from some of the pieces of material in the Seraglio Museum. As a general rule the dress of the *ḥarēm* girls corresponded, as far as the actual articles of attire were concerned, with those worn by the ordinary Turkish lady of standing. The rich brocades made in Brusa were well known, and it is clearly this material that Nicolay represents in his drawings of the Sultan Validé and gentlewoman in her *serail*.[1] There is a special copy of a 1572 German translation of the work at the British Museum;[2] it is elaborately coloured and illuminated. It gives a remarkably good idea of the richness of the brocades. The Sultan Validé is represented as wearing a tunic with the ends tucked up, displaying a long undergarment open at the front and about eight inches from the ground. A broad sash is tied round the waist. The sleeves are tight-fitting, with strips of brocade hanging from the shoulders. The gentlewoman wears a similar tunic with a row of buttons in front. Both the under-chemise and the trousers show, which was not so in the Sultana's costume. The sash and shoulder strips are similar to the above. Each article of clothing should be identified, with its Turkish name, by reference to my list later on in this chapter. As already mentioned, writers on women's costume could give only second- or third-hand information as far as the *ḥarēm* was concerned, and would never be able to see the costumes actually worn by their owners.

There was, however, one exception. Our old friend Dallam, whom we met in chapter ii, actually saw some of the *ḥarēm* girls through a wall grating, and gives this account of his adventure:

> When he had showed me many other thinges which I wondered at, than crossinge throughe a litle squar courte paved with marble, he poynted me to goo to a graite in a wale, but made me a sine that he myghte not goo thether him selfe. When I came to the grait the wale was verrie thicke, and graited on bothe the sides with iron verrie strongly; but through that graite I did se thirtie of the Grand Sinyor's Concobines that weare playinge with a bale in another courte. At the firste sighte of them I thoughte they had bene yonge men, but when

---

[1] Facing pp. 67 and 68 of the French edition and at p. 52 and 54 of the English edition.
[2] C. 55. i. 4. The illumination is the work of the contemporary Nuremberger Georg Mack. See G. K. Nagler, *Die Monogrammisten*, vol. iii. p. 53.

Eines groſſen Türcki-   ſchen heernsweib

THE SULTAN VALIDÉ

A KADIN IN INDOOR COSTUME

I saw the hare of their heades hange doone on their backes, platted together with a tasle of smale pearle hanginge in the lower end of it, and by other plaine tokens, I did know them to be women, and verrie prettie ones in deede.

Theie wore upon theire heades nothinge bute a little capp of clothe of goulde, which did but cover the crowne of her heade; no bandes a boute their neckes, nor anythinge but faire cheans of pearle and a juell hanginge on their breste, and juels in their ears; their coats weare like a souldier's mandilyon,[1] som of reed sattan and som of blew, and som of other collors, and grded like a lace of contraire collor; they wore britchis of scamatie,[2] a fine clothe made of coton woll, as whyte as snow and as fine as lane;[3] for I could desarne the skin of their thies throughe it. These britchis cam doone to their mydlege; som of them did weare fine cordevan buskins, and som had their leges naked, with a goulde ringe on the smale of her legg; on her foute a velvett panttoble[4] 4 or 5 inches hie. I stood so longe loukinge upon them that he which had showed me all this kindnes began to be verrie angrie with me. He made a wrye mouthe, and stamped with his foute to make me give over looking; the which I was verrie lothe to dow, for that sighte did please me wondrous well.[5]

Before giving my own list I should like to include a description by a lady who actually wore the costume. It would be impossible to choose anybody better than Lady Mary Wortley Montagu, who in a letter to her sister on April 1, 1717, writes as follows:

The first piece of my dress is a pair of drawers, very full, that reach to my shoes, and conceal the legs more modestly than your petticoats. They are of a thin rose-coloured damask, brocaded with silver flowers, my shoes are of white kid leather, embroidered with gold. Over this hangs my smock, of a fine white silk gauze, edged with embroidery. This smock has wide sleeves, hanging half way down the arm, and is closed at the neck with a diamond button; but the shape and colour of the bosom very well to be distinguished through it. The *antery* is a waistcoat, made close to the shape, of white and gold damask, with very long sleeves falling back, and fringed with deep gold fringe, and should have diamond or pearl buttons. My *caftan*, of the same stuff with my drawers, is a robe exactly fitted to my shape, and reaching

---

[1] Mandilion—*i.e.*, a soldier's cloak. "A mandilion that did with button meet" (Chapman, *Iliad*, x).
[2] *Scamatie*, derived from the Italian *scamatare*, 'to beat off the dust of wool.'
[3] Muslin or lawn.
[4] The high shoe is still worn by Turkish women.
[5] *Early Voyages and Travels in the Levant*, pp. 74–75.

to my feet, with very long strait falling sleeves. Over this is the girdle, of about four fingers broad which all that can afford have entirely of diamonds or other precious stones; those who will not be at that expense, have it of exquisite embroidery on satin; but it must be fastened before with a clasp of diamonds. The *curdee* is a loose robe they throw off or put on according to the weather, being of a rich brocade (mine is green and gold), either lined with ermine or sables; the sleeves reach very little below the shoulders. The head-dress is composed of a cap, called *talpock*, which is in winter of fine velvet embroidered with pearls or diamonds, and in summer of a light shining silver stuff. This is fixed on one side of the head, hanging a little way down with a gold tassel, and bound on, either with a circle of diamonds (as I have seen several) or a rich embroidered handker-chief. On the other side of the head, the hair is laid flat; and here the ladies are at liberty to shew their fancies; some putting flowers, others a plume of heron's feathers, and, in short, what they please; but the most general fashion is a large *bouquet* of jewels, made like natural flowers; that is, the buds of pearl; the rose, of different coloured rubies; the jessamines, of diamonds; the jonquils, of topazes, etc., so well set and enamelled, 'tis hard to imagine anything of that kind so beautiful. The hair hangs at its full length behind, divided into tresses braided with pearl or ribbon, which is always in great quantity.

As we are now acquainted with several accounts of the dress of Turkish women, both indoor and outdoor, I shall attempt to list all the several articles of clothing in the order worn, giving their modern spellings first, and explain as fully as possible their nature and use. As far as I can gather the mode seems to have altered little during the centuries. Certain articles have had different names at different times, and a word originally applied only to a material was later used for the garment, and so on. But generally speaking altera-tions have been slight. Some of the older words do not appear in modern dictionaries, but I shall add variations of spelling wherever possible.

1. *Gömlek*, formerly *giumlik*. This is a loose shirt or chemise made either of a mixture of cotton and wool or, among the richer, of silk gauze, usually white, but also found in red, yellow, and blue. Formerly it was left open in front as far as the waist, exposing the breasts, but later the fashion was modified, and jewellery closed the garment at the neck and across the bosom. The sleeves are wide and loose, edged with satin or lace (*oya*). It extended only as far as the

knees, and was sometimes tucked into the *dizlik*, or drawers, but apparently more usually hung loosely over them.

2. *Dizlik, dyslik*. This garment, deriving its name from *diz*, 'knee,' and so meaning 'knee-things,' is a pair of linen drawers, cut very wide and drawn close round the waist by an *uçkur* (formerly *outchkoor*), a tape or string passing through the top edge, as in our modern pyjamas. They do not appear to have been always worn as well as the *şalvar*, which latter garment formed the "first piece" of Lady Mary Wortley Montagu's costume. They are short drawers, tied at the knee, and to-day the word is used to express the modern 'shorts.'

3. *Şalvar, shalwar*. These are the outer trousers, or, if the *dizlik* is not worn, the only trousers or drawers. They are very loosely cut indeed, being some three yards wide at the waist. Drawn together at the waist by an *uçkur* (very elaborate and richly embroidered among the well-to-do), they are looped up below the knees, and fall in folds to the ankles. Other varieties reach directly down to the ankles, especially if the *dizlik* is also worn. They are of all materials and all colours. In the Seraglio the women vie with each other in the beauty of their *şalvar*. The finest Brusa brocades, purfled with gold and silver thread, are largely used, and as about eight yards are necessary they can be very expensive garments. The name *kaftan* or *caftan* was applied to the length of embroidered material used, but by extension also to the resulting garment; thus Lady Mary Wortley Montagu employed the word to describe her *entari*, or outer garment. The name *kaftan* was also used for the robe of honour, because of its being covered with embroidery.

4. *Yelek*. This is perhaps best described as a lady's waistcoat, thus corresponding to the men's *yelek*, which is simply an embroidered silk waistcoat. If, however, the *yelek* was provided with arms and trailed on the ground, as sometimes was the case, it practically became an *entari*, the next article I shall try to describe. In all cases the *yelek* fits closely to the figure, and usually has a row of little buttons close together, starting at the bosom and reaching a little below the waist. In the long *yelek* the sides are open from the hips, and the sleeves are tight-fitting, but open at the wrist.

5. *Entari, entary, antery*. This is the gown—the most important article of the *ḥarēm* indoor costume. At the back it fits very tightly,

and has even been described as a corset, while, as we have seen, Lady Mary Wortley Montagu says, "The *antery* is a waistcoat, made close to the shape . . ." It is in reality neither a corset nor a waistcoat, for in either case the garment would have to be laced or buttoned in front. Now the *entari* is wide open in front, and in the days when the open *gömlek* was in fashion the bosom remained entirely exposed. It was joined, however, at the waist by three or four pearl or diamond buttons set closely together, as in men's modern single-breasted evening waistcoats. It was the presence of these buttons that enabled the back of the *entari* to fit tightly, and so to appear (to some writers) like a corset or waistcoat.

The sleeves are tight from the shoulders to below the elbow, at which point they are open and, being very long, hang down nearly to the ground. The sleeve of the *gömlek* is thus exposed from the elbow to the wrist.

At the waist the *entari* becomes fuller, and is open at both sides. It is some two or three feet longer than the wearer, and for walking the ends are tucked up into the waist girdle, or *kuşak*, to be described next. But among the ladies of the *ḥarēm* little walking was necessary, and the ends of the gown would be gracefully draped over the edge of the sofa or divan. The material of the *entari* closely resembled that used for the *şalvar*, the finest embroidered Brusa brocade being used in the old days, while in more modern times damasks, silks, satins, and brocades were imported from Venice, Lyons, and other places by the Greeks, Jews, and especially the Armenians. It was the Armenians who became expert in manufacturing braiding (*arj*) of gold and silk, which added greatly to the richness of the *entari*.

From the above description it will be clearly seen that the *yelek* and the *entari* are practically the same garment. A close inspection of some of the sixteenth-century drawings—*e.g.*, those of Nicolay, Lonicer, Vecellio, Jost Amman, Boissard, Bry and Bertelli—appears to show a simple waistcoat form of the *yelek*, cut low and revealing the *gömlek* underneath modestly closed and slightly gathered, with the *entari* worn as an over-robe. However correct or incorrect these early drawings are, and however much should be allowed for artistic licence and the making of a pretty and acceptable drawing for Western tastes, it is fairly obvious that it was quite possible to dispense with one of the two garments in question, and that only the rich would ever possess both.

6. *Kuşak, kooshak,* the *chussech* of Bassano da Zara. This is a waist-shawl or girdle made of wool, calico, linen, or silk according to the taste or status of the wearer. In the *ḥarēm* it is loose, and worn very wide round the waist and buttocks, or else used as a scarf round the shoulders. Among the 'staff' of the *ḥarēm* it serves its proper purpose of waist-band, and acts as a receptacle for money, handkerchiefs, documents, ink-horns, etc. With the *kadins* its place is usually taken by a jewelled girdle. Apart from the *seiman*, a wadded jacket, and the *kurk*, a fur pelisse only worn in cold weather, there remain of indoor garments but the headdress and shoes to be described. I shall discuss the shoes first.

7. *Şipşip, tchipship.* These are house slippers without heels, pointed and slightly curved at the ends. They are of nearly all materials and colours, and richly embroidered in gold, pearls, and precious stones. Rosettes of pearls, gold cord, and similar decorations are also often added on the instep.

For going out the *pabuç (papoosh)* is worn, which is a strong-soled shoe of yellow leather.

A third shoe, or rather slipper-boot, is the *çedik (tchelik)* of yellow Morocco leather a few inches high in front. For use in the garden these shoes might be made of velvet and other similar material. It would appear that the "Velvett panttoble 4 or 5 inches hie" of Dallam was a particular form of either *pabuç* or *çedik*.[1]

8. *Fotaza.* This is the indoor headdress, and has been well described by Lady Mary Wortley Montagu, except that the *talpock*, or *kalpak*, is an Armenian word, and really refers only to the astrakhan turban as worn by the Armenians. There are many varieties, some being of cloth and only bordered with astrakhan. Just as the turban consists of two separate articles, so does the *fotaza*. First there is a flat-topped little cap (*takke*) rather like a squat fez, made of the finest felt or, especially in former days, of velvet. A blue or gold tassel spreads itself over the crown and falls down to one side. It is worn at a jaunty angle at the back of the head and covered with pearls and

---

[1] For names of other kinds of footwear, used chiefly by men, reference should be made to Evliyá Efendí, *Narrative of Travels*, II, pp. 210, 211.

diamonds, or cheaper jewellery and embroidery among the less rich. In close conjunction, and doubled across the front of the cap, is a beautifully embroidered muslin handkerchief, known as a *yemeni*. It is used partly to keep the cap in place, but mainly as an additional portion of the headdress on which can be fixed more jewellery. Large bodkins studded with diamonds and rubies were largely used by the *kadins,* and other jewellery was fastened in the hair, which hung to one side in long tresses. Out of doors the headdress is completely covered by the upper part of the *yaşmak,* or veil, to which we now turn.

9. *Yaşmak.* This is a veil exclusive to Constantinople, and consists of two pieces of fine muslin or, in more recent days, of tarlatan. Each is folded corner-wise, or else only a single thickness is used. The first piece is placed across the bridge of the nose, and, passing over the mouth and chin and falling on to the bosom, is tied or pinned at the nape of the neck. The second piece is placed over the head, being brought down in front as far as the eyebrows, while the rest hangs behind, and is either tucked in underneath the *ferace,* or outer robe, or else pinned to the other piece of the *yaşmak* at the nape of the neck.

As the veil is very thin the features can be quite clearly seen, although it is highly important that the whole nose should not be exposed, or the lady might be taken for an Armenian—or possibly for a prostitute.

In other parts of the Turkish Empire much heavier and rather ugly veils are worn, one of the most common being the *mahramah,* which consists of a kind of calico petticoat, the upper part of which is thrown over the head and held under the chin, while the face is entirely concealed by a dark handkerchief. So also the *yaşmak* differs from the Cairene *burko,* which is a long piece of black cloth or muslin stretching from under the eyes nearly to the ground. Another form of Muhammadan veil is the *lithām,* or *lisām,* but this word is almost entirely used for the desert mouth-veil of the Tuaregs (Tawāriks) of the Sahara; in a poetical sense it is used figuratively, and Arabian poets describe dawn as "the day doffing its *lisām.*" Examples of all these veils, as well as the face-screen of black horse-hair used in parts of Asia Minor, will be found in the more important works on Turkish and Arabian costume.

10. *Ferace, feridjé, ferigee.* There remains now but to mention the loose-sleeve cloak-like garment worn by all Turkish women in the streets. It is made of black alpaca among the poor, and of a fine broad cloth or light Merino among the better classes, while the rich, or members of the Royal *ḥarēm*, usually have the *ferace* made of silk of some delicate pink or lilac colour. A large square cape hangs behind nearly to the ground. The lining among the rich is often of black or white satin, and further ornamentation with tassels, braiding, and a velvet edging is sometimes worn.

This, I think, concludes all the articles of clothing worn by the Turkish women.[1]

[1] Readers interested in the subject I would refer to the bibliography on costume by René Colas: *Bibliographie générale du costume et de la mode* (Paris, 1933), 2 vols. Turkey and Asia Minor will be found fully indexed at the end of vol. ii—pp. 29, 30 of the " Table Méthodique." Apart from Nicolay I would especially mention the works by La Chappelle, Le Hay, Dalvimart—whose drawings were nearly all reproduced in Shoberl's *World in Miniature* (London)—MacBean, Preziosi, and Hamdy-Bey.

The best text-book on Muhammadan costume is still R. P. A. Dozy, *Dictionnaire détaillé des noms des vêtements chez les Arabes* (Amsterdam, 1845).

CHAPTER VIII

THE ḤARĒM—II

In considering the *ḥarēm* in detail—its *personnel*, method of administration, and general manners and customs—it is imperative to realize at once that we are not dealing with anything so simple as just a few hundred women awaiting the pleasure of the Sultan under the watchful eyes of the black eunuchs. On the contrary, the female hierarchy of the *ḥarēm* was a complicated institution, having a definite and fixed number of officers, with every woman occupying a distinct position according to her age, status, and the point at which she had arrived in her *ḥarēm* education.

The *ḥarēm*, then, must be regarded as a little kingdom of its own, a curious kingdom certainly, but one in which there was a ruler, the equivalent of a Prime Minister, a Cabinet, other less important officials connected with the governing, and finally the subjects—all occupying different positions, but all being given some definite job to do with a chance to improve their position as time went on.

Let us look at conditions as they were when the *ḥarēm* was at its height in the sixteenth and seventeenth centuries.

The ruler of the *ḥarēm* is not the Sultan, nor the head wife or First Kadin (recognized concubine), but the Sultan's mother, the Sultan Validé.

The Turks recognize that a man can have many wives, that he can get rid of unwanted ones and take others at will, but that he can have only one mother, and it is she, therefore, who occupies the unique place of honour that nothing can alter save death. To her, then, are entrusted the most personal and private belongings of her son—his women. The power of the Sultan Validé is enormous, not only in the *ḥarēm*, but throughout the entire Empire. As is only to be imagined, there is ceaseless warfare between the Sultan's mother and his favourite *kadins*. The most ambitious woman in the *ḥarēm* is not she who is content to reach the high position of First Kadin, but she who hopes, plots, and prays to become one day the

Sultan Validé; for then she is not merely ruler of the *ḥarēm* and of the Seraglio, but, if she is strong and her son weak, may even rule the kingdom as well.

No better example of the power and influence a member of the *ḥarēm* might acquire could be given than that of Khurrem, the Russian slave girl, better known in Western Europe as Roxelana. In this case, however, so great was her influence over Suleiman that the question of her becoming Sultan Validé never arose. Bit by bit Roxelana removed all obstacles in her path. About 1541 she had persuaded the Sultan to let her live with him in the Seraglio instead of remaining in the Old Palace, although at this time she was only Second Kadin. After the death of Suleiman's mother only two rivals remained—the First Kadin, Bosfor Sultan, and Ibrahim, the Grand Vizir, who according to some accounts had been the original owner of Roxelana. Plots and counter-plots were laid: Bosfor Sultan was displaced and practically exiled, her son was murdered in a manner that leaves little doubt as to Roxelana's complicity in the business, and Suleiman had the Grand Vizir executed for no apparent reason at all. Although no actual proof was forthcoming to show that Roxelana was again instrumental in this latter crime there is no doubt whatever that he was definitely in her way to absolute power, and she was still afraid of his great influence over the Sultan.

It had been a triumph when she was allowed to move into the Seraglio with her train of slave girls and eunuchs; it was a much greater one when she became Suleiman's legal wife. Not since the time of Bayezid I (1389–1403) had any Sultan contracted a legal marriage, and this strange act of Suleiman was regarded with amazement and concern. In the reign of Selim II (so Bon tells us) so enormous was the sum set aside for the Sultan's wife, being sufficient to build mosques and hospitals, that marriage was not attractive. For the same reason the number of the *kadins* was limited to four. From his whole *ḥarēm*, which might consist of anything from 300 to 1200 women, the Sultan would have his favourites, termed *ikbals*, who would occasionally be honoured by sharing his bed.

In the event of the birth of a male child and the continued and growing affection of the Sultan a lucky *ikbal* might be raised to the coveted rank of a *kadin*. Although they were not actually married the rank of the *kadins* was equivalent to that of a legal wife, and their apartments, slaves, eunuchs, property, dresses, jewellery, and salary were all proportional to the honour and importance of their new position. According to the order of her election, so would the *kadin* be henceforth known. Thus she might be the Second Kadin or Third Kadin, and naturally she would do all in her power to dislodge the one immediately above her—by fair means or foul. In the case of Roxelana, however, the impossible had been achieved, for Suleiman, so far from having other *kadins* after the fall of Bosfor Sultan, actually married off several of his most beautiful women to cement his affection and fidelity to Roxelana.

Melling's drawing of the *ḥarēm* (see plate opposite p. 152) requires a little explanation. As previously mentioned, he had been appointed architect to the favourite sister of Selim III, and in such a capacity had many conversations with the Sultana and her women that were of great assistance to him in his work.

Although his drawing of the *ḥarēm* is entirely fanciful, Melling has not only taken great trouble to introduce into his picture some of the chief members of the *ḥarēm*, but has represented on one story or another all the various daily occupations and customs of the women. In the front centre is one of the more important black eunuchs speaking to the Mistress of the *ḥarēm*. In the right-hand front corner are three women keeping themselves warm with their feet under a *tandir* or pan containing lighted charcoal, which fits under a square tin-topped table covered with tapestry or rugs. Immediately round the corner two Lesbians will be noticed, while in the middle centre is a slave, recognized by her simpler dress. In the left-hand corner a woman of high position is partaking of a meal, while in the main hall seven others are seated round a tray of *pilaf*. On the first floor is the mosque, and here care has been taken to show all the different attitudes of prayer. Immediately above, on the second floor, are some of the bedrooms, and the mattresses are just being put out for the night. During the day they are kept in wall cupboards like that shown on the first floor to the right. Although a slave is represented in the drawing as carrying a water-jug we see no sign of any wall fountain. It seems curious that this has not been introduced, as at least one such fountain was always to be found actually in the bedrooms;

still more would there be one in an enormous hall such as is here represented.

But we must return to the *ḥarēm personnel*. If we look upon the Sultan Validé as ruler of the *ḥarēm* the Chief Black Eunuch, or *Kislar Agha*, must be regarded as her Prime Minister. His duties have already been described in an earlier chapter, but I may repeat here that he was in direct charge of the girls, and could be largely responsible for their being noticed by the Sultan; and he had a very large number of eunuchs to assist him in his duties. He was the *liaison* officer between the Sultan Validé and the girls, and between the Sultan and the outside world. He was, in fact, one of the highest 'men' in the kingdom, and his interests and influence extended far beyond the walls of the Seraglio. With the general running of the *ḥarēm* he was not directly concerned. That was relegated to the female Cabinet, or Privy Council, as it might be called.

This was led by a Lady Controller, Lady Stewardess, or Lady Administrator (*Ketkhuda* or *Kiaya*), who was usually regarded as deputy head of the *ḥarēm*, temporarily acting as a kind of head housekeeper and manageress. Nearly equal to her, and according to some authorities also a deputy head, was the Treasurer (*Hazinedar Usta*), who was responsible not only for the handling of the running expenses of the *ḥarēm*, which were very high and complicated, but for the paying out of the 'pin money' (*paşmaklik*, literally 'slipper money') to all those entitled to receive it, and for the arrangement of pensions paid to those who left the Seraglio for the *Eski Serai*, or Old Seraglio.

Other members of the Cabinet were the Mistress of the Robes, the Keeper of the Baths, the Keeper of the Jewels, the Reader of the *Korān*, the Keeper of the Storerooms, and the Manageress of the Table Service, and so on.

All these positions of trust and responsibility would be occupied by women who had gradually advanced in every part of the *ḥarēm* training, but who had been passed by as far as the chance to become a *kadin* was concerned. This, then, was the compensation for being 'passed over.' Love—at any rate male love—had been denied them, and now all they could hope for was some high position in the *ḥarēm*, which at least would bring them wealth and power to a certain degree.

An indulgent Sultan might even marry them off instead of sending them to end their days in the *Eski Serai*.

So far I have mentioned only the Sultan Validé, her Cabinet, the Chief Black Eunuch, and the four *kadins*. It is now necessary to consider the ordinary member of the *ḥarēm*, what her duties were, how she was trained, and what chances she had of promotion.

Each of the most important women had her own little Court (*oda*), with attendants varying in number according to her rank. At the same time each had a number of pupils studying to make themselves perfect in the particular line allotted to their mistress. Thus, on entering the *ḥarēm* at a tender age the girl would in all probability be immediately attached to one of the *odas* as a novice. In fact, should the Sultan Validé or one of the lesser officials be requiring a new slave or pupil they were at perfect liberty to buy one and train her personally. The new girl, selected from a large number, would be placed under the care of, say, the Mistress of the Robes. There she would serve her apprenticeship, looking upon her tutoress as a mother from whom she would receive all her clothes, money, food, and jewels. The tutoress is to a large extent responsible for her throughout her career, and does all she can to better her condition in whatever way possible. Having made good progress in her own department, the girl may have the chance of entering another *oda* which suits her better. Perhaps she has developed a *flair* for coffee-making or keeping accounts. In which case a few carefully placed bribes may get her the necessary transfer. Perhaps, however, her promotion has been slow and years have passed before she arrives at the head of her particular *oda*. In that case she will probably remain where she is, knowing that her chances of ever being a *kadin* are past, and preferring now to enjoy the privileges of her position.

But, on the other hand, let us take the case of the girl who has started with the Mistress of the Robes, got transferred to the Chief Coffee-maker, and by a lucky chance is present on the occasion of a visit of the Sultan to the Sultan Validé.

It is quite sufficient for the Sultan to glance at her approvingly or make some trivial remark about her. Any such sign of Imperial favour is at once noticed, and the epithet *guzdeh*, or 'in the eye,' is at once given her. This is her first real step towards the envied position of a *kadin*. From this time the girl is 'marked.' She is separated from the rest and is given an apartment and slaves to herself. Meanwhile developments are awaited, and a message to appear before the Sultan may be expected any time. Should this occur great preparations are made before she can enter the room of her Lord. One by one the heads of the different departments are called in to assist. The Keeper of the Baths takes her off first, and superintends her toilet with massage, shampooing, perfuming, and hairdressing. The shaving of the body, dyeing of the nails, and other such details follow. She now proceeds to the Keeper of the *Lingerie*, the Mistress of the Robes, the Head of the Treasury; and so at last she is ready for her Royal lover. And now her chance has come. Every artifice of which the feminine mind is capable is put into play. How can she tell if a male child will be born of the union! But first she must captivate the Sultan's heart, and perhaps several nights will be hers, and anything might happen then.

It has been repeatedly affirmed that when *kadins* or other favoured concubines enter the Sultan's bedroom, which is not allowed until his Majesty has already retired, they approach the foot of the bed, lift up the coverlet, and raise it to their forehead and lips. They then creep in humbly at the foot of the bed, and gradually work their way upward until they are level with the Sultan.

By some this latter custom has been discredited, and when Lady Mary Wortley Montagu mentioned the subject to the Chief Kadin of Mustafa II she was informed that both the choice of a girl by throwing the handkerchief and her creeping in at the bed's foot had no foundation whatever in actual fact.

But I am in no way convinced by this one statement, especially as it only refers to the eighteenth century, and then very possibly merely to the whim of a solitary Sultan. Subsequent writers have simply copied her without question, excepting scholars like d'Ohsson, who did much original research. Now this 'creeping up the bed' was obligatory in Constantinople on a man who had been married to one of the Sultanas. In these marriages the unfortunate husband is entirely ruled by his royal wife, and waits outside until he is summoned. He then timidly enters, kisses the coverlet, and creeps towards his wife by the same 'sliding scale.' The very fact that the custom was thus carried on outside the Seraglio, in the houses of men who before being thus honoured by the Sultan may have occupied very humble walks in life, would considerably add to the opportunities by which such a curious custom would get known and talked about. Furthermore, the 'creeping up the bed' was not confined to Turkish Courts, but was also a well-established custom farther east—in China, for example.

In the authoritative article by Carter Stent[1] we are given the following account of the bedroom ritual, which is similar to that observed in the Seraglio in several particulars. When the Emperor wishes for the presence of any particular concubine in his bedchamber he gives a label or tally, on which he has written the name of the lady, to the eunuch-in-waiting, who takes it to the lady in question, and she is borne in a chair by eunuchs to the Emperor's sleeping apartment, which is named *Yang-hsin-tien*. On retiring to rest the lady does not dare get into the Emperor's bed in the usual manner —that is, from the head, or, rather, side—but it is etiquette to crawl in from the foot till she comes in line with her Imperial bedfellow. Two eunuchs keep watch outside the door, and before break of day they arouse the concubine, and she is borne back again to her own apartment. The circumstance of the concubine's having slept with the Emperor is then recorded in a book, with the name of the lady and the date of the visit. The entry is signed by the Emperor, and the book is referred to to substantiate the legitimacy of the child, in the event of the concubine's giving birth to one.

As to the other custom—that of selecting a concubine by giving or throwing a handkerchief—there is also considerable evidence that, at one time at any rate, it was no 'traveller's tale.'

In the first place it should be remembered that in Turkey the *mendil*, *yağlik*, or handkerchief, holds a position of honour that is probably unique. It is used not only by the Sultan, but by everybody, as a covering for any present conveyed from one person to another. Naturally, in later reigns the introduction of envelopes and cardboard boxes did much to end the custom, but formerly any important letter, sum of money, present of jewellery, or even the gift of fruits, sweetmeats, or clothing, was wrapped up in an em-

[1] *Journal of the Royal Asiatic Society* (*North China Branch*) (1877), pp. 174–175.

broidered kerchief. The richer the wrapper the greater the compliment. It is therefore very possible, if not probable, that the compliment of selecting a favoured girl would be paid by the use of a kerchief.

Furthermore, as we shall shortly see, the reliable Bon definitely tells us that the King throws his handkerchief to the chosen one just before he leaves.[1] In certain situations speech is both superfluous and unbecoming, and so in a Court teeming with etiquette and ceremonial we can well imagine such a custom to have existed. In much the same way the dignified 'throwing the glove' in Western Courts was also a challenge to combat—but of a more serious nature!

Every precaution is taken to make the visit of the concubine as private as possible, and none of the other women may even be aware of the choice, and never will know unless she is made a *kadin* and given a suite of servants of her own. The eunuch on guard outside the Royal bedroom is told of the intended visit, and the portress inside makes the necessary preparations. Care is taken that all doors and windows between the rooms of the girl and those of the Sultan are closed. No one is allowed to appear, and complete silence is maintained everywhere. Although the Sultan almost always receives the girl in his suite within the *ḥarēm* he sometimes honours her by going to her rooms, in which case he is conducted there by one of the black eunuchs, and is received by the lady and her slaves with the most profound respect and obeisance. In the morning he or she returns to their own rooms as silently and secretly as they came.

Speaking of all these matters at the beginning of the seventeenth century, Bon writes as follows:

> . . . if he should require one of them for his pleasure or to watch them at play or hear their music, he makes known his desire to the Head Kadin, who immediately sends for the girls who seem to her to be the most beautiful in every respect and arranges them in a line from one end of the room to the other. She then brings in the King, who passes before them once or twice, and according to his pleasure fixes his eyes on the one who attracts him most, and as he leaves throws one of his handkerchiefs into her hand, expressing the desire to sleep the night with her. She, having this good fortune, makes up as well

[1] In the eighteenth century too we find Flachat describing this same method of selecting a girl in vogue at the tulip *fêtes* of Mahmud I. See later, p. 259.

as she can and, coached and perfumed by the Kadin, sleeps the night with the King in the Royal chamber in the women's apartments, which is always kept ready for such an event. And while they are sleeping the night the Kadin arranges for some old Moorish women, who take it in turn to stay in the room for two or three hours at a time. There are always two torches burning there, one at the door of the room, where one of the old women is, and the other at the foot of the bed; and they change without making a sound, so that the King is not disturbed in any way. On rising in the morning the King changes all his clothes, leaving the girl those he was wearing with all the money that was in the purses: then, going to his other rooms, he sends her a present of clothes, jewels, and money in accordance with the satisfaction and pleasure received. The same procedure holds good for all the others who take his fancy, lasting longer with one than with another according to the pleasure and affection he feels for her. And she who becomes pregnant is at once called Cassachi Sultan—that is to say, Queen Sultana—and if she bears a son its arrival is heralded with the greatest festivities.

This Queen has her own apartment of magnificent rooms, complete domestic arrangements are immediately made for her, and the King allows her a sufficient income to enable her to give away and spend lavishly on anything she may require, and the whole of the Seraglio recognizes her position, extending to her much honour and respect. The other women, even if they have children, are not called Queen, but only Sultana, for having had carnal intercourse with the King; the only one made Queen is she who is the mother of the heir to the throne. These Sultanas, who have lent themselves for the gratification of the King's pleasure, have the further prerogative of being immediately raised above the common level, having rooms and service assigned to them, and receive an honorarium of so many *aspri* a day for their needs, nor do they want for every kind of most lovely garments, making a very sumptuous comparison with the rest.

All these Sultanas intrigue among themselves with much familiarity, and exhibit just as much cunning to avoid indifference on the part of the King, for, being slaves and living in great fear of jealousy for love of his Majesty, each tries to honour him so as to be more favoured and loved than the others. . . . The other women, who have not the luck to be favourites of the King, live an empty life, passing their youth in evil thoughts among themselves, and when old serve as teachers or governesses of the young who arrive every day at the Seraglio. In such bad circumstances they account it a lucky thing for them to find themselves in a position to be sent to the Old Seraglio, because they might get married from there according to the kindness of the Mistress,

THE ROYAL SALOON
[See p. 193]

THE VESTIBULE OF THE FOUNTAIN

[See p. 193]

and to the amount of savings and balance of the allowance and presents received, which may be considerable, because in the Seraglio they are always favoured in many ways by the Sultana in addition to the allowance from the King's treasury.[1]

Here Bon is only referring to the older and experienced women who have never attracted the Sultan in their youth, but how about the girl who has been sent to the Sultan at the discretion of the Mistress and then is not wanted after all? The unfortunate girl has been bathed, perfumed, and decked up like a lamb for slaughter, only to discover that the Sultan has changed his mind, forgotten about her, or never really intended to show any interest in her at all. Immediately she is shorn of her finery, her newly elected slaves are dismissed, and she finds herself once again in her former position.

Besides the *ustas*, or mistresses, the pupils, assistants, and *kadins*, there was an enormous number of women who did the menial work and were nothing more than general servants. The really heavy work, such as cleaning the floors, passages, and walls, was left to the negresses, while the lighter duties included the cleaning and care of the pipes, the repairing and preserving of the sofa cushions, the polishing and preparing of the braziers, the care of the prayer rugs of the mosque, the assisting in the preparation of sherbets, *pilaf*, etc. In some cases a special talent might show itself and be the means of a girl's obtaining a better and more sympathetic employment. Everybody learned to cook, and if the opportunity ever presented itself each prided herself on being able to produce some sugared delicacy or succulent stew to tickle the Royal palate.

As we have seen in a previous chapter, the *selāmlik* contained a large saloon, the *Hünkâr Sofasi* (No. 77 in the plan), where the Sultan sometimes received members of the *harēm* for his pleasure or to witness some entertainment. On such occasions the entire *harēm* might be admitted, and music, dances, and mimic exhibitions would entertain the assembled throng. The massed beauty of these women, their dresses of silk and satin enhanced with jewellery of every description, the richness of the furniture, the brilliancy of the illumination, the silent lines of black eunuchs, and finally the Sultan himself, seated on the throne in scarlet robes edged with sable, a dagger at his waist studded

[1] P. 71.

with diamonds, a white egret in his turban held in place by a cluster
of diamonds and rubies, his bejewelled water-pipe at his side, the
room heavy with the mingled perfumes of the women, the incense
of the braziers, and the amber-scented coffee—all this must have
been a sight to see indeed, and one which rivalled the wildest exaggerations to be found in the pages of the *Thousand Nights and a
Night*, when the glory of Harun al-Rashīd was at its height.

As a relief from the eternal jealousies and bickerings that never
ceased, entertainment of this nature must have been most welcome.
A troupe of dancers and pantomimists was selected and trained,
as well as a band or orchestra. Occasionally, by way of variety,
public dancers from outside the *ḥarēm* were introduced, and the
enthusiasm with which they were received was unbounded. According to several writers the nature of the dances was far from modest,
and we can imagine that the *danse du ventre* and other 'suggestive'
movements played a large part in the entertainment. So also shadow
shows, full of obscenities, resembling those that Montmartre keeps
for inexperienced tourists, were very popular. During the reign of
Selim III a French dancing-master and a number of musicians actually
had permission to enter some outer building of the *ḥarēm*; and there,
in the presence of several eunuchs, they gave lessons to the girls who
had been selected to act in their next 'show.' Such girls were usually
those who had not yet embraced the Muhammadan religion, as the
law frowned on exhibitions of this nature.

Except for such diversions as these and occasional trips up the
Bosphorus, life in the *ḥarēm* must have been dull indeed.

In the foregoing pages I have attempted to show how a girl could
'better herself,' and how there always was a possible chance of her
being seen by the Sultan or even getting married outside the Seraglio
altogether.

Ex-*kadins* of late Sultans sometimes married from the *Eski Serai*
and finally severed all connexion with the Seraglio. No better
example of the freedom of a "retired" *kadin* could be given than that
of *La Sultana Sporca*. She had received this uncomplimentary nick-
name, "the Filthy Sultana," owing to her ill mode of life, which was
nothing more nor less than that of a procuress and bawd. Originally
one of Ibrahim's *kadins*, she was sent to the *Eski Serai* and married a

Pasha. When this man died she was at liberty to live where she liked. Being an expert in the arts of vice and debauchery through long practice in Ibrahim's ḥarēm, she felt it a pity that all her knowledge was being wasted, and so to relieve the boredom of old age she became the most sought after and exclusive procuress in Constantinople. Her particular line was to buy young girls, give them a very complete training in singing, dancing, and general coquetry, and then hire them out to rich Pashas and young bloods of the town. The story of how she refused one of the girls to the Sultan (Muhammad IV) and subsequently caused a Bosnian captain to be executed for having made her his mistress when the Sultan wanted her himself has been told by Rycaut,[1] with a less satisfactory version in the diary of Dr John Covel.[2]

It must not be supposed, however, that all the women in the ḥarēm were content to live an uneventful life without trying for something better—and sometimes getting it.

The Bosphorus can tell many tales of what happened to women who tried—and failed. But there were also the few who tried and succeeded. Curious as it may seem, the ḥarēm had an attraction for some women. To them it was not only the place of mystery, silence, boredom, and incarceration; it was also the place of intrigue, opportunity, luxury, and riches. In fact, in the sixteenth and seventeenth centuries Italian and Sicilian women were willingly sold into the ḥarēm with the sole purpose of intrigue.

The full story of those countless ḥarēm intrigues will never be told, nor will the number of women drowned in sacks be known. From all accounts it appears that the stories of this nature, which once shocked the entire civilized world, were in no way exaggerated. The drowning of one or two women would attract no notice at all, and everything would be carried out with silence and dispatch. The *Kislar Agha* takes them to the *Bostanji-bashi*, under whose direction the hapless females are placed in sacks weighted with stones. The *bostanji*, to whom the duty of drowning them is committed, board a small rowing-boat to which is attached by a rope a smaller one in which the women are placed. They then row towards the open

---

[1] *History of the Turkish Empire, 1623–1677* (London, 1687), pp. 259-260.
[2] Under July 17, 1676, for which see *Early Voyages and Travels in the Levant*, pp. 160-162.

water opposite Seraglio Point, and by several dexterous jerks of the rope cause the boat to capsize. A eunuch accompanies the *bostanji* and reports to the *Kislar Agha* the fulfilment of his orders.

At times, however, a mass drowning would take place on the discovery of some plot to depose the Sultan or similar grave offence. As many as 300 women have been drowned on such an occasion. The most terrible case was during the reign of Ibrahim, who after one of his debauches suddenly decided to drown his complete *ḥarēm* just for the fun of getting a new one later on. Accordingly several hundred women were seized, tied up in sacks, and thrown into the Bosphorus. Only one escaped. She was picked up by a passing vessel and ultimately reached Paris.

A strange tale is told of a diver who was sent down after a wreck off Seraglio Point. Almost immediately he signalled to be drawn up again, and explained in a voice quaking with terror that at the bottom of the sea was a great number of bowing sacks, each containing the dead body of a woman standing upright on the weighted end and swaying slowly to and fro with the current.

But there is the other side of the story to be told as well. We have seen how Roxelana was the first woman to move into the Seraglio with her train of servants and eunuchs, and how gradually she obtained complete ascendancy over the Sultan and ruled supreme in the *ḥarēm* until her death in 1558. This was the beginning of the Reign of Women (*Kadinlar Sultanati*), which lasted about a hundred and fifty years, till the death of the Sultan Validé Tarkhan, mother of Muhammad IV. During this long period it was the *ḥarēm* that ruled the kingdom, a continual battle being ceaselessly waged between the Sultan Validé, the Chief Kadin, and sometimes the *Kislar Agha*. The whole *ḥarēm* became a hotbed of intrigue, bribery, extortion, plots and counter-plots. While the Sultans were indulging in orgies of drink or vice, according to their tastes, it was the women who crept to the secret grilled window of the Divan, listened to State secrets, and played their cards accordingly.

Following Suleiman, Selim II kept his entire *ḥarēm* in the Seraglio, and as his drunkenness increased so did the power of the Chief Kadin, Nur Banu Sultan. When her son became Murad III she assumed the title of Sultan Validé, and as such her power increased even more than before. Meanwhile intrigue was ripe in the *ḥarēm*, and the fight for the envied position of First Kadin had begun. It was won by a beautiful Venetian woman of the noble house of Baffo. She had been captured by a Turkish corsair in her early youth, and by her beauty and cleverness soon won the heart of Murad to the exclusion of all other women. But his mother, the Sultan Validé Nur Banu, got alarmed and gave orders for the cream of the slave markets to be sent to the Seraglio. So successful was she that, so far from keeping true to his one love, Murad plunged into a continuous orgy of licentious indulgence. The price of women went up, and slave-dealers and even powerful members of the *ḥarēm* joined in the procuring of fresh virgins to quench the Royal flame of sensuality. So for a time the power of the Venetian—known as Safieh, Safiye, or Baffa, after the name of her family—was eclipsed. But this was only so far as Murad's couch was concerned. Safieh had bigger fish to fry, and was already in secret correspondence with Catherine de' Medici to prevent Turkey from attacking Venice. She it was who directed the movements of the Ottoman fleets and armies, while Murad was still wallowing in the delights of the *ḥarēm*. She also corresponded with the Venetian Ambassador by means of a Jewess named Chiarezza, who used to sell jewels and other similar articles to the Seraglio. Apart from the determination to keep Turkey from having a war with Venice she had but one desire, to the fulfilment of which everything would be sacrificed, and that was to place her son on the throne, and thereby herself become the Sultan Validé. When in 1595 the time came she never hesitated for a moment, and was instrumental in the appalling murder of Muhammad III's nineteen brothers. Thus her object was achieved, and for a time she continued to govern the country. She even sank so low as to corrupt her own son and encourage his habits of debauch in order to leave her a freer hand in State affairs, and although he was persuaded against his will to lead the janissaries against the Hungarians and Austrians in 1596 he immediately returned to the seclusion of the *ḥarēm*, leaving the government in the hands of Safieh. But her turn came later, and one day she was found strangled in her bed.

The Reign of Women continued, and Ahmed I was entirely under their influence. His successor, Mustafa I, was a lunatic, while when

Osman II began to show interest in State affairs he incurred the dis-
favour of the janissaries and was immediately killed. All this time
the country was virtually ruled by another woman—Kiusem (Kiosem
or Kieuzel) Sultan, the mother of Murad IV and Ibrahim. Murad
who came to the throne in 1623, actually threw off the influence of
the *ḥarēm*, at any rate temporarily, and was the last Sultan to lead
his army in the field. His intemperate habits, however, proved fatal
and after an attack of fever, provoked by drink and terror at seeing
an eclipse of the sun, he died at the early age of twenty-eight. One
of his last acts was to order the execution of his brother Ibrahim
thus making the Ottoman race extinct, and giving the throne to his
favourite, the *Silihdar* Pasha.

But once again the *ḥarēm* triumphed, and Kiusem falsely reported
Ibrahim's death. At the news Murad grinned a ghastly smile, and
tried to rise from his bed to gloat over his brother's dead body.
His attendants, knowing that their lives were at stake in the event of
the discovery of the truth, held back the dying man in his bed. The
end came almost at once, and Kiusem, seeing a further period of
government in store for her, rushed off to the *Kafes* to tell Ibrahim
the good news.

As we shall see in the next chapter, he was too terrified to open the
door, thinking the incessant knocking to be merely the arrival of the
mutes with the bowstring whose coming he had daily feared for the
last eight years.

And so, free at last, Ibrahim mounted the throne, and soon proved
himself the most depraved, selfish, cruel, rapacious, and cowardly
man that even the Ottoman Empire had produced. His Grand
Vizir, Kara-Mustafa, sought to check his excesses, but he fell out
with a member of the *ḥarēm*, and his execution soon followed. His
successor decided to give the Sultan's debauchery and follies full rein
and so gross were some of his orgies that even the *ḥarēm* murmured
in indignation. All the best offices of State were sold to the highest
bidder or given to worthless favourites, taxes were increased, and
every resource possible was drained to supply the demands of his
excesses.

Ḥarēm scandal caused a report that he was impotent, used up by
his unwearied debauches, but the birth of a son in 1642 and two more

the following year soon put an end to that rumour. At the same time his vicious life in the *ḥarēm* continued, and historians tell us curious tales of the happenings in the Seraglio. One of his chief passions was a morbid craving for perfumes, especially for ambergris, with the exotic heavy scent of which he drenched his beard, clothes, and room hangings. Another craving he had was for furs. One night he had listened to a tale in the *ḥarēm* about a king who was dressed in sable skins and whose sofas, couches, walls, and floors were covered with the same skins. Ibrahim thought he would also like to be a 'sable king,' and in the morning he summoned the Divan and ordered a general collection of sables to be made all over the Empire. Both an ambergris and a fur tax were imposed, and indignation grew at these stupid and useless extravagances. Demetrius Cantemir[1] gives a terrible description of Ibrahim's life in the *ḥarēm*: how when nature was exhausted he fortified himself with aphrodisiacs and covered his room with mirrors to stimulate the passions. Every Friday a fresh virgin was presented to him (usually by his mother!), and anyone who suggested some new form of orgy was certain of a personal triumph. One of his little games was to strip all his women naked and make them pretend to be mares, while in a similar condition he would run among them acting the part of stallion as long as his strength lasted.

The extravagances of the women were nearly as bad as his own, and he allowed them to take anything they liked from the shops and bazaars without payment. One of these women happened to say she preferred to shop at night, and so the shopkeepers were made to stay open and provide sufficient torchlight for their wares to be clearly seen. Another woman told Ibrahim that he would look nice with jewels in his beard! No sooner said than done, and he actually appeared like this in public! The superstitious Turks regarded it as a very bad omen, because the only other King who had acted in this way was Pharaoh of the Red Sea incident.

Many are the stories told of Ibrahim's depravity, lust, and cruelty, but the tale of the *Kislar Agha* and his slave girl as related by Rycaut is worthy of repetition, if only to show how an incident in the *ḥarēm* led to a war which lasted over twenty years.

[1] *History of the Ottoman Empire* (London, 1734), p. 254.

It appears that the Chief Eunuch, the *Kislar Agha*, chanced to cast his eyes upon a fair slave put up for sale by a Persian merchant. So enamoured of her did he become that he decided to buy her for himself and add her to his *ḥarēm*, which, useless though it was, pride and tradition made him support. Although he bought her as a virgin she soon proved to be with child, and the justly indignant eunuch was greatly offended and confined her to the house of his steward. However, when the child was born curiosity got the better of indignation and the eunuch went to see the babe, and was so delighted with it that he resolved to adopt it at once. Now it was about this time that Ibrahim's first son, Muhammad, was born, and, the child being in want of a nurse, the slave girl of the *Kislar Agha* was chosen, who accordingly entered upon her duties in company with her own son.

Ibrahim at once preferred the slave's son to his own, who was pale and anæmic, and passed hours playing with him in the gardens of the Seraglio. This roused the jealousy of Muhammad's mother, who developed a hatred for the girl, her son, and the *Kislar Agha*. One day she attacked Ibrahim about the matter, who in his rage snatched Muhammad from his mother's arms and flung him into a near-by cistern. He was saved from drowning, but bore a scar on his forehead for the rest of his life.

But by this time things had got too hot for the *Kislar Agha*, and he suddenly decided that a trip to Mecca might be followed by a retirement to Egypt. Matters were arranged at once, and three ships were filled with the Chief Eunuch's *ḥarēm*, treasures, and goods of every description. Contrary winds compelled them to put into Rhodes, and hardly had they continued on their course when six Maltese galleys approached and opened fire. After a long and bloody fight the Turkish vessels were overpowered, and the *Kislar Agha* died fighting like a man. So enormous was the booty that the voyage was regarded as no ordinary trip, and the young boy found on board was at once taken to be the Sultan's son on his way to Alexandria to be educated. The presence of the *Kislar Agha* had confirmed this belief and the Grand Master of the Knights of St John treated the boy with the honours due to a future sovereign, and all Europe believed the story. The child was educated, and after being dragged about in various countries ended by becoming a monk, and was known as Father Ottoman.

But when the news reached Ibrahim he became mad with rage, executed his Captain Pasha, and swore to be revenged not only on the Maltese, but on the Venetians who had harboured them in Crete. Although war was openly declared against Malta the secret objective was Candia, or Crete. A formidable fleet set sail in 1645 with the declared object of attacking Malta, which had been busy strengthening its fortifications and making ready for a long siege. But the Turkish fleet changed its direction and sailed to Canea, the western extremity of Crete, which it reached late in June. Canea and then Retimo fell into its hands, and in 1648 the siege of the capital began, and lasted for twenty years!

Meanwhile at home the *ḥarēm* still ruled the country, but Ibrahim had gone too far, and his deposition was sought to save the country from ruin. The Sultan Validé, Kiusem, was diplomatically sounded as to her views, and, still smarting from the gross indignities she had suffered at her son's hands, she agreed to receive a deputation from the army and the people. After useless remonstrances she yielded to their demands, Ibrahim was deposed and sent back to the *Kafes*, and the young Muhammad placed on the throne in his stead. And now Kiusem had another, and younger, Sultan Validé to reckon with, Tarkhan or Turkhan by name, who proved to be more than a match for her elder rival. As the imprisoned Ibrahim still tried to get back his lost throne and the Spahis demanded his death the *mufti* yielded, and amid the blasphemies and curses of the wretched man the bow-string ended his miserable life.

Now more than before did Kiusem see her power slipping away, but she decided to make one last effort by plotting with the *Agha* of the janissaries, whom she had won over to her side, to depose Muhammad IV and put Suleiman, his younger brother, on the throne in his stead. At first everything went well. The *Agha* collected troops, and the Grand Vizir, being surprised at night, was obliged to attend the meeting. Feigning to agree with their plans, he asked leave to go to the Seraglio to call the Divan, but once he was safely inside the doors were locked, and the rest of the night was spent in arming all available troops and barricading the Palace. Tarkhan

Sultan was awakened, and an oath of allegiance was taken to serve and defend the young Muhammad, who was still but a child. The *mufti* declared by a *fetva* that Kiusem must die, and a decree was drawn up by the Vizir and signed by the trembling hand of the young Sultan. It was now the hour of Tarkhan's triumph, and a search was made in Kiusem's suite without result. At last the wretched old woman was discovered hidden in a clothes-chest and dragged out to her death. Every atom of respect was forgotten in the terrible scene that followed. Her earrings and bracelets were torn off her, the money she scattered on the ground as a bait was ignored, her rich robes were torn in a thousand pieces, and, in spite of all the orders her oppressors had received to respect the body of their Sultan's grandmother, the hapless woman was stripped of her clothes and dragged by the feet naked to the gate of the *harēm* known as the Gate of the Aviary (No. 40 in the plan). There she was strangled, and her partisans were killed later. Tarkhan was now in command of the situation, but was wise enough to entrust the power of government to Muhammad Kiuprili, the first of the three Grand Vizirs of the name who ruled Turkey so successfully. With the death of Tarkhan the Reign of Women was virtually ended, and hopes for the Empire began to revive.

CHAPTER IX

THE SELĀMLIK

As already explained in the introductory chapter, the *selāmlik* was that part of the house reserved for the men only, the word actually meaning 'place of greeting.' In the case of the Seraglio, however, it was used in its widest sense, as it included the large Throne Room into which women were often introduced, and also the Hall of Circumcision. The Corridor of the Bath and the Golden Road linked it closely with the *harēm*; in fact, as time went on the barrier between these two important units of the House of Felicity grew less and less, and, as already mentioned in the first of the *harēm* chapters, it is no easy matter to-day to trace where the two divide.

The Vestibule of the Hearth, *Ocakli Sofa* (No. 70 in the plan), was built after the terrible fire of 1665 as a connecting link between the Court of the Sultan Validé and the *Hünkâr Sofasi*, or Royal Saloon, sometimes known as the Throne Room Within. It leads into the anteroom of the Royal Saloon, the Vestibule of the Fountain (*Çeşmeli Sofa*), which is even more ornate than the *Ocakli Sofa*. As can be seen from the plate opposite p. 183, it is a tall room completely tiled from floor to ceiling. The chimney-piece and the doorway leading to the vestibule of the suite of Murad III are both surmounted by deeply carved Cufic reliefs. The shutters to the cupboards on either side of the fireplace are inlaid with mother-of-pearl, and resemble designs in the Hall of Ambassadors at the Alhambra, Granada.

Passing on into the huge domed Royal Saloon, one is immediately struck by the mixture of Oriental and French forms of decoration. An elaborately carved French dado is surmounted by another one of Cufic characters, and rococo ornamentation is much in evidence in the large array of chairs and grandfather clocks. The room was used for the larger *harēm* entertainments, the women being seated in the raised portion of the room behind the pillars. The musicians, heavily blindfolded if engaged from outside the Seraglio, sat in the gallery above the women.

The Royal throne was a simple structure to the right, surmounted by a canopy upheld by four pillars. Of official ceremonies held here the only one recorded appears to be the first meeting of the new Sultan with his complete *ḥarēm* before the ceremony of " the Girding of the Sword" at Eyyūb, which corresponds to our coronation.[1] The modern painted treatment of the pendentives and supporting arches is of little artistic value, and is reminiscent of much similar work in many of the larger Constantinople mosques. In the far left-hand corner is the Corridor of the Bath (*Hamam Yolu*), having the Royal baths on the left and the bedroom of Abd ul-Hamid I and a room used by Selim III on the right. Abd ul-Hamid's room is so overloaded with rococo decoration that not an inch is free from some type of scroll-work in gilt or marble. The fountain, chimney-piece, cupboards, and daïs are all replete with the writhing eccentricities of the worst Louis XV excesses. In fact (except for the chimney-piece, which is, if possible, even more rococo and of the proscenium type), it is a relief to pass on to the more sober room of Selim III, lined on three sides by low sofas upholstered in silk and satin brocades embroidered in pleasing floral designs. A row of windows on the north and west sides affords a fine view of the gardens beyond.

Through a long passage running by the side of Selim's room access is obtained to the wall kiosk of Osman III and the adjoining rooms.

Here again the French influence predominates, as is at once noticed by the much-overloaded façade, which faces a large paved courtyard with a rectangular pool in the middle and a trellis vine along the eastern side.

Basically the kiosk is Italian in design in its use of the orders, but the Eastern influence is retained in the usual wide-spreading roof eaves, which, together with its supporting cornice, rise in waves from each end of the façade to the centre over the doorway. The doorway itself is framed by a pair of columns supporting an undulating entablature capped by a mass of writhing sculptural forms; and on either side of the doorway are two windows, each separated by pilasters, heavily grilled, and surmounted by a comparatively chaste little string-course, over which in turn are rectangular panels filled

[1] For an account of this interesting ceremony see F. W. Hasluck, *Christianity and Islam under the Sultans* (Oxford, 1929), vol. ii, pp. 604–622, " The Girding of the Sultan."

THE KIOSK AND COURTYARD OF OSMAN III

[See p. 194]

THE WALL KIOSK OF OSMAN III : A VIEW LOOKING UP FROM THE
SERAGLIO GARDENS

with intricate carving. The wall treatment on either side of the centre bay is again divided by pilasters, the intervening spaces here being decorated with the characteristic wall fountains, and also with views painted in sharp perspective—reminiscent of Pompeian wall frescoes of the Fourth Style.

The external side of the building as seen from the Seraglio gardens presents a strong contrast in its severity of design, and the high, beetling side of the walls, with the projecting kiosk at the top, appears like a prison or medieval fortification. Decoration has been kept to a minimum, and the whole effect is fine and pleasing in character.

From the windows of the kiosk itself a magnificent view is obtained of the Golden Horn and the Bosphorus, and before the erection of the ugly station buildings the near distance was occupied by gardens stretching to the water's edge.

Internally the kiosk is divided into three main rooms leading out of each other, the wall kiosk itself being part of the centre one, which is twice as large as either of the other two. Each room is most lavishly decorated, so that barely a square inch of wall or ceiling surface remains uncovered. The walls are panelled and decorated in various ways, with carved and painted floral designs of a most fantastic nature, and with frescoes showing views in perspective of Italian landscapes. Some panels are filled with tiles set in most intricate patterns, while others are pierced to form niches to hold pipes, trays, etc., and resemble similar niches to be seen in the chamber of Murad III and the Baghdad Kiosk. The furniture and mirrors are French, of the Louis XIV and Louis XV periods, heavily carved and gilded, and upholstered with rich brocades and silks.

The whole effect of these rooms is so rich in its wealth and profusion of decoration and riot of colour as to appear almost gross and vulgar. At the same time the kiosk is a remarkable example of later Turkish art, and of the most lavish rococo style then prevalent in so many countries in Europe.

The courtyard separates the kiosk of Osman III from the back windows of the Royal Saloon, to which it is now necessary to return in order to reach the rooms of Murad III and Ahmed I and Ahmed III. Room 86 in the plan forms the vestibule or hall to the large chamber of Murad III. It is entirely covered with tiling, having many fine floral panels surmounted by several cornices of alternate Cufic and floral designs. Both the cupboard shutters and the door are inlaid with mother-of-pearl.

Except for the Royal Saloon, the chamber of Murad III is the largest in the *selāmlik*. It has a high dome which can be clearly seen in one of my photographs of the Courtyard of the Princes (opposite p. 198). It is a pleasing room, and the tiling is relieved by several series of wall niches in sets of three, an elaborate wall fountain of the cascade type, and two canopied thrones or beds on the chimney side. The chimney-piece itself is very fine, having a pointed canopy over twenty feet high resembling the top of a minaret, or, to the Western mind, the point of a giant pencil. A very beautiful, deep Cufic cornice surrounds the room at a height of some eight feet.

Leading out of this room are two small chambers both full of charm and interest. The first is the Library (*Kütüphanesi*) of Ahmed I, and the second (the smallest room in the whole Seraglio) the dining-room (*yemek odasi*) of Ahmed III.

The general scheme of the library resembles that of the large room of Murad III, the tiling, however, being chiefly in the upper part, since all the lower half of the room is devoted to cupboard book-shelves closed by double panelled doors beautifully inlaid with various geometrical designs. A charming tiled skirting surrounds the room, and gives a touch of lightness which one would hardly expect in a library. The pendentives contain large circular inscriptions, with two small ones above and one below. The usual ball and tassel is suspended from the centre of the dome. The books and manuscripts have been transferred to the New Library, in the Third Court.

The little dining-room of Ahmed III leads out of the library to the left and is unique in character. It is panelled in wood and gaily painted with vases of bright flowers and dishes of fruit of various kinds. An inlaid tray in the centre of the room supports a glass bowl for preserved fruits and the usual two spoons used in eating. A small side-door gives access to that part of the Royal Saloon where the members of the *ḥarēm* sat.

And so in this hurried survey (hurried partly because all these rooms are open to the public) we have covered practically all the *selāmlik*. There yet remains, however, the most interesting, if the grimmest,

THE CHAMBER OF MURAD III

[*See p. 196*]

THE DINING-ROOM OF AHMED III

THE KIOSK OF OSMAN III : ONE OF THE SMALLER ROOMS

part to be seen. I refer to the *Kafes*, or Cage. It can be reached by means of the Golden Road and along a corridor known as the *Jin Müşaveret Mahalle*, or Consultation Place of the Jinn, or else from the hall of Murad III's room. It is not open to the public, and owing to this fact and to its morbidly interesting nature I shall deal with it in some detail.

The *Kafes* has been the scene of more wanton cruelty, misery, and bloodshed than any palace room in the whole of Europe. To its institution are due the weakness, vices, and imbecility of so many of the Sultans and, to a large extent, the gradual decay and fall of the Ottoman Empire.

The enormous *harēm* of Murad III had produced 103 children for him, and at his death twenty sons and twenty-seven daughters were still living. On his recall to the capital the eldest son and heir, the future Muhammad III, put his nineteen brothers to death and sewed seven of his father's pregnant concubines into sacks and had them thrown into the Marmora, just to be on the safe side in case a possible claimant to the throne was born! But this was the end of such drastic measures, for henceforth it was decided not to kill the Princes—at least, not at first—but to keep them safely locked up in a building in the Seraglio which soon came to be known as the Cage. It was a two-storied building hidden away in the very heart of the *selâmlik* and surrounded by a high and dismal wall. It was not until the time of Osman III (1754–57) that the wall was lowered and more windows were unblocked. These unhappy men were kept without knowledge of the outside world, or even of public affairs of the Empire. Their education was entirely neglected, except for what they could learn from their companions, who consisted of deaf mutes and a handful of sterile women who were allowed to form a *harēm* to amuse the Princes. Although every care was taken to make these women barren—either by the removal of the ovaries or simply by the use of pessaries, made by the Seraglio physicians, of such ingredients as musk, amber, bezoar, aloes, cardamom, ginger, pepper, cinnamon, and cloves—yet mistakes did occur, and the child (and sometimes the mother as well) was immediately drowned.

It is hard even to imagine what such a life must have been like. The only thing that can be compared with it is the 'solitary confinement' as enforced in certain State prisons of to-day. But such men at least have lived in the world, their brains and bodies have been allowed to grow and develop. But some of the Princes, such as Ibrahim, had been in the Cage from the age of two. Others, such as Osman III, were immured for fifty years, or thirty-nine years in the case of Suleiman II. When they came out they had all but lost the power of speech, and their minds and bodies were like vegetables. And yet these men—these few 'lucky' men, who had escaped the bowstring of the deaf mutes—were expected to take up the reins of government at a moment's notice and rule over one of the most difficult and extensive kingdoms in Europe. No wonder, then, that excesses occurred. Only a miracle could produce a normal man after such experiences. By some the particular form of 'revenge' would be sought in the over-indulgence of every conceivable kind of vice that a half-crazed brain could devise; for others a ruthless use of the scimitar and an endless flow of blood would help to blot out the past.

But there were exceptions, among them Suleiman II, who during his thirty-nine years' confinement had learned calligraphy and spent all his time copying out *Korāns* and praying; and when finally he came to occupy a turbulent and disquiet throne many a time did he wish himself back in the quiet solitude of the Cage. Very bloody were some of the happenings that occurred here. I shall give but two examples.

Ibrahim grew up in the *Kafes*, never knowing from day to day when the door might slowly open and the mutes enter with the fatal bowstring ready to do its deadly work. When the day came that the reigning Sultan, Murad IV, died the Seraglio attendants hastened to tell Ibrahim the good news and to proclaim him Sultan. He heard the noise of the approaching crowd just in time to barricade the door with the help of his concubines, and, crazed with fright, could see nothing but lies and traps in the explanations shouted through the door. Still he would not believe, until the door was broken down and the dead body of Murad was flung at his feet. For a moment he stood transfixed with a feeling of mingled joy and fear, and then, realizing the truth, danced round the corpse in hideous triumph, crying out, "The Butcher of the Empire is dead at last!"

But Ibrahim had not done with the *Kafes* yet, for after his ignoble and vicious reign of nine years the nation rose and flung him back

THE KAFES, OR CAGE : THE NORTH-WESTERN PORTION OF THE BUILDING

THE CORRIDOR "WHERE THE JINN HOLD THEIR CONSULTATIONS,"
LEADING TO THE KAFES

into it again. There he waited, hoping daily to be restored to the throne. Then one day the door opened and the expectant ex-Sultan and his concubines prepared for the good news. But the Sultan Validé had abandoned him, and this time it *was* the bowstring.

In more recent days, when the janissaries mutinied in 1807, Selim III anticipated their demands by voluntarily exchanging places in the Cage with his cousin Mustafa. The new Sultan soon proved his incompetency, and when Bairakdar marched to Selim's aid Mustafa in his turn ordered Selim to be killed. The murderers entered the Cage, and after a terrific fight for his life Selim was strangled. When Bairakdar reached the gate he thundered on it and called aloud for Selim. " Here is he ye seek! " they cried, and threw out the body of the Sultan. Mustafa was dragged off the throne and put back into the Cage, and Mahmud II became Sultan.

These and similar happenings give to the *Kafes* an historical background that creates for this strange building of the *selāmlik* an interest all its own.

It has been described as a two-storied building, without windows in the lower story, consisting of twelve magnificent apartments all exactly similar to one another and all luxuriously furnished. How true this was once I cannot say, but it certainly is not correct as far as the building that remains to-day is concerned—except that it is two stories high. Few architectural changes appear to have been made here, so it seems probable that the information was purely guesswork. It is not clear, nevertheless, how the heir to the throne, with a *harēm* of some two dozen women (Melling gives the number at forty, but this may be intended to apply to the *Kafes* as a whole), as well as several brothers, each with his separate *harēm*, not to mention eunuchs, mutes, buffoons, etc., could get into a building of this size. For it consists of four rooms only. True, they are fine rooms with the usual ornate rococo decoration, showing French early eighteenth-century influence, and so must have undergone considerable alterations in the course of their history, yet there is no sign of structural alterations such as can be clearly seen in other parts of the Seraglio. It may be then that, whereas the *Kafes* rooms were used exclusively by the Princes, the *harēm* and other members of the Cage had their rooms across the court on the first floor of that part of the buildings that backs on to the Golden Road. I was lucky in obtaining three photographs of the *Kafes* and courtyard, so that the whole extent of the area can be studied.

In the photograph reproduced opposite p. 198 we see, first, the outer, or north-western, part of the building. The whole façade is tiled, windows are heavily barred, and a broad overhanging roof runs right round the building. To the right is the domed room of Murad III, and beyond that a glimpse can just be obtained of the courtyard of Osman III. A section of the arching below is also visible. It is probably somewhere in this lower part, now a waste overrun with wild fig, acacia, and other trees, that the original *Kafes* wall had its foundations. The fine pierced balustrade is exactly the same as that which surmounts the Imperial Gate, and doubtless dates from the same period (nineteenth century). In the second photograph in the same plate we get a good view of the other half of the *Kafes*, and here the tiling is much clearer. A long oriel window will be noticed, below which is the entrance from the corridor "where the Jinn hold their consultations," connecting with the Golden Road. In the illustration opposite can be seen the other side of the courtyard, and exactly how closely connected with the *Kafes* the rooms on the mezzanine and first floor are. It is here that I suggest the 'staff' of the *Kafes* would be housed. In fact, the only other place where such a comparatively large number of women could live would be in the buildings, long since gone, on the opposite side of the courtyard, beyond the pierced balustrade. Only a thorough inspection of the ruins hidden by the heavy undergrowth would help to reveal the possibilities of such an alternative suggestion, and this unfortunately I have not had the opportunity of doing.

So also I cannot say what other buildings once existed between the *Kafes* and right away in a northerly direction to the extreme point of the outer Seraglio walls near the Baghdad Kiosk. It is, however, in this wide empty area that some of the *selāmlik* buildings described by such early visitors as Nicolas de Nicolay, Dallam, and Bon, and even in later years by Flachat (1750), must undoubtedly have been situated. When inspecting the outer wall surrounding this area I noticed three doorways filled in with bricks, the centre one, double the width of the other two, being surmounted by a stone lintel with

THE COURTYARD OF THE CAGE, SHOWING THE BUILDINGS ON THE SOUTH-EASTERN SIDE

mutules, or projecting slabs on the soffit, or under-surface, as in a Doric cornice.

The only other exit from this part of the *selãmlik* is through a double-leafed iron-studded gate leading to the outer gardens by the Goths' Column. It seems probable that it was through this gate that the early visitors to the *selãmlik* made their entrance.

Apart from the Baghdad and Revan Kiosks and the Pavilion of the Holy Mantle, which are treated elsewhere, there remain only the reception-room of the *selãmlik* (the *Mabeyin Hümayun*) and the Hall of Circumcision (*Sünnet Odasi*) to be discussed. Of the former I can say nothing as to its origin and use, except that it was built by Selim, and appears to have been connected with the Pavilion of the Holy Mantle in some way or other. Dr Miller,[1] quoting from Ahmed Rasim, tells us that at a later period the Sultans regularly received the pages of the Palace School in these rooms (which she calls the Rooms of His Presence) following the first prayer of the morning, and upon rare occasions they also received there the members of the Secret Council, and the Grand Vizir, the *mufti*, the two judges of the Army, and the Minister of Foreign Affairs.

We are now approaching the L-shaped pillared hall which flanks the Pavilion of the Holy Mantle on its two outer sides. The terrace looking into the gardens is bounded at one end by the *Mabeyin Hümayun* and at the other by the *Sünnet Odasi*.

There appears to be some doubt as to whether this latter building was really used for the circumcision of the Princes, but an inspection of it leaves little doubt that this was indeed the case, as should be evident from my description. There are several approaches to the Hall of Circumcision. Personally I entered it through the small door near the Revan Kiosk and across the pillared hall where Dallam erected his organ. It can also be reached *via* the Golden Road past the *Mabeyin Hümayun*, and lastly from the terrace of the Baghdad Kiosk through a small door at the side of the fish-pond.

The Hall of Circumcision was built by Ibrahim in 1641, and is a square room with a small carved iron door leading from the pillared hall. It is beautifully tiled, and at first glance the domed ceiling appears to be tiled as well, but a closer inspection shows it to be painted

[1] *Beyond the Sublime Porte*, p. 242.

to match the walls. The tiling is of various dates, but of especial interest are four panels with identical designs and colourings on each side of the door. They measure no less than four feet by one foot six inches, and earthenware plaques of this size are unknown elsewhere.

In the lower part of these panels is a design of two deer which, so the Director affirms, is unique. Between the windows on the two outer sides are deep recesses fitted with a kind of leaden sink and running water used in connexion with the function of the room. The white and gold carved work at the sides should especially be noticed. A heavily embossed brazier occupies the centre of the room.

Immediately next the Hall of Circumcision is a small outhouse, now used as a lumber-room. It appears to be of fairly recent construction, and I could find out nothing about it. The terrace, now enclosed by a glass partition, was clearly once open to the pillared hall, which was doubtless protected by awnings such as are described by Dallam (see p. 33).

And here the *selāmlik* merges into the buildings of the Pavilion of the Holy Mantle, which forms part of the chapter on the Third Court.

CHAPTER X

THE BATHS

1. The Baths of the Seraglio

To so great an extent does the bath enter into the life of every Turk, both male and female, from the highest to the lowest, that the subject cannot be dismissed with the curt information that the Seraglio had many baths once, but that to-day hardly any remain.

The subject merits a chapter to itself. In order to appreciate what the large baths used by the pages and *harēm* girls were like we must go to the public baths in the city for descriptions of eyewitnesses. Doubtless in some cases the Seraglio baths were more elaborate and luxurious, but as far as one can judge the differences were trifling.

With regard to the personal baths in the Seraglio we are more lucky, and two adjacent baths, known as those of the Sultan and Sultana, remain intact save for the elaborate hangings, sofas, cushions, and suchlike that the disrobing rooms once contained.

I shall describe them in detail shortly; but apart from these none of the baths remain in any good state of repair. Some have been converted into rooms for other purposes, and can only be recognized by the perforated domes or general shape of the building.

The number of baths in the Seraglio was always considerable, owing to the fact that, apart from the Sultan and the Sultan Valide, each *kadin* had her own suite which included a bath; and each separate division of both the *selāmlik* and the Court of the Divan had one also. Naturally the number of baths varied considerably, but on an average it must have totalled some thirty or more. All baths were heated by water introduced under the floor on the Pompeian system, or else merely distributed to the various wall fountains on different sides of the room. The boilers were usually of copper, like those which could once be seen at the Alhambra, in Granada. As far as can be ascertained, the boiler-rooms were on a level with the baths, but where space was a consideration it seems probable that they were underneath in the basement, where there was plenty of room, not only for the boilers, but also for the storing of the immense quantities of wood which were used for the fires.

In some cases so great is the state of ruin that a few broken pieces of marble and the cock of a fountain are all that remains among the *débris* to show where a bath once existed.

But let us take the whole Seraglio court by court and see exactly what survives to-day. When we have done that we can turn to some of the few early accounts that have come down to us, which will help to give life to the cold marble and clothe the dressing-room once again with the rich hangings and luxurious sofas which once adorned it in such grand profusion.

In the First Court was the bath of the infirmary, immediately to the right of the Imperial Gate. The entire building has long since disappeared, but no special interest would attach itself to a hospital bath of the Outer Service, so we can at once proceed to the Second Court. To the left is the bath of Beşir Ağa, but it is now merely a ruin. To the right in the kitchen quarters several fountains and water-cocks can be found among the ruins, but no sign of any bath on a large enough scale to serve the complete kitchen staff exists. The wall fountains were sufficient for ablutions before prayer, and it seems highly probable that these members of the Inner Palace service would use the public baths in the city.

With the halberdiers, on the left of the court, things were different, for, as we have already seen (p. 110), their duties were largely connected with the *ḥarēm*, and the service was kept complete with its courtyard, mosque, eating-room, dormitories, and baths. A glance at the plan will remind us that the halberdiers' baths lay to the right at the bottom of the stairs. The wall fountains were of white marble, as can be seen from the few that remain, but so great is the *débris* that nothing can be said about the decoration or even the general scheme of the rooms. A second chamber leads off the main one, and apparently served as the *tepidarium*. The latrines are built against the outer side.

Of the baths in the *ḥarēm* itself, apart from the Sultana's bath, the only remaining ones are those leading off the courtyard of the *ḥarēm* girls (No. 44 in the plan), and similar ones I 'discovered' hidden away among the ruins of the so-called girls' hospital (No. 58 in the plan).

Here again any detailed description is impossible. The former are in far the better condition, and remains of marble decoration on the walls give us a slight idea of what they were originally like. The rooms are very narrow, allowing of no central plunge basin, but merely a series of wall fountains. It seems probable, however, that a massage marble slab once adorned the middle of the main room. The same applies to the hospital baths, but the state of these rooms is really too bad to permit any further description.

As already mentioned, the Sultan's bath and the Sultana's are the only ones in the Seraglio in good repair to-day, and these we shall now consider in detail. It was at these baths that the *haremlik* and the *selāmlik* met. A corridor, known as the *Hamam Yolu* (Corridor of the Bath), connected the Sultana's suite with the *Hünkâr Sofasi* (Royal Saloon), and from the corridor itself access was gained to both baths. The Sultan's bath (*Hünkâr Hamami*) is the more important of the two, and is, moreover, the only one open to the general public, so I shall describe that first.

It consists of the usual three rooms, the general scheme throughout being one of brightness and lightness, white marble and tall narrow columns with stalactitic capitals being employed. On entering from the corridor one finds oneself in a small room almost entirely devoid of decoration, so that it is difficult for the imagination to clothe the walls with gorgeous golden hangings encrusted with myriads of pearls like those still to be seen in the Seraglio Museum. Heavy Persian rugs covered the floors, and low sofas upholstered in gold and silver embroideries and piled up with cushions lined the walls. A bejewelled *nargileh* and coffee-set practically completed the furniture of the room, in which one at once recognizes the undressing- and rest-room of the baths. In 1934 a rather pathetic attempt was made to enable tourists to recognize the original function of the room by the installing of a sofa with white hangings along the right-hand side.

On the left is a small lavatory of the usual Turkish type, to the right of which another doorway leads into the *Hünkâr Sofasi*.

The second room is the *tepidarium*. From a central corridor small rooms lead off either side, the entrance to each being flanked with slender white columns. That on the left contains a marble wall fountain.

A lavish use of white marble, relieved by the introduction of gilt iron-work, makes the third and last room—the *calidarium*—the most beautiful of them all. Here there is little call on the imagination, as everything being of marble or iron has remained *in situ*. Passing in through a finely wrought iron-gilt door, one is at once attracted by a really beautiful cascade wall fountain immediately opposite at the end of the room. A closer inspection will show that the boiling water was introduced from a boiler in a room behind. The water fell into a marble bath beneath, which, raised on a marble step, stretches the entire breadth of the central part of the wall. The bath itself is narrow and long, like ordinary Western baths, and at each end is a seat with a high back and a single arm-rest facing the room, displaying a conventional decoration in a panelled surround. All is in white marble. In front of the bath is a movable concave stepping-stone, also of white marble. In each corner of the room on either side of the bath is a beautiful wall fountain enclosed by four tall pillars similar to those in the second room, the only free one, however, being that nearest the centre of the room.

To the left of the entrance is the chief wall fountain, where the more intimate operations of the bath were carried on. It is raised on a semicircular platform, and is divided from the rest of the room by a pierced gilt partition with a door in the centre. A small window to the right looks into the left-hand corner fountain-room between the four pillars. On the opposite side is a similar, though much less important, wall fountain. It has no separate partition, but a small window commands a view of the *tepidarium*.

Thus we see that the three-room arrangement of the ordinary public baths was closely followed in the Royal *selāmlik*. The hottest water would be in the long bath, and the wall fountains would be regulated at varying temperatures according to the purposes they served. In the second room the water would be much cooler, for use in closing the pores of the skin in preparation for the most wonderful part of the bath—the relaxation in the rest-room to the accompaniment of the soothing *nargileh*, the slices of melon covered with snow, the steaming black coffee in the bejewelled *finjan*, the crystal glass of delicately perfumed sherbet, or whatever else Royal fancy might dictate.

The Sultana's rooms lie exactly parallel to those of the Sultan, and are so similar as hardly to merit a separate description. The entrance is not direct from the Corridor of the Bath, but is through a narrow passage leading off on the *harēm* side. The first room is quite bare, being entirely stripped of the gorgeous hangings and sofas that once made it a rest-room worthy of its Royal occupant. Unlike the corresponding room in the Sultan's bath suite, it has a small window looking out into the corridor. The small lavatory lies in the left-hand corner of the first room as one goes in.

The second room closely resembles that in the Sultan's suite, and has a marble wall fountain and small window looking into the third room, which one now enters. It is at once noticed that the bath is not centred along the end wall, but stretches flush with the right-hand wall. It is broader than the Sultan's, has no side-seats and only one fountain, to the left of the bath. The rest of the room is similar to the adjoining one, having a gilded wrought-iron partition and a wall fountain on each side.

It is quite possible that other baths once existed in the ruined portion of the *selāmlik* beyond the library of Ahmed I (No. 88 in the plan), but if so no trace remains, and no account has come down to us. Records exist of the building of at least two baths during the reign of Murad III (1574–95), but except that the work was carried out by Greek workmen nothing further appears to be known.

I shall now turn to the only other remaining baths in the Seraglio, the so-called baths of Selim II, situated on the right-hand side of the Third Court. As can be seen in the plan (Nos. 103 and 104), there are several rooms of varying shapes and sizes in this part of the court. The main room, supported by fourteen heavy stone pillars, was used as one of the halls of the Palace School, and known as the Hall of Campaign (*Seferli Koğuşu*), but the proximity to water is obvious from the fact that the pages of this hall were entrusted with the washing of the Sultan's linen. Leading out of this room was a second one of equal length, but not so broad, described to-day as the "Rest-room of bath of Selim II," while a small adjoining chamber contained

the large copper boilers. Farther to the right are two square rooms
of equal size and closely resembling each other in architectural detail.
These rooms at once suggest both by their massive type of stonework and by their high vaulting that at one time they all formed
part of a large and elaborate *hamam*. Yet from the time of Selim I
(1512–20) the farthest one had been used as a treasury, and its twin
was simply described as "Dressing-room of bath of Selim II." To-
day this latter room houses the silver and crystal-ware of the Palace,
while the other rooms have been altered to display the famous
porcelain collection.

The difficulty of assigning these rooms to their original uses as part
of the baths of the Palace School may possibly be somewhat cleared
up by a reference to Tavernier's chapter on "The Baths of the Seraglio." At any rate, it will give readers the opportunity of drawing
their own conclusions, while the actual description of the rooms
affords a very good idea of the elaborate system of marble and faïence
tiling:

> I come now to the Great Bath, which is adjoyning to the Chamber
> of the *Hamangibachi*, who is the chief Overseer of it, and which makes
> part of the Appartment of the *Seferlis*, or the Grand Seignor's Laundry-
> men.[1] The place where they put off their Cloaths is a spacious Louver,
> or Banquetting-house of Freestone, high enough, and in one of the
> most eminent parts of the Seraglio. The Floor is pav'd with a very
> delightful kind of Marble laid in squared pieces, and it has two large
> Windows jutting out upon the Gardens, somewhat like Balconies,
> from which you have a Prospect of the two Seas. In the midst of that
> *Domo* or *Louver*, you find a Fountain, the water whereof is receiv'd
> into two Basins, or Cisterns: The former, which is the highest, and
> withal the least, is of one piece of White Marble, having in it a little
> intermixture of Red and Black Veins, and pierc'd through at six
> several places, for the reception of so many small Pipes of Copper,
> through which the water falls down into the other Basin, which is also
> of Marble, of several pieces, and several colours. . . . On one side of
> the Fountain, which is in the midst of the *Domo*, there is an entrance
> into the bath, and near that is the Hall, where they uncloath themselves

---

[1] The significance of the word *Seferli* appears to have been twofold—referring to both
expeditions and laundries. The word *seferî* actually means 'on a war footing' or merely
'appertaining to a journey.' The pages attached to the *Seferli Oda* were responsible for
washing the Sultan's clothes both before and after campaigns and journeys. Hence,
apparently, the connexion.

in the Winter-time. A little Gallery which lies on the left hand, leads to the places design'd for the easing of nature, and every seat has a little Cock, which supplies them with water to wash themselves, after they have done. . . . At the end of the Gallery, there is a door which gives you passage into three Chambers, which are so many Baths for the use of the Grand Seignor's Quarter. There is adjoyning to the last of those Chambers a spacious place pav'd Checquerwise with Marble of different colours, and there the *Ichoglans* are trimm'd. This place has a little eminency in the midst of it, from which there is a gentle descent of all sides, that the water wherewith the Barbers wash their Heads and Beards may the more easily be carried off, and the place be alwaies kept clean. On both sides of the Wall, whereby it is enclos'd, there is a great double Cock, with two Keyes belonging to it, which, at the same mouth, supplyes them alternately with either hot water, or cold, and that falls into a Basin or Receptacle of White Marble, wherein three or four men may bathe themselves without any inconvenience, or trouble one to the other. There is also at one of the ends a little Room of Black and White Marble, and there the Barbers, who have no knowledge of any other Profession, put up all their necessary Utensils and Instruments, as Razors, Hones, Balls, and those Irons wherewith they pare their Nails. . . . Opposite to the Chamber of the Barbers, there are three other Rooms arch'd with Marble, the largest whereof much surpasses in Beauty those that are adjoyning to it. The Floor of it is of white and black Marble, and the Walls are done about with square pieces, that are white and blew, and in every one of them you find a Flower in emboss'd Work, done to the Life, and which a man would take for enamell. Little Lamines or Plates of Gold cover the junctures of those square pieces, and there cannot any thing be imagin'd more pleasant and divertive than that Chamber is. In the Roof of it, there are several round holes, of about half a foot diameter, over which there are little Glasses made in the fashion of Bells, order'd as the Venice-Looking-Glasses are, lest any one should have the curiosity to get up to the Roof, and laying himself upon his belly think to see what is done in the Bath. The place has no light but what it receives by the means of those holes, and while some body is in the Bath: But especially when they go out of it, the door is shut, the better to keep in the heat, and to prevent their being seen; which might be, if instead of those forementioned holes in the Roof, there were Windows below, according to our Mode. All the other Baths have their Structures after the same manner, and having no light but what comes at little glaz'd holes, there is not any passage into it, but that of the door, to the end that being presently shut, the heat might the better be kept within the Bath, and to prevent their being seen who

are in it. The Second Chamber is another Bath, but as to Beauty, it
is much inferiour to the other; And as for the third, there is something
in it which is singularly remarkable. The Floor of it is layd as with a
sort of small stones, so as that the foot cannot slip, though it be wetted
at their departure out of the Bath: And the whole Room is done all
about with square pieces, having in them flowers of emboss'd work,
done to the Life, and covered with Gold and Azure. This is the place
into which the Grand Seignor enters, when he comes out of the Bath;
and he alwaies goes into it alone, when he intends to shave himself in
those parts, which are not to be nam'd without immodesty.[1]

This interesting, if somewhat muddled account, was written about
1666 from information received during Tavernier's sixth voyage, and
describes the Seraglio baths in the time of Muhammad IV (1648–87).
A shorter, but much clearer, account was given in 1635 by Evliyá
Efendí when he was personally received into the private rooms of
Murad IV (1623–40):

> On the night that I read the Koran I had the good fortune to see the
> imperial bath, with which no other in the world can be compared.
> The four sides of it are assigned to the use of the pages, and in the centre
> there is an inclosed bath for the emperor. Water rushes in on all sides
> from fountains and basins, through pipes of gold and silver; and the
> basins which receive the water are inlaid with the same metals. Into
> some of these basins, hot and cold water run from the same pipe.
> The pavement is a beautiful mosaic of variegated stones which dazzle
> the eye. The walls are scented with roses, musk, and amber; and aloes
> is kept constantly burning in censors. The light is increased by the
> splendour and brilliancy of the windows. The walls are dry, the air
> temperate, and all the basins of fine white marble. The dressing-
> rooms are furnished with seats of gold and silver. The great cupola of
> the first dressing-room, all of bright marble, may be equalled by that
> of Cairo only. As this bath stands upon a rising ground it towers to
> the heavens: its windows all look towards the sea, to Scutari and
> Kazi-koi. On the right of the door of the dressing-room is the room
> for the musicians (motrib-khān) and on the left, the cupola of the inner
> treasury (Khazāneh Khās).[2]

And with those two descriptions of the baths of the Sultan and
his pages we shall have to be content. It seems to be fairly obvious
that individual taste of each Sultan would be sufficiently responsible

[1] *New Relation*, p. 41 *et seq.*   [2] *Narrative of Travels*, I, p. 181.

for any alterations such as the building of additional rooms or the dividing up of a large hall into several compartments. It was only in later years when the *selāmlik* began to encroach more and more on the *harēm* that the Royal bath was built side by side with that of the Sultana.

2. OTHER ROYAL BATHS IN THE CITY

At the commencement of the nineteenth century the Sultans began to tire of the Seraglio as the Royal residence, and their eyes turned more and more to the wider spaces on the Bosphorus. The most beautiful sites were selected for palaces, which varied in size and style of architecture according to the taste of the Sultan. Naturally every palace had large and costly baths, but as time went on the tendency was to abandon the three-room variety, and concentrate in rococo marble decoration in a single room based more upon European models, particularly as the introduction of large mirrors demanded a flat wall rather than a curved surface.

Thus the bathroom at Dolma Baghtche is composed entirely of veined Egyptian alabaster, with clusters of pillars, heavy cornices, and dadoes of the same material. The whole is surmounted by a dome of coloured glass through which the light lends added brilliance to the polished floor and silver fittings of the room. Similar rooms, though less elaborate, were built between 1853 and 1874 at other palaces, such as Beylerbey, Tcheragan, and Yildiz. The palace at Beylerbey was built by Abd ul-Aziz in 1865, but it replaced a former one erected by Mahmud II (1808–39) in which the old three-room bath could still be seen, and therefore can be regarded as the link between the two varieties. Luckily we have a good description of this bath which, coming from the facile pen of Miss Pardoe, is well worth reproducing:

Passing a crimson door, surmounted by a crescent-shaped cornice of rich gilding, the visitor enters a small hall, in which stands a basin of fine white marble, occupied by two swans, wrought in the same material, and appearing to sport in the limpid water; which, escaping from this charming fountain, falls through concealed pipes into the basins destined to supply the bathers. The cooling-room, opening from this dim apartment (where the light only penetrates after struggling through stars and crescents of painted glass, inlaid in the marble roof

like clusters of jewels), is hung with draperies of silk, richly embroidered; and the large mirror which occupies the wall at the lower
end of the divan, is set in a frame-work of gold and enamel, surmounted
by the Ottoman arms, skilfully executed; while the divan itself,
formed of gay-coloured satin, is wrought in silks until it resembles a
flower-bed; and the cushions which are scattered over it are of the
same beautiful and costly description. The bath is a vast hall, of the
most elegant proportions, lined, and roofed, and paved with marble.
It is lighted like the cooling-room, and surmounted by exquisitely-
imagined fountains; and gives back a long and subdued echo at every
footfall which disturbs its deep and dreamy silence.[1]

3. The Public Baths

So far we have examined only the private baths for the use of the
Sultan, his household, and other members of the Palace service.
But unless we get a good idea of the public bath we shall miss many
things that would lead to a better understanding of the manner in
which the great majority of the Palace *personnel* spent such a large
and, to them, important part of their lives. As the present work is
chiefly concerned with the *ḥarēm*, more attention will be paid to the
women's baths, for detailed descriptions of which we are almost
entirely dependent on the nineteenth-century accounts of lady travellers. But this is not so bad as it sounds, because, firstly, ladies who
followed Lady Mary Wortley Montagu, such as Miss Pardoe and Mrs
Harvey, were shrewd observers and descriptive writers, and, secondly,
the public baths have changed little, if at all, during the centuries.
Their traditions have remained unaltered, and the description (given
at p. 215) of a bath that Bassano da Zara had about 1520 can equally
well apply to my own experiences in 1934. And as regards the female
baths, what differences can time effect in the behaviour of a hundred
naked women out to enjoy every moment of their temporary freedom with idle chatter or scandalous gossip!

But before we come to individual descriptions it would be as well
to realize that, like so many other things in Turkey, the baths are in
no sense 'Turkish,' but merely Byzantine baths adapted or rebuilt—
while they in their turn were taken from the still earlier Greek and
Roman originals. The whole subject is immensely interesting, because

[1] *Beauties of the Bosphorus*, p. 14.

THE BATHS OF ESKI KAPLIJA, AT CHEKIRGE, NEAR BRUSA

THE FEMALE PUBLIC BATHS

THE WOMEN'S BATH

the history of 'Turkish' baths is the history of the blending of East and West, and, as Urquhart rightly said, "Rome was indebted to her strigil as well as to her sword for the conquest of the world." In an institution that formed part of the daily life of millions we can see reflected not only the development of art and architecture, and the manners, customs, fads and fancies, of the ordinary citizen, but the rise and fall of nations, the growth and decay of empires.[1]

Take, for instance, the most famous of all the ancient baths in Constantinople—those of Zeuxippus, situated near the site of the public gardens between Sancta Sophia and the mosque of Ahmed, near the Hippodrome. The very name is romantic. It was here that Hercules yoked the steeds of Diomed, and in the neighbouring grove he raised an altar to Jupiter. There are many other versions given to account for the name of the baths, but the etymological one is as good as the others and much more poetical! At all events this was the spot chosen by Septimius Severus to build the most magnificent baths ever erected outside Rome. They were intended as a peaceful gesture in expiation for his reckless destruction of Byzantium in A.D. 196. The proportions were vast, and the famous collection of bronze statues there was without rival. Old Gyllius gives us a list of most of them, and tells us more of their subsequent history. After falling into decay and neglect the baths were rebuilt by Constantine, and restored again later by Justinian after the Nika revolt of 532 to even greater magnificence. When Muhammad II entered the city they were in ruins, but so rich was the material, abounding in every known variety of marble, granite, and porphyry columns, severed capitals, and general *débris*, that he used it all for the building of his mosque on the summit of the Fourth Hill.

But if Hercules was connected with the Zeuxippus he had a great and highly pertinent rival at the once celebrated bath described by Agathius in no less a person than Venus herself, who was not the

[1] A full and complete history of the 'Turkish' bath yet remains to be written. There is a modern work in French (Paul Négrier, *Les Bains à travers les ages*, Paris, 1925), but its scope is rather too wide. We must still refer to the excellent articles in Daremberg *et* Saglio, *Dictionnaire des antiquités*, and Smith's *Dictionary of Greek and Roman Art*, under *Balneum*, and to Pauly's *Real-Encyclopädie* under *Bäder*. Much useful information is to be found in Becker's *Gallus* and *Clarikles*. See also D. Urquhart, *Pillars of Hercules*, vol. ii, pp. 18–88; Erasmus Wilson, *The Eastern or Turkish Bath* (London, 1861); and the works on Pompeii by Gell and Mau.

tutelary goddess, but just one of its customers! Gyllius also tells us of another bath, called Didymum, in which both sexes bathed together, as they did in the luxurious days of Imperial Rome.

Other Byzantine baths, hardly less famous in their day than Zeuxippus and all teeming with historical associations, included those of Anastasia, Achilles, Arcadius, Blachermæ, Carosia, and Constantine. Of all these only the last survived destruction, and after its renovation by Muhammad II was known as the *Chukur Hamami*, or Sunken Bath, either owing to its position in a depression on the Fourth Hill, near the famous church of the Holy Apostles, or else because it was said to be built on the site of the cisterns of Arcadius. The subsequent history of this bath was curious. As time went on it was gradually built over, and was entirely lost sight of until its rediscovery by M. Texier in 1833. He inspected it carefully, and gave a full account in his *Byzantine Architecture*.[1] But its reappearance was brief, and in 1889 it was built over again,[2] and will probably now continue its rest undisturbed for ever. At the same time this is to be regretted, from both an architectural and an archæological point of view, because not only is it the oldest bath in the city, but it was built almost exactly in accordance with the plans as laid down for a Roman bath by Vitruvius.

Byzantine Constantinople conquered the invading Turks with its baths just as it did with so many of its other institutions and customs. Several of the old foundations were used again, and much of the ruined material was employed in the new structures. In the seventeenth century Evliyá Efendí[3] tells us there were some 300 baths, and 4536 counting the private ones. The number of public ones decreased, and by the end of the nineteenth century there were only about 130. To-day the number is rather less. In view of the fact that nearly every traveller has given a description of his experiences in a 'Turkish' bath,[4] it will be sufficient here to translate extracts

---

[1] London, 1864, pp. 159–164. See also vol. iii of the manuscript collection of his drawings at the Royal Institute of British Architects, 66, Portland Place, London, W. 1.

[2] Apparently the last man to see it was E. A. Grosvenor, who says in his excellent work *Constantinople* (vol. i, p. 360): "In August 1889, I visited the only room that could still be entered. With a rope for ladder, I descended to a vaulted room, twelve paces long, from which every trace of ornament had disappeared. This chamber . . . was itself sealed up the following week." [3] *Narrative of Travels*, I, p. 181.

[4] Among numerous descriptions of the baths may be mentioned Nicolay, *Quatre premiers*

from one of the earliest accounts in existence (that of Bassano da Zara) and discuss briefly any points of interest that may arise from it. In order, however, to bring the subject up to date I shall quote my own experiences when discussing the hot baths at Brusa (pp. 229–232).

During the time that Bassano was in the employ of the Seraglio he took many trips in all parts of Turkey and visited many baths, and so was able to make comparisons and get a good idea of all the shapes and sizes. He chooses for his detailed description one of the large ones, apparently in Constantinople, and says:

> The design of these baths seems to me, especially as far as the domes are concerned, to be copied from the Thermæ of Diocletian in Rome, although very much smaller. At the entrance is a room shaped like a church, but round and domed with lead, large and commodious, almost like the Rotunda at Rome. . . . In the middle of this there is usually a beautiful basin of fine marble, with a fountain of four jets, around which are seats made of brick three cubits long and so high from the ground that a man sitting there could not touch the floor with his feet. All the vaulting of this first room is of marble slabs. The above-mentioned seats are all partitioned by a small wall a cubit in height, or by a wooden shutter of a considerable size so that they are divided up and allow one to lean on one's elbow. Each of the seats is about four cubits wide, and those who wish to bathe can undress there. The seat is covered first with a mat, on which is placed a rug or tapestry. On wishing to enter and take a bath one must first speak to the custodians of the bath, who are stationed around the walls of this room, and then to the cashier, who sits in a corner on a stool just as our lawyers do. When this is done you may undress on one of those seats . . . you must be careful not to show any immodest parts, for shameless ones are beaten and thrown out of the baths. When undressed you make your clothes into a bundle and place it on the seat with your hat, cap, or turban which you wear, on top. Your clothes will not be safe unless you have a servant to guard them, because the custodians of the baths themselves will steal your purse and other belongings.[1] Before you take your shirt off they will give you a

Livres, p. 59 _verso_ and p. 60 and _verso_ of the English edition, pp. 72–74 of the French; Grelot, _Relation nouvelle_, pp. 187–192 of the English edition; Thévenot, _Travels into the Levant_, pp. 31–32; Tournefort, _Voyage into the Levant_, vol. ii, pp. 314–316; White, _Three Years in Constantinople_, vol. iii, pp. 296–313; A. Slade, _Records of Travels in Turkey, Greece, etc._ (1854), pp. 398–401; C. Oscanyan, _The Sultan and his People_ (London, 1857), pp. 320–339; E. de Amicis, _Constantinople_ (London, 1896), pp. 160–163.

[1] _Cf._ Thévenot, _Travels into the Levant_, p. 31: "Having pull'd off your shirt, you put it with your cloaths in the napkin you sate upon, leaving them there without fear that

long ample towel to cover yourself—that is to say, if you haven't got one of your own—and others to dry yourself with. . . . Having then covered your privities with the towel, all the rest of you being bare, you enter the first room of the bath, where there are always about fifteen servants varying with the size of the bath, some shaving, some kneading the bones, some washing, so that all are busy at their task set them by their master. From this you pass through several rooms all of different kinds, each hotter than the last, adorned with fine marble and porphyry all round, like the vaulting; and in each are two water-pipes, one hot and the other cold, which flow into marble basins, and the water which overflows on to the ground escapes through holes in the floor. From here you enter the main part of the bath, which is usually spacious and covered with marble so smooth that it is hard to stand upright. This place, like the other rooms, is domed and has several glass windows tightly shut, the whole being covered above with lead. The dome in the middle is very high. In winter the baths are heated at midnight (in summer every one washes in cold water), thereby consuming vast quantities of wood. They use pine-trees four or five cubits long, thicker than a man's thigh, and also a small amount of oak. In the centre of this room, which we have called the heart of the baths, there is a square stone of marble, porphyry, and very fine serpentine, a palm thick, longer than the height of a man, and two palms from the ground. It is set on four beautiful marble balls. As soon as anybody arrives they are invited to stretch themselves on this stone body downward, and one of the servants mounts with his feet on your back and pulls out your arms in a certain manner peculiar to them. But it never pleased me, and I would never lie down there, although they often begged me to do so.

Then, when they think they have massaged and pulled you about enough on one side, they make you turn over with your body upward and then start pulling your arms again until you might well imagine it was an exhibition of the strength of Hercules. When you get off this stone you go into another room (whichever you wish) if it is un-occupied, either colder or warmer according to your taste. For they are not all of the same temperature (as has been said) and there are some so hot that they make you sweat, and others moderated to suit your wishes, for in the heart of the baths there are many little rooms like cells all round, but well made and ornamented, and in each is a marble basin into which two pipes lead from the wall, one furnishing hot and the other cold water. You let as much water as you want run

anybody will touch them, for the Bagnios are places of liberty and security, as though they were sacred, and there is no cheat ever committed in them, for if any were the Master of the Bagnio would be obliged to make good what was lost or embeziled."

into the basin, and after getting it to the required temperature you stop up the pipes. And this method obtains throughout the baths. After this you lie on the ground close to the basin and one of the servants throws water over you from a bowl, while another washes you, covering the opening of the little room with a towel. If the servants are busy one does both the washing and throwing, while in the case of a poor man he has to do both for himself because the servants hasten to serve the rich as they are eager for tips [literally 'drink-money']. To rub you down they use a kind of bag made of a thick dark cloth; no soap is supplied if you don't bring your own. If you want your head, beard, or other hairs shaved a man who specializes in that business will attend to you. So also if you want to get rid of your hair in any part without shaving they give you a paste, in a different room from the others. The Turks use this paste a great deal, for they consider it a sin to have hairs on their private parts, and you never find any of them, either man or woman, who have any. And in this matter the women are more superstitious than the men, and as soon as they feel the hairs coming they hurry off to the baths. When you have finished washing you change the towel you have been wearing, which they call *futà*, in the bath, and on coming out a servant approaches from behind with a basin to wash your feet again. You then return to the first room where you left your clothes, which is very slushy from the constant flow of water. Here there is always a good coal fire, especially in winter, to dry several shirts at once as well as towels for the bathers. When you have sat down the servant washes your feet, and as an act of courtesy you are expected to show your appreciation by placing your right hand on his head and then putting it to your mouth, as is the custom with us in presenting letters. When you are dressed it is up to you to recompense the servant as you leave, so you go up to the grill where the cashier of the baths has his place and give him what you think fit. There is no fixed charge, some give him one Aspro, some two, others three, but most people give four.[1]

The above account is fairly comprehensive, and calls for little comment. We might, however, enlarge on two points—the lack of any mention of pattens for the feet and the custom of shaving the body.

It would appear quite certain that in Bassano's day wooden pattens were not used in the baths. They are not mentioned either by Grelot or by Thévenot. It seems quite possible that they were introduced to Constantinople from Venice, where they had been in use

[1] *I Costumi et i modi particolari de la vita de Turchi*, pp. 2–4.

for centuries. Bassano's omission could not have been merely an
oversight, because in the first place he says how difficult it was to
stand upright, and secondly he mentions the slushy state of the floor
and how the servant had to wash the feet again on the bather's
return to his dressing-room. Pattens have several uses. In baths
heated from below they are most useful in preserving tender feet
from the heated marble. They also stop slipping on the wet floor.
When I attempted to walk round the marble basin in one of the
Brusa baths on bare feet I discovered it was both difficult and risky,
but once pattens were worn progress was unhindered. Lastly, they
keep you well above all flowing water and far less pure liquids that
from time to time pollute the floor. This fact was very clearly brought
home to me in the Turkish lavatory of my 'hotel' at Brusa, when
suddenly without any warning the dirty water from other parts of
the house flowed under my feet, which luckily were shod in high
wooden pattens!

By the seventeenth century shops of patten-makers were common.
The pattens (*nalin*) were of plain walnut or box, with a leather strap
nailed to the hollow each side. More costly ones were of rosewood,
ebony, sandalwood, or other rarer woods, studded with silver nails,
with a strap of coloured leather embroidered with gold. In the Royal
ḥarēm the pattens of the *kadins* were even more luxurious, being inlaid
with mother-of-pearl and tortoiseshell, with straps studded with
pearls and turquoises. There is something coquettish in the use of
high pattens, and in the seventeenth century the Venetian chopines
were sometimes half a yard high.[1] They were in common use in
Naples in the sixteenth and seventeenth centuries, and appear constantly in the literature of the period.[2] In England patten-makers are
mentioned as early as 1400, and became a separate fraternity in 1469.
Until well into the eighteenth century the uncleaned and unpaved
roads made pattens for ladies a real necessity, and their adoption in
Constantinople seems to have come from the West, the ordinary
clog-like shoes of the Arabs and Persians not being sufficiently high
to suggest a new use in the baths.

[1] See Thomas Coryat, *Crudities* (London, 1611), vol. i; p. 400 of the 1905 edition.
[2] See, for example, Basile's *Pentamerone* (1634) in the Penzer-Croce edition (London,
1932), vol. i, p. 60 *n.* 2.

With regard to the removal of hair from the body, we find a much more detailed and interesting account of the depilatory given by Thévenot in 1656:

> . . . having shaved your chin, and under the arm-pits, he gives you a razor to shave yourself everywhere else; and you go into one of the little chambers that are made in the intervals betwixt the sides, and being there, you take off your napkin and hang it upon the door, that so every one that sees it may know there is somebody within, which will hinder them from coming in, and there you may shave yourself at your leisure: If you be afraid that you may hurt yourself with a Razor, they give you a bit of Paste, made of a certain mineral, called *Rusma*, beat into a powder, and with lime and water made up into a Paste, which they apply to the parts where they would have the hair fetcht off, and in less than half a quarter of an hour, all the hair falls off with the Paste, by throwing hot water upon it: They know when it is time to throw on water by trying if the hair comes off with the Paste; for if it be left too long sticking on the place, after it had eaten off the hair, it would corrode the flesh. *Rusma* is a mineral like to the rust or dross of iron; it is much in use in *Turky*, and sold in so great quantities, that the Custom of it yields the Grand Signior a considerable Revenue. In Malta they use instead of *Rusma*, *Orpiment*, which they mingle with lime for the same use.[1]

This *rusma* is apparently the same as the Syrian *dowa*[2] and Egyptian *nūrah* mentioned by E. W. Lane in his excellent chapter on the Cairene bath[3] and by Burton.[4] It is obvious that *rusma* contained arsenic, as several accounts mention the danger of its " corroding the flesh " unless watched very carefully. In Europe to-day the use of depilatories containing sulphide of arsenic has been almost entirely abandoned as being dangerous, and in their place sulphides of calcium, strontium, and barium are substituted. The advantage of a depilatory over a razor is that the paste removes the hair at the neck of the follicle, while shaving only levels it with the surface of the epidermis and it soon grows again—if anything, rather stronger than before.

The use of tweezers to pluck out the hairs, although both painful

---

[1] *Travels into the Levant*, pp. 31–32. See also de La Motraye, *Travels through Europe*, vol. i, pp. 95–96, and Flachat, *Observations sur le commerce*, vol. i, pp. 443–444.
[2] See Alexander Russell, *Natural History of Aleppo* (second edition, London, 1794), pp. 134, 378–379.
[3] *Modern Egyptians* (London, 1860), pp. 336–343.
[4] *Nights*, original edition, vol. iv, p. 256 n. 1. See also vol. ii, p. 160 n. 3.

and laborious, appears to have been largely favoured by women, especially in Persia. "The Ladies," says Tavernier,

> not regarding the prohibition of Mahomet, employ their Female Slaves for the performance of that Office; and with a small kind of Pincers and twitchers, such as those wherewith we take off the hair of the mustachoes, they do with a little more trouble, but less hazard, what that earth [*rusma*] does in less time, but with more danger. Our *Sultanesses* are yet too delicate to imitate the Ladies of Persia; nay the men themselves, in *Turkey*, are not very forward to have that twitch'd off with pain, which the Razour can take off without any trouble.[1]

The removal of the pubic hair was even more indispensable to the Muslim woman than is that of the axillary hair to the 'smart' woman of to-day. But it was not only these regions that had to be freed of any superfluous growth, but every portion of the body, particularly the orifices, including the nostrils and ears. Consequently this practice resulted in the most detailed inspection, duly carried out by the slave, or possibly by a female friend, who in her turn would submit to a similar scrutiny of her body. Such great intimacy between women has very naturally given rise to charges of Lesbianism, which in many cases seem to have been fully warranted.

Writers are constantly telling us that no husband who wishes his wife to remain pure and chaste would dream of allowing her to attend a public bath, but unless his means allowed him to install a private one at home he would find it well-nigh impossible to forbid her the former—on both religious and sanitary grounds. It will be interesting to see what Bassano da Zara has to say on the subject in his description of the women's baths early in the sixteenth century:

> Although men own the baths they do not do the washing themselves, for being most particular on this point they employ women who wash those who come without a slave or servant. But most of the women go in parties of twenty at a time and wash each other in a friendly manner—one neighbour with another, and sister with sister. But it is common knowledge that as a result of this familiarity in washing and massaging women fall very much in love with each other. And one often sees a woman in love with another one just like a man and woman. And I have known Greek and Turkish women, on seeing a lovely young girl, seek occasion to wash with her just to see her naked

[1] *New Relation*, p. 44.

and handle her. And many women go to baths outside their own neighbourhood to do this, although the custom is to go to the baths in one's own district. This and many other dishonest things originate from women's washing. They often stay together at the baths (if they go early in the morning) until the dinner hour, and if they go after they stay nearly until evening. I will not omit to mention that well-bred women do not go to the public baths, but have very fine ones of their own at home in their *serragli*. . . . I will now tell you in what manner the middle-class woman goes to the bath, and how often a week. This type of woman, then, visits the baths, many of them four times, many three times, but every one goes at least once, otherwise she would be known as devoid of delicacy and dirty. But there are two reasons why none would miss going. In the first place they cannot pray in church unless they have washed, and secondly because as they are otherwise not allowed to go out it serves as an excuse for leaving the house. With this excuse they can do so, saying they are going to visit the baths, when in reality they go elsewhere. . . . It is the custom with Turkish women to have two or three Christian slaves, or slaves who once were Christians but have renounced their faith. On the head of one of these slaves is placed a copper pot, not very big but high and broad like a chamber-pot.[1] Inside it they put a chemise of cotton which reaches to the ground; they are worth four or six *scudi* each according to the fineness of the weave, and even men use them, putting them on as soon as they have washed, instead of a shirt, to draw off all moisture from the flesh and leave the body dry so that they can put their shirt on top immediately and get dressed.

They also have a white chemise, clean hose, and as many towels as they want. Then they cover the bowl with a linen cloth embroidered with silk and golden foliage; and they take a handsome fine-woven carpet and a beautiful cushion. On arriving at the baths they first spread out the carpet over that provided by the baths, and remove their silk cloaks. The pot is placed on the ground in one of the little rooms, with the base uppermost, so that the mistress can sit on it. And when she has sat on it the slaves start to wash her, standing one on either side. When she thinks they have washed her enough she retires to rest in one of the moderately warm rooms, while the slaves wash each other. When they have stayed as long as they wish, they put the chemises and other garments back into the basin and go home, paying the same amount as the men. There are some women who take with them a rich repast, and eat it at the baths with the appetite that the baths naturally give.[2]

---

[1] See plate to chapter xxii of Nicolay's *Quatre premiers Livres*.
[2] *I Costumi et i modi particolari de la vita de Turchi*, pp. 5–6.

Bassano must have got his information from reliable sources, for eighteenth- and nineteenth-century accounts of lady eyewitnesses can add little, unless it be to visualize the scene more clearly for us by the aid of a facile pen and highly developed power of vivid description. In 1717 Lady Mary Wortley Montagu writes as follows:

> The first sofas were covered with cushions and rich carpets, on which sat the ladies; and on the second, their slaves behind them, but without any distinction of rank by their dress, all being in the state of nature, that is, in plain English, stark naked, without any beauty or defect concealed. Yet there was not the least wanton smile or immodest gesture amongst them. They walked and moved with the same majestic grace which Milton describes of our general mother. There were many amongst them as exactly proportioned as ever any goddess was drawn by the pencil of Guido or Titian—and most of their skins shiningly white, only adorned by their beautiful hair divided into many tresses, hanging on their shoulders, braided either with pearl or ribbon, perfectly representing the figures of the Graces.
>
> I was here convinced of the truth of a reflection I had often made, that if it was the fashion to go naked, the face would be hardly observed. I perceived that the ladies with the finest skins and most delicate shapes had the greatest share of my admiration, though their faces were sometimes less beautiful than those of their companions. To tell you the truth, I had wickedness enough to wish secretly that Mr. Jervis [Charles Jervis, the Irish portrait painter and writer] could have been there invisible. I fancy it would have very much improved his art, to see so many fine women naked, in different postures, some in conversation, some working, others drinking coffee or sherbet, and many negligently lying on their cushions, while their slaves (generally pretty girls of seventeen or eighteen) were employed in braiding their hair in several pretty fancies. In short, it is the women's coffee-house, where all the news of the town is told, scandal invented, etc.

Some hundred and twenty years later Miss Pardoe gives us a similar description, from which the following lively scene is taken:

> For the first few moments I was bewildered; the heavy, dense, sulphureous vapour that filled the place, and almost suffocated me— the wild shrill cries of the slaves pealing through the reverberating domes of the bathing-halls, enough to awaken the very marble with which they were lined—the subdued laughter and whispered conversations of their mistresses, murmuring along in an undercurrent of sound —the sight of nearly three hundred women, only partially dressed, and

that in fine linen so perfectly saturated with vapour that it revealed the whole outline of the figure—the busy slaves passing and repassing, naked from the waist upwards, and with their arms folded upon their bosoms, balancing on their heads piles of fringed or embroidered napkins—groups of lovely girls, laughing, chatting, and refreshing themselves with sweetmeats, sherbet, and lemonade—parties of playful children, apparently quite indifferent to the dense atmosphere which made me struggle for breath—and, to crown all, the sudden bursting forth of a chorus of voices into one of the wildest and shrillest of Turkish melodies, that was caught up and flung back by the echoes of the vast hall, making a din worthy of a saturnalia of demons, all combined to form a picture like the illusory semblance of a phantasmagoria, almost leaving me in doubt whether that on which I looked were indeed reality, or the mere creation of a distempered brain. . . . When at length they venture into the outer hall, they at once spring upon their sofas, where the attentive slaves fold them in warm cloths, and pour essence upon their hair, which they twist loosely without attempting to dislodge the wet, and then cover with handsome headkerchiefs of embroidered muslin; perfumed water is scattered over the face and hands, and the exhausted bather sinks into a luxurious slumber beneath a coverlet of satin or of eider-down. The centre of the floor, meanwhile, is like a fair; sweetmeat, sherbet, and fruit-merchants (old crones, who frequently have as many *billet-doux* as bowls of *yahourt*—coagulated buttermilk—in their baskets), parade up and down, hawking their wares. Negresses pass to and fro with the dinners, or *chibouques* (pipes) of their several mistresses; secrets are whispered—confidences are made; and, altogether, the scene is so strange, so new, and withal so attractive, that no European can fail to be both interested and amused by a visit to a Turkish Hammām.[1]

Another account is to be found in Mrs Harvey's *Turkish Harems and Circassian Homes*,[2] but sufficient has now been said to enable us to form a very good opinion of what a crowded woman's bath was like.

There remains, however, to speak of the Bride's Bath, a ceremony in which a procession of naked virgins plays an important part, and one which a virgin destined for the Sultan's bed would go through in a form probably differing little from that witnessed personally by Lady Mary Wortley Montagu:

Those that were or had been married placed themselves round the room on the marble sofas; but the virgins very hastily threw off their

---

[1] *Beauties of the Bosphorus*, pp. 15–16.   [2] London, 1871, pp. 71–81.

clothes, and appeared without other ornament or covering than their own long hair braided with pearl or ribbon. Two of them met the bride at the door, conducted by her mother and another grave relation. She was a beautiful maid of about seventeen, very richly dressed, and shining with jewels, but was presently reduced by them to the state of nature. Two others filled silver gilt pots with perfume, and began the procession, the rest following in pairs to the number of thirty. The leaders sung an epithalamium, answered by the others in chorus, and the two last led the fair bride, her eyes fixed on the ground, with a charming affectation of modesty. In this order they marched round the three large rooms of the bagnio. 'Tis not easy to represent to you the beauty of this sight, most of them being well proportioned and white skinned; all of them perfectly smooth and polished by the frequent use of bathing. After having made their tour, the bride was again led to every matron round the rooms, who saluted her with a compliment and a present, some of jewels, others pieces of stuff, handkerchiefs, or little gallantries of that nature, which she thanked them for by kissing their hands.

The more intimate details of this charming ceremony, such as the depilatory, are omitted, but can be supplied from a manuscript diary of one John Richards, and now in the British Museum:

> Upon Solemne Occasions, when a Virgin does prepare herselfe for her husbands bead, they make a feast in the Baths to which they Invite their ffriends, att w.h time she takes of the Haire of her body w.h she never does before, and is allways practised afterwards in these Hot Countrys, w.th how much modesty this is done I cannot tell, but I am told that it is very Expensive.[1]

From the above accounts of Lady Mary Wortley Montagu it would appear that it was the custom for the women to bathe in a state of complete nudity, or nearly so. And if we are to believe artists who have attempted to represent the "Harem Bath" there is no doubt whatever about the matter. But whether this was indeed a fact is a question that is, of course, quite impossible to answer. At the same time it would be interesting if we did know, because if no clothing at all was worn it would be entirely contrary to the usual custom among Turks, not merely when in public baths, but when several bathe together in a bath whether it be public or private. This applies equally to men and women. In view of this it is interesting to

[1] Stowe MSS., 462, f. 42b.

read a curious tale about Mahmud I (1730–54), who apparently was in the habit of amusing himself with members of the *harēm* in various ways. According to Flachat[1] one of his little jokes was as follows: having stationed himself secretly in a window overlooking the baths, he would await the arrival of the girls, who would all be given a chemise *according to custom*, imagining that they were the same as usual. But the wily King had had all the stitches removed and the material tightly glued together. The doors were then locked, and the King watched developments as the heat and moisture did their work. Some of the girls laughed with surprise as the dress fell away in pieces, but others were very angry. This tale might well be true, as Flachat undoubtedly had it from his friend the Chief Black Eunuch, to whom the Sultan would be certain to relate such an amusing experience. Although the *harēm* consisted of so many nationalities it must be remembered that their training was strict, and all Turkish customs were closely observed. Quite apart from this, an assumed modesty, occasioned by the ever-present factor of competition, might well produce a reluctancy to disrobe completely before those who were, after all, nothing but rivals for the Sultan's preference.

But we should hesitate to accept as fact what may be merely the product of the artistic imagination.

On the other hand there is a manuscript of the *Zanān-nāmeh*,[2] by Fāzil (Yildîz 2824–73), in the library of the university of Istanbul, which contains a plate showing the interior of a Turkish women's bath. This illustration is reproduced opposite p. 224 of the present work. It will be seen that the women are almost entirely nude, and no attempt whatever is being made to conceal the privities. The attendants wear a cloth round the waist, leaving the breast bare. Attention should be drawn to the exaggerated pattens worn by a visitor in full costume.

4. THE HOT BATHS OF BRUSA

We have now examined such baths as still exist in the Seraglio, and given a brief description of Royal baths in other palaces. We

---

[1] *Observations sur le commerce*, vol. ii, pp. 28–29.
[2] For a French translation of the *Zanān-nāmeh*, or *History of Women*, see that by J.-A. Decourdemanche (Paris, 1879), especially the section headed *Les Baigneuses*, pp. 127–133.

have also considered the history of the public baths at different periods.

There still remain, however, the natural hot baths at Brusa to be discussed, not merely because of their general interest from several points of view, but because Brusa played a distinct part in the history of the Seraglio as the city to which Sultans retired to 'take the cure' when tired out with the excesses of fighting or debauchery, or visited with acute attacks of rheumatism and kindred ailments.

Brusa, too, was the city in which the Turks first learned to appreciate the bath. When their capital was changed to Adrianople they were already fully initiated, and as cleanliness is so strongly enjoined in the *Korān* the 'Turkish' bath had come to stay. But at Brusa the way was made easy: it was not necessary to rediscover the hypocaust of the Romans; nature had already supplied the boiling water, and it merely remained to divert it to the desired baths and basins, cool it to different temperatures, and cover the area with some kind of building.

Although Brusa has suffered terribly at the hands of invaders, and to-day is but a ghost of its former mighty self, the baths still remain in perfect working order, and one still can swim in the marble bath of Rustem Pasha and enjoy the beauty of the Byzantine and Turkish arches and magnificent coloured faïence.

For some reason or other few people go to Brusa nowadays (perhaps it is because the Hôtel d'Anatolie is no more!), and as recently as 1934 the Mayor triumphantly produced from his private drawer a book containing about sixty calling cards to prove to me that people *did* still come to the city! Whatever misfortune may have fallen to its lot during the long centuries of its history, its charm and beauty still remain, and, primitive as the life and the accommodation are to-day, nobody should go to Constantinople without including a visit to Brusa. Even if the baths have no interest for them, the glories of the Green Mosque and the tombs of the early Sultans more than repay any trouble or expense to which the traveller is put.

Let us therefore first glance briefly at its past history, and then I shall add a detailed account not only of the baths themselves, but of the actual experiences and sensations that these "Royal Waters" afford to-day.

Brusa (also spelled Broussa, but known to the Turks as Bursa) was founded by Prusias, King of Bithynia, when Hannibal was seeking refuge with him after the defeat of Antiochus at Magnesia in 190 B.C. The city was named Prusa after its founder, and for many years was the seat of the Bithynian Kings. After the defeat of Mithridates it fell into the power of the Romans, and was but a second-rate town under the capital of Bithynia, Nicomedia. However, it continued to flourish under Roman rule, and its baths began to attract attention. About A.D. 111 Pliny the Younger was appointed Governor of Bithynia, and did much to beautify Prusa by the erection of public edifices. Among these were the public baths, and Pliny devotes a letter to Trajan on the subject,[1] and says what an ornament to the city the proposed baths will be. Although Nicomedia still remained the most important town, the fame of the hot springs spread, and a temple of Æsculapius and Hygieia was erected near the principal spring whither in the third century patricians came for treatment.

In the reign of Constantine the baths began to acquire a great reputation, and several Byzantine Emperors went to Prusa for the cure at the "Royal Waters." Justinian erected the first baths on a really large scale, and built a palace and khans for visitors. The area of the hot springs was known as Pythia, but later, under Constantine Porphyrogenitus, was changed to Soteropolis (town of the Saviour) in gratitude to the healing powers of the waters. Among important people who benefited by the baths was the Empress Theodora, wife of Justinian. In 525 she journeyed to Brusa with a *cortège* of 4000 attendants in golden litters, and is said to have taken a fortnight on the journey, being persuaded of the baths' curative powers by the good they had already done Justinian.

Brusa continued to flourish under Roman and Byzantine rule, until in the middle of the tenth century, after a year's siege, it was captured by Saif al-Dawla of Aleppo. It was, however, soon retaken by the Greeks, who restored the town and strengthened the walls. By this time the eyes of the Seljuk Turks were turned in its direction, and the town fell into their hands at the close of the eleventh century. They evacuated it after the capture of Nicæa by the Crusaders in 1204, and did not recapture it until 1326, after a

[1] Book x, ep. lxx.

ten years' siege under Orkhan. From that moment Brusa increased in strength and importance. The Osmanli Sultans had found a new capital, and after their life of wandering and fighting settled down to make the city a worthy centre of a new empire. Artists, poets, architects, historians, and soldiers flocked to the new capital from all parts of the Middle East. The Turks learned the value of the bath, and the unwashed days stretching back to Ghengis Khan were over. Bit by bit the traditions and culture of the Greeks were to be absorbed by their conquerors, until finally, when Constantinople became the capital in 1453, with the adoption of everything Byzantine—the secluded Palace, the veil, the ḥarēm, eunuchs, ceremonial clothes, the weekly visit to the mosque, leaden roofs, red ink for State documents, and a hundred other things—the transformation was complete.

But much was to happen before then, and Brusa was not destined to enjoy peace for long. Murad I had changed the capital to Adrianople in 1361 merely as a means of extending his father's European conquests. The hearts of the Osmanlis were still in Brusa, where all their first mosques and schools had been built, and where the remains of all their early Sultans lay. But the blood-soaked Tamerlane was on the way, and after the defeat of Bayezid in 1396 Brusa was sacked and reduced to ruins early in the fifteenth century. Only ten years were to pass before it was sacked again by the Prince of Karaman. Fires and earthquakes played further havoc in modern times, destroying many of the restorations made by Selim I and Suleiman. But in spite of all these vicissitudes the famous baths of Brusa remain, and once we are inside their time-honoured walls past and present have no meaning, and the centuries roll back to be halted at our will, whether it be in the days of Suleiman the Magnificent, Orkhan the Conqueror, or Justinian the Lawgiver.

The baths of Brusa lie about a mile and a half out of the town in the direction of Mudania in or near the little village of Chekirge ('locust'), which, as we have already noticed, was once called Pythia. The whole district is impregnated with sulphur and iron from some half-dozen springs originating in sources on the lower slopes of Mount Olympus.

There are two main iron springs which supply Eski Kaplija and

Kara Mustafa, and two sulphur springs feeding Yeni Kaplija and Beuyük Kükürtlu. On leaving Brusa in a north-easterly direction you follow the Mudania road for nearly a mile, when you see in front of you a most picturesque group of curiously domed buildings, "the biggest of which is magnificent, and has four great Domes cover'd with lead, bor'd like a Skimmer; and all the Holes of these Domes are clos'd with Glass-Bells like those the Gardiners use to cover Melons withal."[1]

This is the Yeni Kaplija, built, or restored, by Rustem Pasha, Grand Vizir and son-in-law of Suleiman, as a thank-offering for the Sultan's cure of the gout. The temperature is very considerable, as the spring rises at 195 degrees. Immediately to the right is the small Kainarja bath for women, while the Kara Mustafa lies only a few paces to the left. On the southern side of the road are the Beuyük and Küçük Kükürtlu sulphur baths, the spring of which rises at 178 degrees. This completes the group, and now we must branch off on the forked road to Chekirge, where the Eski Kaplija stands alone. The mosque and *türbeh* of Murad I are close by, and remind us of the importance of the baths in the early Ottoman period, but according to tradition it was these very baths to which Justinian and Theodora came in the sixth century. The water comes down at a temperature of 117 degrees Fahrenheit, and consequently does not need such a dilution of cold water as is required at the Yeni Kaplija. In general architectural details the baths differ but little. In all cases the first room is by far the largest, the second room the smallest, and the third, and hottest, room of medium size. The Eski Kaplija is interesting on account of its fine Byzantine capitals, from which the arches spring with an impost. The Yeni Kaplija is famous chiefly for its beautiful coloured faïence and typical Turkish arches. I have spent many happy hours in both the baths, and the following account of my experiences therein can apply to both equally well.

On entering the first room I am at once conscious of a curious change of atmosphere, due not merely to the difference of temperature, which is not so noticeable on a warm day, but to other factors which at first are hard to determine. But on starting to look round I begin to realize what they are. Space is undoubtedly the first

---

[1] Tournefort, *Voyage into the Levant*, vol. iii, p. 310.

factor—vast empty space, occasioned by the two large cupolas and high walls. Then there is the silence, and perhaps it is this that has subconsciously impressed me most. Then the weird array of towel-clad figures, looking like so many mummies awaiting burial, doubtless adds to the strange atmosphere of the place. The only sounds to break the silence are the splash of the water in the marble fountain in the centre and the occasional shuffling of some bather on his wooden pattens as he makes his way to the warmer room, to which I myself am shortly to be introduced. A further inspection of the hall shows it to be surrounded with low couches and cubicles, for the use of the poorer and richer customers respectively. At the far end of the hall are huge wooden towel-drying frames, and if custom has been good additional lines of towels stretch high up right across the hall.

I retire to a cubicle and undress. There is no need here to wrap one's clothes in a bundle; no one will intrude. But on the long benches I notice two soldiers who make their clothes into a neat bundle and put their caps on the top exactly in the manner described by Bassano about 1520. I now wrap a towel round my middle, and, having put my feet into the strap of the pattens, shuffle my way into the second room—the *tepidarium* of the Romans. Here the rise in temperature is very noticeable, and although a certain amount of steam is present one soon gets used to the atmosphere. In the middle is a fountain of hot water, with large copper bowls for pouring the water over one's head. I am told, however, that it is for use after the bath and not now. So I pass on round the room, which is only half the size of the first and domed with a single cupola.

To the right and left small rooms lead off—some for massage and the depilatory, while others serve as latrines. The bather who determines to 'do the thing properly' calls for a *masseur*, who immediately leads the victim to a place apart. In the Eski Kaplija a corner between the Byzantine columns is usually chosen, while in the Yeni Kaplija space is not such an important factor, and a small room can be selected at will. I am at once put into a small marble bath, where I boil for about twenty minutes in water I can hardly bear. I am then conducted to a marble slab, and the massage begins in real earnest. It consists of two distinct parts, massage with the glove and massage with the bare hand. The first is quite pleasant,

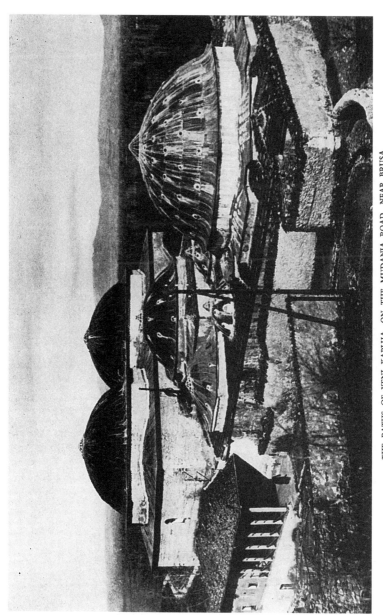

THE BATHS OF YENI KAPLIJA, ON THE MUDANIA ROAD, NEAR BRUSA

THE ARZODASI, OR THRONE ROOM

THE HALL OF CAMPAIGN, WHICH NOW HOUSES PART OF THE
PORCELAIN COLLECTION

and the novice is intrigued by the rolls of dried skin and dirt that are triumphantly shown him by the *masseur*. The glove having been discarded, the manual massage starts—with a severity that would make the feeble collapse. The powerful fingers are worked in between the shoulder-blades till they crack, and the backbone is pressed so hard that one can only just endure without calling out or trying to do something by way of revenge. For by this time I had ceased to regard the *masseur* as a friend, but rather as a fiend who for some reason entirely unknown to myself was determined not to leave a whole bone in my body if he could help it. But the torture continues. The arms are now pulled out to their furthest extent, likewise the legs, and both are submitted to such a drastic treatment that I was surprised to find they hadn't been wrenched from my body. One certainly has a greater fellow-feeling for victims of the Inquisition than one ever had before.

But the worst is over, and the next process comes as a great relief, consisting of a complete lathering of the body from head to foot. I am now left to recover, which, to my own surprise and satisfaction, I gradually do; whereupon I am informed that I can now proceed to the third and hottest room. In the Yeni Kaplija the temperature is really excessive, especially as there is no outlet for the steam. Immediately on entering I experience the most strange feelings— a mixture of curiosity and shyness, if not actual fear. Everything seems different. The atmosphere has now become heavy. Figures lie or move slowly, like shadows in the underworld. With Ulysses or Æneas I wonder who these strange and silent spectres are that appear and disappear in the steam-laden gloom. Suddenly the clank of a copper bowl, the noise of shuffling pattens, or the splash of a swimmer recalls me to my senses, and as I gradually accustom my eyes to this strange element in which I find myself living for the first time I begin to examine the room and get an idea of what it contains and what I should do next myself. For nobody is with me. I was just pushed in and left!

But try as I will it is impossible to be rid of the illusion that I am in some unearthly place, and a nervous fear seizes me, lest by some erroneous movement or action I betray myself and hollow, vaporous laughter proclaim my ignorance or clumsiness. But all is pure imagination, and as I penetrate into the room and gradually make my way round the circular marble rim of the central basin I pass naked bodies lying prone on the floor, or crouching in odd corners, or seated near one of the side-baths, or bending over a wall fountain looking for all the world like figures from a Greek vase magnified to life-size by some magician's art. Time stands still, and, like the lotus-eaters of old, I take no thought of to-morrow, and begin to enjoy that strange feeling of warm contentment and relaxation that only these baths can give. It is with a Herculean effort that one moves at all, but gradually I creep towards the basin and slowly lower myself into the water and experience the curious sensation of swimming in nearly boiling water. The effort wakes me from my stupor, and when I return to the second room it seems almost cold by comparison. Here I gradually cool off with the help of bowls of tepid water and proceed to a far corner of the room, where I discard the red towel I have worn up till now and receive three fresh towels round my body, a fourth being wrapped round the head like a turban, and a fifth put in my hands to mop the perspiration that still pours from my face.

And now comes the reward of the bath—that feeling of bodily satisfaction, cleanliness, and freshness that transcends the ken of mortal man and elevates one to heights ethereal. I lie like a king on my couch and, clapping my hands in true Oriental fashion, call for cigarettes and coffee. Troubles and trials are forgotten, and as my smoke curls upward to the great space above I only hope this modern burnt offering will reach the throne of Olympian Zeus, at the foot of whose mighty home I lie.

CHAPTER XI

THE THIRD COURT

Roughly speaking, the Third Court is only half the size of the Second. It includes the various buildings of the Palace School (now the Museum), the Inner Treasury, the Pavilion of the Holy Mantle and Sacred Relics, and the mosque (now the New Library); there are also the two detached buildings—the *Arzodasi*, with which we are already familiar, and the *Kütüphanesi*, or Library, of Ahmed III.

I shall discuss these two latter buildings first.

The *Arzodasi* is a rectangular building of a single story with an overhanging roof supported by a pillared marble colonnade running completely round the building. There are twenty-two pillars in all, the majority being marble, but some of granite.

The gentle slope of the ground away from the Gate of Felicity necessitates steps at the far side of the *Arzodasi*. They descend in a double flight of some dozen steps each. Although the building underwent restorations during the reigns of Mustafa II, Ahmed III, and Abd ul-Mejid, the general scheme of the structure as built by Muhammad II has been preserved, and portions are said to date from the fifteenth century. The interior is divided into two unequal parts, the larger, on the *harēm* side, being the actual Audience or Throne Room; the smaller one, originally panelled with sheets of gold and silver, apparently acted as an anteroom for the use of ambassadors and important personages seeking audience with the Sultan. The walls contain much good second-period tiling, and attention should be drawn to the lovely chimney-piece which Bon described as being "entirely covered with sheets of silver purfled with gold." There is also an interesting cascade fountain, so arranged, according to Palace tradition, that the noise of the water falling from one basin to another should cover conversations not meant to be heard by the attendants. As already mentioned in a previous chapter, the throne can best be described as a low four-poster bed. It still displays some of the ornate decorations on the pillars and canopy, which once was heavy with gold and jewels, and with elaborate jewelled silk tassels, which hung down over the Sultan's head. It is situated in the left-hand corner of the room, with the fireplace to the left and the cascade fountain to the right.

According to Tavernier[1] there were eight separate coverings for the throne, all kept in the Treasury until they were wanted. The first was of black velvet embroidered with pearls, the second of white velvet with rubies and emeralds set in bezels or collets, the third of violet velvet with turquoises and pearls, the next three of velvets of other colours embroidered in gold, while the last two were gold brocades. The particular covering chosen differed with the status of each ambassador.

Mention should be made of the charming wall fountain in the passage between the two rooms, with a fine panel of tiling, surmounted by the royal *tuǧra*, or monogram, to the left.

Immediately beyond the *Arzodasi*, but slightly to the left, or *ḥarēm*, side, is the *Kütüphanesi*, or Library, of Ahmed III. Several authorities state that it was erected in 1767 by Mustafa III, but possibly an earlier one occupied the same site. It is a cruciform building approached by a double flight of stone steps, which leads through a fine bronze door into a vestibule which occupies one of the arms of the building. The opposite one is a windowed recess lined with a low sofa and with tiling above. The lateral arms, somewhat larger than the others, are also tiled and occupied by large bookcases with glass doors. Twelve marble columns support the high dome, from which a huge lantern depends. A brazier, *Korān*-stands, odd chairs, and stools, two or three book-cupboards, a large carpet, and several rugs complete the furniture of the library. With regard to the library itself many wild statements have been made, but recent inspection of the manuscripts (of which there are some 5000 in all) has failed to discover any treasure of outstanding value.[2] According to Gaselee the best manu-

---

[1] *New Relation*, p. 38.

[2] See F. Blass, "Die griechischen und lateinischen Handschriften im alten Serail zu Konstantinopel," *Hermes*, vol. xxiii (Berlin, 1888), pp. 219–233; Stephen Gaselee, *The Greek Manuscripts in the Old Seraglio at Constantinople*, a pamphlet of fourteen pages (Cambridge, 1916); C. P. Vegleres in the quinquagenary number of the Ἑλληνικὸς Φιλολογικὸς Σύλλογος, pp. 172–182; and especially D. A. Deissmann, *Forschungen und Funde im Serai* (Berlin and Leipzig, 1933).

script was that by Critoboulus, being the only original Greek account of the fall of Constantinople.

In a general account on the library written in 1845 Charles White[1] says that it is more diversified than any other in the capital. Its contents embrace all subjects, including a magnificent edition of the *Romance of Antar* upon metallic paper, and another of the *Gulistān* of Sadi. It possesses *Korāns* transcribed by divers Caliphs and a collection of portraits of Sultans painted upon a broad roll of canvas, which are taken from a quarto volume containing the original portraits of the Sultans and many of their children, with a preface and short panegyric of each.

The library is closed to the public, and, as far as I could see, contains very few printed books at all. These are now housed in the building just across the court (No. 98 in the plan) which was originally the mosque of the Inner Service. I shall return to it later.

In 1719–20 it appears that Ahmed III founded a private library somewhere between the mosque and the courtyard of the *Kafes*, and it was here that the rarer manuscripts were kept. Whether this has any connexion with that of Ahmed I (No. 88 in the plan) I cannot say.

There seem to have always been two main libraries in the Seraglio, one for the Sultan and the other for the general use of the pages.

The first account I can find of two separate libraries in the Seraglio is contained in the manuscript of Hierosolimitano (1611), to which reference has already been made in chapter ii. One of these libraries is described as "public," on the men's side, while the other was private and "further inside." It seems to have closely resembled that of Ahmed III in its general arrangement. "On both sides," writes Hierosolimitano,

> are two cupboards with glass doors, and there are always kept in these cupboards some two dozen illuminated volumes such as he [the Sultan] wishes to read; and the cupboards are low so that a person squatting in Turkish fashion can see the books which are visible through the transparent glass and conveniently take them out and read them. Above each of these cupboards is an open shelf on which every Wednesday morning are placed three purses full of coins, one of gold and two of silver, all freshly minted, for donations and alms.

[1] *Three Years in Constantinople*, vol. ii, p. 192.

In the library which is behind where the attendants and pages dwell are books of every kind and language, and of great beauty. In particular there are 120 works on Constantine the Great, each two ells in breadth (that is to say, three spans each) and over three in length—of vellum as thin as silk. There are manuscripts of the Old and New Testaments, other histories, and lives of the saints all in letters of gold and bound in silver gilt, tooled and inlaid with jewels of inestimable value. And nobody at all is allowed to touch them.[1]

At one time many other smaller libraries existed in the Seraglio, as each *oda* had its own library. Until comparatively recently quite a large number of books and manuscripts were to be seen in the antechamber of the *Arzodasi*. A few years ago it was decided to collect all the books together into a single library and furnish it on modern lines.

The disused Palace School mosque (*Ağalar Camii*), which juts out sideways into the Third Court, was chosen for this new library (*Yeni Kütüphane*), while the adjacent little mosque of Ahmed (*Sultanahmet Camii*) was converted into an excellent reading-room (*Mütalea Salonu*), where students are allowed to study from any of the 12,000 volumes which this new composite library is said to contain. The building is of red brick, rectangular in shape, and surmounted by a cylindrical vaulted roof. It is well lighted by two floors of windows. At the western end a low cement enclosure, with an old fountain in the middle, has recently been built.

According to Halil Edhem,[2] who examined the building from an architectural point of view, the plan was originally square and not rectangular, and had a centre cupola flanked by a smaller one each side on a lower level.

Immediately behind the New Library is the *ḥarēm* mosque, with a latticed window connecting the two.

With the exception of the group of buildings known collectively as the Pavilion of the Holy Mantle and the Treasury, the rest of the Third Court was devoted to the Palace School, with its various halls, dormitories, classrooms, baths, etc.

So great have been the alterations in such buildings of the Palace School as *do* remain that, unless he has previously made himself

---

[1] F. 104.   [2] *Nos Mosquées de Stamboul* (Istanbul, 1934), p. 54.

familiar with the history of this extraordinary military School of State, the student will find it difficult to reconstruct it architecturally by what he sees to-day. To put it briefly, the sites of the different *odas*, or chambers, of the school are to-day occupied by the collections of porcelain, glass, costumes, etc., or else by the Museum directorate. Even if an inspection of them all is obtained, modern partitions, the heightening of rooms by the demolition of an upper floor, and many other similar renovations make it impossible to recognize anything from early descriptions—except possibly the so-called Baths of Selim II. At the same time it is necessary to have some rough idea of the working of the Palace School, which formed so important a part of the Seraglio and was the one good influence that to a large extent counteracted the pernicious effects of *harēm* rule. The best modern accounts are undoubtedly those of Professor A. H. Lybyer[1] and Dr Barnette Miller,[2] and embody the sixteenth-century accounts of such men as Spandugino, Junis Bey, Ramberti, Geuffroy, Navagero, and Menavino.

The earliest description is that of Angiolello (1473–81), but the fullest account is probably that of Bobovi (1665).[3] In view of the above, therefore, I shall give here only the briefest description of the Palace School, paying most attention to the buildings which still exist in the Third Court.

In chapter iv I explained the true origin of the corps of janissaries, showing that the distinctive feature of the system was the recruitment of the corps from a levy of Christian children, who were forcibly converted and specially trained for their profession. This could not come into being all at once, and the earlier Sultans maintained a kind of bodyguard of bought or captured slaves, which as it grew in size was organized and trained, not as a single unit, but as several distinct divisions, in each of which the individual exhibited that state of bodily condition or mental capability that caused his inclusion in the particular division to which he was detailed.

Thus boys of pleasing appearance, bodily perfection, and of good

---

[1] *The Government of the Ottoman Empire in the Time of Suleiman the Magnificent*, pp. 71–89, 126–128.
[2] *Beyond the Sublime Porte*, pp. 47–71, and the article on "The Curriculum of the Palace School of the Turkish Sultans," in the *Macdonald Presentation Volume*, pp. 305–324.
[3] British Museum, Harl. MSS., 3409.

birth and education were at once indicated for training as pages in the Sultan's Court, or as *spahi-oghlans*, or recruits in the highest corps of standing cavalry. The rest became *ajem-oghlans*, members of the Outer Service of the Seraglio and janissary recruits. The schools for the Royal pages were originally at Adrianople and possibly Brusa, but after the capture of Constantinople and the building of the Palace on Seraglio Hill Muhammad, the most highly educated man of his time, decided to establish a great School of State, which in its curriculum would combine a thorough intellectual education with a full military training and perfect development of the body. No better patron or personal example could have been chosen than Muhammad himself, who was not only a first-class linguist and student of history and philosophy, but excelled in archery and horsemanship, as well as being a recognized master in strategy and the management of munitions and the commissariat. And so was formed this State School of Royal pages, with a curriculum that at the time had not its equal in Europe.

Several factors stand out as unique in the history of education with regard to the Palace School that deserve special mention. In the first place, there was not a single Turk in the whole establishment. The boys were Austrian, Hungarian, Russian, Greek, Italian, Bosnian, Bohemian, and even German and Swiss, as well as Georgian, Circassian, Armenian, and Persian. But the point to stress is that they were all slaves, and henceforth had no nationality, no family, and no future except that offered them by the only lord and master they were now to know—the Sultan. Once loyalty to the throne had been clearly established it soon became evident how valuable this highly trained body of youths was proving itself, not only to fill official posts in a continually enlarging empire, but as a support to the throne against the janissaries, who were yearly becoming more difficult to handle.

In the second place, not only was the training long and arduous, but the interest of the School in its pupils was for life. After the modern undergraduate has graduated from one of our universities he passes on to some profession or business, and practically severs all connexion with the Varsity. If his education has stopped after his leaving the public school about the only tie he has left is the old school tie. If he decides on an Army or a Navy career he will go into Sandhurst or Dartmouth, where his general, religious, and cultural education has to look after itself. But in the case of the Palace School the education was continuous and all-embracing—both mental, physical, and religious. It was private school, public school, Varsity, and military or naval college combined, and as such is probably unique in the history of education. But there was not room in the Seraglio for all the pupils. It housed only some 500 to 800 of the *iç-oghlans*, or Inside youths as they were called. The palaces at Adrianople and Galata were used as 'outhouses,' so to speak, and each contained some 300 or 400 students. These students apparently ranked lower than those in the Seraglio, and their schools can be regarded as preparatory schools whence the *iç-oghlans* would pass on if they had made sufficient progress. At the same time two of the Seraglio halls were also of a preparatory nature—the Great and Little Halls—so it would seem rather as if the 'outhouses' catered for students of a secondary standard who might never pass into the Seraglio, but merely graduate direct to some minor official position.

The *odas* in the Seraglio were four in number during the reign of Muhammad, but had increased to six before the end of the reign of Ahmed I (1617). Their names and functions were as follows:

1. *Has Oda*, Royal Chamber (*has*, or *khas*, meaning 'proper,' 'pure,' or 'private,' and so 'Royal'), the highest and most exclusive unit, consisting of 39 members only, the Sultan himself making the fortieth. From the time of Selim I they were made custodians of the Holy Relics in the Pavilion of the Holy Mantle.

2. *Hazine Oda*, Chamber of the Treasury. This was under the Inside *Hazinedar-bashi*, a white eunuch, and numbered 60 or 70. The duties were the care of the Sultan's treasure, making all payments, and keeping accounts.

3. *Kiler Oda*, Chamber of the Pantry. This was under the *Kilerji-bashi*, who controlled the kitchen service of the Seraglio. The numbers of this hall seem to have varied, but the average was between 70 and 100. Their duties consisted in supervising the Sultan's food, and they rode with him whenever he left the Palace.

4. *Büyük Oda*, Great Chamber, originally called *Yeni Oda*, or New

Chamber, the change of name being apparently due to the creation of the *Küçük Oda*, or Little Chamber, founded by Suleiman. Both these chambers were concerned only with the education of the pages, the honorary positions in the higher *odas* mentioned above being awarded according to merit.

5. *Küçük Oda*, Little Chamber. Additional to the above. Both halls were under the *Ikinji-Kapi-oghlan*, or Eunuch of the Second Gate. The numbers in the Great Chamber were originally between 100 and 200, and rose to 400, at which time the Little Chamber housed some 250 *iç-oghlans*. Both chambers had been abolished by the end of the eighteenth century.

6. *Seferli Oda*, Chamber of Campaign. Founded by either Ahmed I[1] or Murad IV, about a dozen years later.[2] This chamber actually came immediately after No. 3, the *Kiler Oda*, in order of seniority, and maintained its strength (from 70 to 150) by drawing from the Great and Little Chambers. The pages of the *Seferli Oda* combined the duties of laundering the Sultan's clothes for campaigns and running the military band. I have already referred to the connexion of this *oda* with the so-called "Baths of Selim II." These last three *odas* appear to have been under the general command of the *Sarai Aghasi*, who was the Assistant Director of the entire School.

Apart from the auxiliary schools already mentioned as existing in Adrianople and Galata, a third one was founded by Ibrahim Pasha, Grand Vizir of Suleiman, and named after him. Both this and that at Adrianople were abolished by Sultan Ibrahim, while the Galata School is still flourishing. The total number of pages in the Seraglio was never less than 300 or more than 900. The usual course of study, extending for no less than fourteen years, included Turkish, Arabic, and Persian in all their branches, while 'side-lines' such as leather-working, the manufacture of bows and arrows and quivers, falconry, dog-breeding, music, shampooing, manicuring, haircutting, and turban-dressing were selected largely at choice. Rewards in the form of pay were always given, so that every encouragement to progress

[1] Dr Miller, *Beyond the Sublime Porte*, p. 56.
[2] Lybyer, *The Government of the Ottoman Empire in the Time of Suleiman the Magnificent*, p. 128, *n.* 1.

was extended. "These boys," says Menavino, in speaking of the *Yeni*, or *Büyük*, *Oda*,

> have a daily allowance of two aspers during the first year, three during the second year, four during the third year, and thus their allowance increases each year. They receive scarlet garments twice a year, and some robes of white cloth for the summer.[1]

Discipline was severe, but the use of the bastinado was allowed only once a day. The pages were watched day and night by the white eunuchs, and every precaution was taken to prevent unnatural relationships. That several of the Sultans preferred boys, or took them in addition, to women is well known, and the following entry from the archives of the Bank of St George at Genoa leaves little doubt on the subject:

> They [the white eunuchs] look for all the world like mummified old women, and are, for the most part, very thin and shrivelled. Their duty is to attend upon the Grand Signor when he goes out in State, and also to keep order among the white pages, mostly Christian lads, stolen from their parents, to the number of about 300 to 400 each year. Some of these boys are very good-looking and wear magnificent dresses. Their cheeks are plump, and their painted eyebrows meet. Very strange things are told of them, but these things are common hereabouts, and nobody thinks much about them.

Rycaut devotes a short chapter to the subject, and says that the pages invented a language of signs among themselves which they used to express their passions, but that in the event of discovery they were nearly beaten to death and expelled from the Seraglio. It will be remembered that the *harēm* did not begin to move into the Seraglio until about 1542, so until that date all the buildings in the Third Court were devoted to the Sultan and the Palace School, which fact may account for the position of the *harēm* in its crowded position away from the main courts.

Each of the six chambers of the Palace School had its own hall, dormitory, and classroom, and the number of buildings was further increased by a conservatory of music, two mosques, a common room for the staff and chief pages, offices of administration, the Baths of Selim II, and the Library of Ahmed III. The majority of these

---

[1] *Trattato de costumi*, p. 91.

buildings disappeared after the fires of 1655 and 1856, but a glance at the plan will show exactly what remains to-day.

Apart from the library already discussed and the Pavilion of the Holy Mantle, to which I shall refer later, the oldest hall still standing is the *Seferli Koğuşu* (No. 103 in the plan), the Hall of Campaign (*koğuşu* being the modern word for 'hall,' *oda* meaning rather 'chamber' or 'school'). This room, with the one behind it, was part of the baths, and to-day houses the famous collection of Chinese porcelain (*Çini Hazinesi*). The next room (No. 104) was also part of the baths, and is now devoted to the silver and glass collection (*Gümüş ve Billûr Salonu*). The other five rooms in this corner of the court constituted the Royal Treasury, for a very detailed account of which I must refer readers to the gem expert Tavernier.[1] To-day they have been turned into the Seraglio Museum, and contain *objets d'art* of every conceivable kind, from the Persian and other thrones of gold covered with pearls and rubies to teapots, coffee sets, clocks, desk furniture, daggers, pipes, cigarette-holders, toilet sets, chessmen, ink-horns, specimens of Oriental calligraphy, needlework, ivory carvings, tortoiseshell inlay, and a host of other articles too many to mention. Although this is not the place to give any detailed account of the different collections, a word or two about the famous ceramic collection may be allowed.

Many contradictory statements have been made concerning it, and it is only in recent years that we have been in a position to realize the true state of affairs. This is due to the publication in 1930 of *Meisterwerke der türkischen Museen zu Konstantinopel*,[2] by Professor Zimmermann, who personally supervised the arrangement of the collection. A commission was appointed for this purpose after the Balkan War in 1912, but owing to the World War the installation was not completed until 1925. The next description was a brief one included in the official guide-book of the Seraglio.[3] Finally, in 1934 two articles dealing with the collection appeared in the *Transactions of the Oriental Ceramic Society*, the first by R. L. Hobson and the second by Sir Percival David. These are most interesting, and it is from them that the few following remarks are chiefly taken.

---

[1] *New Relation*, pp. 45–51.   [2] Two vols., Berlin and Leipzig.
[3] *Topkapi Sarayi Müzesi Rehberi*, pp. 68 et seq.

The Oriental ceramics in the Seraglio form the third largest collection in the world. First, and entirely unrivalled, was that in the Forbidden City in Pekin, and secondly comes the Johanneum in Dresden. Therefore any serious student must visit Istanbul to complete his education, as he will discover many unique and wonderful specimens.

According to Sir Percival David, the earliest record of Chinese ware in Istanbul occurs in an inventory of the Palace made in 1504, during the reign of Bayezid II. It lists twenty-one specimens, nearly all plates. Another inventory was made under Selim I in 1514, and listed sixty-two specimens said to have been brought from the Heshtebesht Palace, in Tabriz. It was not, however, until the accession of Suleiman the Magnificent (1520–66) that the collection really began to assume large dimensions. This was due to the personal interest of the Sultan in Chinese porcelain and the great additions made by conquest and received as gifts from foreign emissaries seeking his favour. No further mention of the porcelain appears to have been made until 1680, when there is reference to a larger collection of Chinese ware as being stored partly in the *Hazine* (Treasury) and partly in the *mutfak't* (kitchen).

In the reign of Abd ul-Mejid (1839–61) the collection was stored in the cellars of the Treasury, and some of it was removed to Yildiz by Abd ul-Hamid II (1876–1909). On his deposition, however, everything was returned to the Seraglio. To-day the collection consists of some 10,000 pieces, out of which 1300 are celadons, 2600 Ming wares other than celadon, and the rest Chinese and Japanese porcelains of post-Ming date. The conquests of Persia, Syria, and Egypt naturally added largely to the collection, and the numerous specimens of blue and white bear witness to this. Of interest is the large number of green celadon plates which were in daily use in the Seraglio. The colour was specially chosen as, according to a Near Eastern superstition, it disclosed the presence of poison in the food.

Although by far the greater portion of the collection is Ming (1368–1643), there are many fine specimens of both Yuan (1280–1368) and Sung (960–1279) dynasties.

Continuing our inspection of the buildings of the Palace School, we come to two very large structures, which together take up nearly the entire far, or north-eastern, side of the court. The first of these is the *Kiler Koğuşu*, or Hall of the Pantry, now used as the office of the directorate of the Seraglio. I have been in it only twice, but the Director has himself kindly drawn in the divisions of the building in my plan. Restorations have entirely altered the original interior decoration, which must have been of a simpler nature altogether. "Here were stored," says Dr Miller, quoting from Menavino, Badoaro, and Bobovi,

> a full assortment of drugs, above all of potent antidotes for poisons; the rare and costly spices, perfumes, and aromatics brought from Egypt, Arabia, and the Indies; the huge candles brought from Wallachia for lighting the Selamlik, Harem, and palace mosques; vast quantities of jams, marmalades, and other sweetmeats; a supply of drinking water from the two Chamlijas and from the spring of St. Simon in the Old Palace; the delectable syrups manufactured to order in 'Grand Cairo' which were the foundation of many of the royal drinks; and the great pieces of ambergris sent by the pasha of the Yemen which was one of the ingredients of a favourite variety of sherbet.[1]

The next building, separated from the first by a passage connecting the Third and Fourth Courts, is the *Hazine* (also written *Khazine*) *Koğuşu*, or Hall of the Treasury. As previously mentioned, this was the hall of the highest *oda* after the *Has Oda*. To-day it is used as a sorting-room and museum store, and naturally is not open to the general public.

The northern corner of the court is taken up with the *Emanat Hazinesi* (Treasury deposit), used formerly by the *Kiliçdar* (or *Silihdar*), the Sword-bearer, and later as the Treasury of the Pavilion of the Holy Mantle, which itself is the large square building divided into four chambers in the extreme corner. I shall return to it soon. Next to this, and extending as far as the New Library (No. 98), are the *Hasodalilar Koğuşu* (Hall of the Royal Chamber) and connecting rooms. The original building was situated near the Revan Kiosk, the present one being rebuilt in the middle of the nineteenth century by Abd ul-Mejid. The main hall is a large rectangular room supported by six pillars, having a connecting passage to the Pavilion of the Holy Mantle. There are several adjacent rooms, which included

[1] *Beyond the Sublime Porte*, p. 213.

a small suite for the chief officer of the *oda* and a hospital used only by members of the Royal Chamber, while the other pages were accommodated in the larger one in the First Court.

This completes the buildings of the Palace School, but we have yet to consider the Pavilion of the Holy Mantle.

Although the treasuring and veneration of relics, being a form of idolatry, is hardly consistent with the spirit of Islām, the temptation to cherish and reverence tangible memorials of the Prophet has not been entirely resisted. Such relics, however, are very few in number (as compared, for instance, with those of the Buddha), and are to be found, not in Arabia, but in other countries which have adopted Muhammadanism, either entirely or in part. Thus in India Bijāpur, in the Deccan, venerates two hairs from the Prophet's beard, which are kept in a box that is never opened. Then at Rohrī, in Sind, is a single hair kept in a jewelled case of solid gold in a shrine erected specially for the purpose in 1745. This hair is exhibited once a year, and by a clever trick mechanism is made to rise and fall by itself. Still more hairs, this time three in number, are said to be preserved in the famous "Mosque of the Barber," which lies a little north-west of Kairwān (Qaïrowan, or Kaïrouan), the most interesting town in Tunisia. It is dedicated to Abû Zemaâ el Beloui, who was not a barber at all, but merely one of the Prophet's followers, and the correct name of the mosque is "Mosque of Sidi the Companion." The three hairs are buried with him, one in each eyelid and the third under his tongue. As he always carried them with him when alive he has by some curious mistake been described as the Prophet's barber. As we shall see later, the rest of Muhammad's beard is in the Seraglio.

Reputed footprints of the Prophet, like those of the Buddha, exist in many parts of India, and appear to vary considerably in size and shape. But apart from these comparatively unimportant relics there existed in Cairo the regalia of the Caliphs,[1] consisting of the Prophet's standard and mantle, and, according to some accounts, his sword as

---

[1] *I.e.*, the titular Caliphs of 'Abbasīd descent who were allowed to hold a shadowy Court at Cairo under the Circassian Mameluke rulers. The title 'Caliph' (more correctly *khalīf*, in Arabic *khālifa*, and never *khalif*, meaning 'lieutenant,' and so 'representative') was first borne by the four successors of Muhammad. The title then descended to the thirteen Umayyad Caliphs of Damascus, then to the thirty-seven 'Abbasīd Caliphs of Baghdad,

well. Now when in 1516–17 Selim I had completely subdued Syria and Egypt, finishing up his victories by a bloody massacre of 50,000 of the inhabitants of Cairo, he not only obtained the title of Caliph, but possessed himself of these sacred relics. His appalling cruelties as a conqueror were only equalled by his religious humility and contrition as a worshipper, and all his time was spent in the mosques and other religious institutions in Egypt. The Prophet's standard, *Sancak Şerif*, was dispatched to Damascus in order that it might be taken on the annual pilgrimage to Mecca,[1] but the other relics (exactly what they were is uncertain) were taken to Constantinople, where they have remained to this day.

They were taken at once to the Seraglio, and a special building was made to receive them which became known as *Hirkai Şerif Odasi*, the Pavilion (or Chamber) of the Holy Mantle, since, until the sacred standard was added seventy-seven years later, the *Hirka* was the most important of the relics.

As mentioned above, there has always been considerable doubt as to what relics there actually were. All accounts seem to agree on the mantle and the standard. It is with regard to the lesser articles that differences occur, and it seems uncertain as to whom they belonged —whether to the Prophet himself or to one or other of the "four companions," Abu Bekr, Omar, Osman, and Ali. The best seventeenth-century account, and, in fact, the only reliable one, is that by Tavernier, who got his information from two men who had served many years in the Treasury. One of them was actually Head Treasurer, and in this capacity was present at the ceremonies connected with the relics. Tavernier describes the mantle, the standard, the seal, and two swords. Of modern accounts I think that by White is the best. His list includes the mantle, the standard, the beard, tooth, and footprint, the last of which he saw personally. I shall now take them one by one and give further details about them.

1. *The Hirka Şerif, or Holy Mantle.* It is believed to have been presented by the Prophet to a pagan Arab named Ka'b ibn Zuhayr, one

whose dynasty fell before the Mongols under Hulaku (brother of Marco Polo's Kublai Khan) in 1258. The titular Caliphs of Egypt continued to support a hollow sovereignty in Cairo, until in 1517 Selim I compelled the last of them, Mutawakkil, to abdicate in his favour, and obtained the title for himself and his successors.

[1] It reached Constantinople at the end of 1595 (see later, p. 248).

of six men whom Muhammad wished to convert. He defied them to write anything more beautiful than the *Korān*. Five of them acknowledged their inability to do such a thing and became converts. But Zuhayr persisted in criticizing the holy book, and fled to the desert, hiding in a cave. Later he repented and wrote a poem which proved such a masterpiece that the Prophet took from his own shoulders the mantle he was wearing, one that had been woven in the *harēm*, and put it upon the poet's shoulders. The poet, being converted, became one of the Prophet's most devoted adherents, and his poem has been handed down to posterity under the title *Bānat Su'ād*. The mantle was sold by the poet's children to Mu'awiweh I, founder of the Ummayid dynasty, and, passing to Baghdad with the 'Abbasīds and then to Cairo, finally fell into the hands of Selim I, and so came to Constantinople.

It has been described as a green, black, white, and striped garment, while Dr Miller was assured by several Palace attendants that it is in reality cream-coloured.

Tavernier says it is a garment of a white camlet made of goat's hair, with large sleeves. His description of the ceremony connected with it is as follows:

> The Grand Seignor having taken it out of the Coffer, kisses it with much respect, and puts it into the hands of the *Capi-Aga*, who is come into the Room by his Order, after they had taken the Impressions of the Seal. The Officer sends to the Overseer of the Treasury, for a large golden Cauldron, which is brought in thither by some of the Senior-Pages. It is so capacious, according to the description which they gave me of it, as to contain the sixth part of a Tun, and the out-side of it is garnish'd, in some places, with Emeralds, and Turquezes. This Vessel is fill'd with water within six fingers breadth of the brink, and the *Capi-Aga*, having put *Mahomet's* Garment into it, and left it to soak a little while, takes it out again, and wrings it hard, to get out the water it has imbib'd, which falls into the Cauldron, taking great care that there falls not any of it to the ground. That done, with the said water he fills a great number of *Venice*-Chrystal Bottles, containing about half a pint, and when he has stopp'd them, he Seals them with the Grand Seignor's Seal. They afterwards set the Garment a drying, till the twentieth day of the *Ramazan*, and then his Highness comes to see them put [it] up again in the Coffer.[1]

[1] *New Relation*, p. 74.

The day after the ceremony the bottles of water were sent to the Sultanas and important personages of Constantinople, together with a piece of paper wrapped up and bearing the imprint of the Prophet's seal (to be described later). They soaked the paper in the water, and then drank the lot. Bobovi (as quoted by Dr Miller) adds that the water was dew gathered by the pages of the Commissariat in the month of April, and was regarded as a remedy against fever and other ills, and was put into the mouth of the dead as a talisman against the torments of the sepulchre. As time went on the ceremony became very simple, and is considered to have been more in accordance with the original practice of the sixteenth century.[1]

2. *The Sancak Şerif, or Sacred Standard.* According to some Arabian historians this standard originally served as a curtain for the tent entrance of Ayesha, the Prophet's favourite wife. The usually accepted tradition is that it was the turban-winder of one of Muhammad's converted enemies, a man named Buraydat.

During the Flight he was sent against Muhammad at the head of a body of horse by the chiefs of Mecca. But instead of attacking he threw himself on his knees, unwound his turban, and, fixing it to his lance-point, dedicated it and himself to the Prophet's service and glory. Like the mantle, it ultimately came into Selim's hands, and, as mentioned above, was sent to Damascus, where it was deposited in the great mosque and carried every year to Mecca at the head of the pilgrims. Realizing its political possibilities, Murad III had it sent to Hungary as an incentive to his army. At the end of the campaign it was conveyed to Constantinople by Muhammad III, who had just (1595) ascended the throne. Henceforth the standard became the symbol of Ottoman domination, and was exhibited only when either the Sultan or the Grand Vizir joined the field army in person, or in the case of national emergencies (as in 1826) or on declaration of war, the last occasion being in 1915 when a holy war was proclaimed against the Allies.

It would appear that the standard is detached from the pole and enclosed in a rosewood coffer, inlaid with tortoiseshell, mother-of-pearl, and precious stones. It is sewed within another standard, said to be that of Omar, and this again is enclosed in forty different cover-

---

[1] See, further, White, *Three Years in Constantinople,* vol. i, pp. 214, 215.

ings of rich stuffs, the innermost being of green silk embroidered with golden inscriptions.

Whether there is any significance in the number of wrappings, corresponding with the number of members of the *Has Oda*, who were the custodians of the relics, I cannot say. White adds that the mantle had also forty wrappers, but the account may be incorrect on this point. The keys of the coffer were kept by the *Kislar Agha* in virtue of his office as inspector and administrator of the holy cities (see p. 129). White actually saw the pole or staff resting against the angle of the wall. It was surmounted by a hollow globe of silver gilt enclosing a copy of the *Korān* said to have been transcribed by Omar. Another copy, transcribed by Osman, is folded in the second standard. D'Ohsson[1] describes the receptacle as being in the shape of an apple and containing a *Korān* by Osman and the key of the Ka'aba presented to Selim by the Sherif of Mecca. Tavernier says the standard was kept in a cupboard in the Sultan's bedroom adjoining the *Hirkai Şerif Odasi*.

3. *The Mühür Şerif, or Sacred Seal.* The only account of the seal and the ceremonies connected with it appears to be that by Tavernier:

Towards the feet of the said Bed [the divan in the 'Winter chamber,' or chief room of the relics], there is a kind of Neech [niche] made within the very Wall, in which there is a little Ebony Box, about half a foot square, and in that is lock'd up *Mahomet's* Seal. It is enchac'd in a Crystal, with a Bordure of Ivory, and taking all together, it may be four inches in length, and three in breadth. I have seen the Impression of it upon a piece of Paper; but he who shew'd it me, would not suffer me to touch it, only upon this score, that he look'd on it as a great Relick. Once in three months this Chamber is made clean, and the Carpets are chang'd, the Pages of the Treasury being employ'd in that Office. And then it is, that the *Chasnadar-bachi* opens the Box, and having in his hands an embroider'd Hand-kerchief, he takes out the Seal, with great respect and reverence, whilst the Senior of the Pages holds a golden Cup, garnish'd with Diamonds and blue Saphirs, on the top of which there is a kind of Perfuming-Pot, out of which there comes an exhalation of all sorts of sweet scents, whereby the whole Room is in a manner embalm'd. The Page holds that cup in both his hands joy'nd together, and lifting it up higher than his Head, all those that are present immediately prostrate themselves to the

[1] *Tableau général*, vol. i, p. 265.

ground, as an acknowledgement of their veneration. As soon as they are up again, the Page brings down the Cup, lower than his chin, and the principal Officer of the Treasury, holding the Seal over the smoke, all those who are in the Room, come and kiss the Chrystal which covers one of the most precious Relicks, that they have of their Prophet.[1]

Tavernier was unable to obtain a description of the seal itself, as to its material and engravings. On the 14th day of *Ramaḍān* fifty pieces of paper were stamped with the seal "with a certain gummy Ink, which is prepar'd in a Pourcelain Dish, whereinto he [the Sultan's Sword-bearer] thrusts his finger, and rubs the Seal with it, and keeps all those Printed Papers" to send them to important personages together with the mantle water, as explained above.

4. *The Sakal, or Beard.* This is said to have been shaved from the Prophet's chin after death by his favourite barber, Salman, in the presence of Abu Bekr, Ali, and several disciples who performed the ceremonial fumigations. It is said to be about three inches long, of a lightish brown colour, without grey hairs. It is preserved in a glass reliquarium, hermetically sealed, and richly ornamented. The location of various hairs from the Prophet's beard has already been mentioned.

5. *One of the Prophet's Teeth.* This tooth was one of the four which were knocked out of his mouth by a blow of a battle-axe during the battle of Bedr, where, 'tis said, the Archangel Gabriel fought on the Prophet's side at the head of 3000 angels. Two of the teeth have been lost, and the fourth is said to be in the *türbeh* of Muhammad II.

6. *The Footprint of the Prophet.* This was actually seen by White. It is the impression of a foot upon a square fragment of calcareous stone. It is believed to be that of the Prophet, indented by him at the moment he was assisting the masons to raise a heavy stone for the building of the Ka'aba. According to another tradition it was made when Muhammad placed his left foot in the stirrup to mount his famous horse Borak.

As mentioned above, Tavernier also describes two swords. One is "a very homely kind of Cuttelas" in a scabbard covered with green cloth, and is said to have belonged to Omar. The other is a short

---

[1] *New Relation*, pp. 73–74.

sword venerated because "it some time was the Sword of a certain person named *Ebou-Nislum*, with which he cut to pieces, those, who had spread a Heresie in the Law of *Mahomet*."

Tavernier gives an account of several of the rooms which formed part of the suite of the Pavilion of the Holy Mantle, but owing to demolitions and rebuildings it tells us but little. The main entrance is under the colonnade in the Third Court next to the Mounting Platform through a highly ornate gate known as the *Şadirvan Kapisi*, or Gate of the Fountain. Access is immediately obtained to the southernmost of the four square domed rooms, which appears to be a kind of reception-room with a fountain in the centre. Of the remaining three I have personally seen only the most northerly, and then just a brief glance through the grilled windows that look out into the L-shaped pillared hall. As far as I could judge the entire walls were covered with exquisite tiling, and heavy hangings hid from view what may have been show-cases containing some of the lesser relics. Lanterns hung from the ceiling and rich carpets covered the floors. There was little light, and as I was really being conducted to the Hall of Circumcision my furtive glances were but momentary. I made my exit the way I had come—namely, by a small door at the top of a short flight of steps in the corner of the Fourth Court behind the *Emanat Hazinesi* (No. 109 in the plan). Both this latter building, the *Has Odasi*, and the kiosks leading off the pillared hall were all connected ceremonially and architecturally, combining together as the Pavilion of the Holy Mantle. Exactly what part each played at different times is impossible to say. I shall have occasion to add a few words about the Revan Kiosk in the next chapter, as this really forms part of the Fourth Court.

CHAPTER XII

THE FOURTH COURT

ALTHOUGH to-day the remaining part of the Seraglio is known as the *Dordüncü Avlu*, or Fourth Court, the term is really used for convenience, and even so is applied more to that part near the kiosk of Abd ul-Mejid than to the whole area.

Moreover, the buildings connected with the Pavilion of the Holy Mantle and the marble terrace leading to the lovely Baghdad Kiosk in no way constitute part of another court, while the kiosk of Abd ul-Mejid, being a late Louis-Philippe erection, hardly comes into the history of the Seraglio at all.

With its unrivalled views of the Marmora, the Bosphorus, and the Princes' Islands, this part of the Seraglio was proclaimed by nature to be a garden, and as such successive Sultans have vied with one another to make it more lovely. From the very foundation of the Palace kiosks were built on the highest points amid the trees and flowers. Here every passing breeze would be caught, and, freed from the cares of State, or even from domestic troubles, the Sultans could enjoy perfect peace and privacy. That it was a private garden can at once be realized by a glance at the plan. It was entirely cut off from the other Seraglio buildings. Only the back windows of the *Kiler Koğuşu* and the Treasury looked on to it, and on those occasions when members of the *harēm* were allowed to walk in the garden, or in the event of a garden *fête*, every window was securely barred and all doors were closed. Connexion with the *harēm* was cut off by the Pavilion of the Holy Mantle, and the pages of the Palace School were safely kept in the Third Court. As we have already seen in an early chapter, it was through a door leading into this garden that surreptitious visitors were introduced, and some of the buildings mentioned as existing in the most northerly part of the gardens were obviously summer kiosks which fell into ruins as time went on, or else were pulled down to make room for the Baghdad Kiosk in 1639, or for the adjoining marble terrace, known as the *Sultan Ibrahim Kameriyesi*.

THE REVAN KIOSK, ADJOINING THE PAVILION OF THE HOLY MANTLE

THE BAGHDAD KIOSK, FROM THE TERRACE OF SULTAN IBRAHIM

The vast space of undergrowth hiding foundations of long-forgotten buildings which stretches from the Hall of Circumcision and the Baghdad Kiosk to the outer wall of the Seraglio has already been mentioned (p. 200).

Before speaking of the tulip gardens of Ahmed III which became so famous in the first quarter of the eighteenth century I shall deal briefly with such buildings as still exist in this so-called Fourth Court. As mentioned in the previous chapter, the Revan Kiosk was really connected with the Pavilion of the Holy Mantle. It occupies the highest point of the whole Seraglio, and from the time of Muhammad II this hill undoubtedly supported some building or other which formed a summer retreat close to the *selāmlik*. Here the sweet scents of the garden and one of the world's most lovely views could be continually enjoyed.

In the spring of 1635 Murad IV set out on his Anatolian campaign, expelling the Persian heretics from those cities in the Ottoman Empire they still occupied. Revan (Persian *Riwan*, English *Erivan* or *Irwan*), the capital of the Government of the same name, in Transcaucasia, to the north of Ararat, was conquered, and on the march back all provincial governors convicted of the slightest neglect were severely punished. At Revan the Sultan is said to have seen a kiosk which pleased him exceedingly, and on his return to the capital orders were given to have it copied in the Royal garden. The site on the most prominent part of the Seraglio was selected. Although named after the scene of Murad's victory, Revan, it also became known as the *Sarik Odasi*, or Room of the Turban. It is cruciform in shape, and could be described as a smaller edition of the Baghdad Kiosk. But owing to the fact that it is no longer 'free,' but has been joined to the back of the *Emanat Hazinesi* by a wall pierced with large windows, a wrong impression of its original form is obtained. It consists of a domed chamber lighted by a double row of rather narrow mullioned windows. A roof with widely overhanging eaves affords shade to the centre chamber as well as to the balconies between the arms of the kiosk. A small bay, or window divan, has been built into what was once the balcony overlooking the tulip garden. The upper part of the exterior is tiled, while the inside closely resembles that of the Baghdad Kiosk, being covered with second-period tilings and fine examples of the calligrapher's art.

In 1638 Murad IV made his final and greatest expedition against the Persians, which culminated in the capture of Baghdad. Suleiman the Magnificent had taken the town in 1534, and now Murad recaptured it, thus upholding the curious tradition in the East that the great city of Baghdad, the ancient city of the Caliphate, can only be taken by a sovereign in person.

Murad always had an eye for architectural beauty, and this time he saw a building which seemed to him the most perfect of its kind in the world. After his triumphal return to Constantinople orders were given to build a kiosk near the other one on the model of that in Baghdad.

The plan is cruciform, like the Revan Kiosk, but the surrounding arcade, with its broad overhanging roof, forms an outer cross which gives the effect of an octagon by the addition of small balconies or bay-windows between some of the arms. Other additions have also tended to alter the original plan. For instance, when facing the kiosk from the marble terrace we see that the arcade to the right, or garden side, is filled in, the tiling and traceried windows being continued in exact replica of the main kiosk, thus forming a kind of external anteroom. It was used at one time as a library. To the left the arcade is open, but on walking round in this direction we soon reach a point when it becomes closed with glass panelling, and extends thus until it meets the anteroom on the south side. A glance at the plan will supplement this description.

Taken together, the Revan and the Baghdad Kiosks are examples of the supreme works of the Turkish architectural style based on Persian originals of the seventeenth century. The tilework has reached its zenith, the outside of the latter is covered with tiles from the base to the eaves, while, as mentioned above, that of the former is tiled half-way up, but the general external effect is one of harmony and symmetry, to which a grace and lightness is imparted by the slender columns with capitals displaying the lotus *motif*. In the Baghdad Kiosk the voussoirs to the arches are in coloured marble with serrated edges, and the spandrels between the arches are decorated with circular medallions inlaid flush with the white marble surface

A gilded dome, with a tall lantern above, is carried by arches which span the openings to the four arms of the cross. A gilt ornate ball (at one time a lamp) hangs on a long chain from the centre of the dome. The interior tiling is of the highest order, the shades of colour especially noticeable being green and both dark and light blue on a white ground. The designs are mainly floral. The pomegranate flowers and large-leafed foliage in two-handled vases in panels on each side of the fireplace are magnificent. The bird designs are also deserving of special mention, the red beaks affording a striking note of bright contrast against the lighter background.

The handsome bronze fireplace is of the usual canopied style, and is built low to give warmth to people sitting on sofas and divans. Bassano tells us that the logs were placed upright, and not across as is usual with us, the idea being to create an upward draught and avoid smoking. A tall minaret-shaped chimney pierces the roof at one side of the dome. A broad Cufic cornice runs right round the room into the recesses, which are lined with magnificently embroidered divans. Behind and at the sides of these divans are cupboards, the doors of which are inlaid with ivory and mother-of-pearl. Similarly inlaid niches display Chinese porcelain, and were probably used for pipes, perfumes, and similar articles. Traceried windows occupy the upper part of the kiosk, in pairs within the recesses and singly in the intervening wall spaces. A table or brazier is usually placed in the centre of the room, but this is a purely modern arrangement for decorative purposes. The kiosk has had many uses during the centuries, being in turn a smoking-lounge, a library, a reception-room, and a prison.

Between the Baghdad Kiosk and the Hall of Circumcision stretches the wide marble terrace, with the *havuz*, or pool, on the left stretching down to the Revan Kiosk. To the right, as one faces the Hall of Circumcision, is a finely wrought canopy in gilded bronze raised on four slender columns. According to an inscription, it bears the name of *Iftariye*, from *Iftar*, the meal taken after sunset during a fast, because it was here that Ibrahim took his evening meal during *Ramadān*. It was here also that this same Sultan gave alms as part of the celebrations of his sons' circumcision, and the official guide-book to the Seraglio has two most interesting pictures (facing p. 128), the

255

first of which shows the Sultan standing in front of the *Iftariye*, while several men are on their knees picking up the *bahşiş* which has been thrown down near the *havuz*. In the second picture the *havuz* and the grovelling men still appear, but behind the line of nine officials we see the Royal Princes resting on divans, apparently after the operation, while the Sultan holds some high official, probably the Chief Physician, in conversation. The *havuz* itself is all that now remains of the 'water-garden' which early writers have described as existing in this part of the Seraglio. It is open on the terrace sides, and bounded on the other two sides by the windows of the Hall of Pillars and the Revan Kiosk. There is a charming pyramidical marble fountain in the middle, and the reflection of the gleaming white marble balustrade and surrounding columns in the waters of the pool beneath lends a coolness and serenity to the whole of these upper terrace buildings that is both restful and dignified. Passing down from the terrace by a short flight of marble steps at the side of the Revan Kiosk, one reaches the gardens. They extended, on various levels, throughout the whole of the Fourth Court, being broken to the north-east by the kiosk of Mustafa Pasha (No. 118) and the truncated tower chamber known as the *Hekimbaşi Odasi*, or Chamber of the Chief Physician (No. 119). As far as I can ascertain, the tulip gardens lay between the Revan Kiosk and the *Hekimbaşi Odasi*—i.e., Nos. 113 and 119 in the plan—while an orangery was planted on the lower level behind the kiosk of Mustafa Pasha, extending northward as far as the rectangular sunken marble pool which lies just under the Baghdad Kiosk.

Another, and smaller, pool separates the kiosk of Mustafa Pasha and the *Hekimbaşi Odasi* on the lower level.

The former of these buildings consists of two chambers of uneven sizes with a long flight of steps between them leading to the orangery. They rest on slender marble columns which can only be seen from the lower gardens. The origin of the building and the name of the architect appear to be unknown, and it was only later restorations that attached to it the name of the Vizir Mustafa Pasha. The earliest date known in connexion with it is 1704, when it was first restored by Ahmed III, as is recorded on an inscription. The name *Sofa Köşkü*, or Kiosk of the Sofa, is also applied to this building, but the

THE BAGHDAD KIOSK : A VIEW OF THE INTERIOR

THE KIOSK OF MUSTAFA PASHA, IN THE FOURTH COURT

reason for this alternative name remains unexplained. Certainly the chief attraction of the kiosk is the huge sofa window looking out on gardens beneath, and the word *sofa* is used in this sense as well as to denote an anteroom. The general decoration of the kiosk is Louis XV, and need not detain us further. It is said that the seal of the Grand Vizir was kept here.

The neighbouring *Hekimbaşi Odasi* is a two-storied building looking more like a prison, with its row of heavily barred windows right at the very top, immediately underneath a triple cornice, than the Chamber of the Chief Physician. As previously mentioned, it is said to be the lower part of an early tower, and Palace tradition dates it back to the time of Muhammad II.

A collection of early medical instruments can still be seen in the cupboards within.

In striking contrast are the *Üçüncü Kapi*, or Third Gate, and the Abd ul-Mejid Kiosk (*Mecidiye Köşkü*), in the south-eastern corner of the court. They both seem quite out of place here, and would be much more at home in Versailles. The kiosk, or New Pavilion as it is sometimes called, was built by a French architect in the middle of the nineteenth century on the site of two earlier kiosks—the *Çadir*, or Tent, and the *Üçüncü Yeri*, or Kiosk of the Third Estate. It houses a strange collection of French furniture of every period, that of the Second Empire predominating.[1]

Numerous gilt clocks, elaborate silver-gilt centrepieces, candelabra, inlaid caskets, reproductions of famous triumphal columns, etc., stand on Louis XV marble mantelpieces, ormolu commodes, or else occupy positions in the centre of the rooms. There is also a collection of paintings of the Sultans, which is not on view to the public as yet. It is needless to say that the view from the kiosk is unsurpassed. In latter years the kiosk was used as the reception-room for important visitors to the Seraglio, and here it was that coffee, cigarettes, and rose-leaf jam were served before the inspection of the courts began.

The only other buildings in the court consist of a little kiosk called *Esvap Odasi*, or Chamber of Robes (which apparently was used for

[1] For further details see the modern Turkish guide-book, *Topkapi Sarayi Müzesi Rehberi*, p. 150.

donning ceremonial robes for receptions held in the *Mecidiye Köşkü*), and the *Sofa Camii*, or mosque for the servants of the Pavilion of the Holy Mantle.

There remains but to speak of the gardens and to give a short account of the famous tulip *fête* as held during the reign of Mahmud I. Most of the Sultans were really interested in the Seraglio gardens, and each made some addition either by laying out an entirely new garden or by the introduction of some hitherto unknown plants or trees. Ibrahim was particularly fond of tulips, while Muhammad IV favoured the Ranunculus genus, having roots and seeds sent by his Pashas from all parts of Syria and the islands in the Mediterranean. But other flowers, such as the rose, the carnation, the hyacinth, and the lilac, were also cultivated to a large extent, and not only in this garden, but in that of the Summer Palace, near Seraglio Point, as well; and at one time they must have been a marvellous sight to behold.

To-day no trace of the past glory remains, and a box-hedge and a few scattered trees are all that is left.

It was, however, in the reign of Ahmed III that the tulip reached its height and actually began to interfere with State business and to prove a drain on the national resources by the reckless extravagance of the *fêtes*, which seemed to be regarded as even more important than the great national festivals themselves. In the next reign, that of Mahmud I, the tulip cult was still continued, but in a lesser degree; and it was during this period that Flachat made his observations. He has left us a detailed account of a tulip *fête* which well deserves inclusion here:

> It takes place in April. Wooden frames [or 'galleries'] are erected in the courtyard of the New Serail, on both sides of which rows of shelves are arranged for the setting out of the vases containing the tulips in the form of an amphitheatre. Alternating with the vases are lamps, and from the topmost shelves cages of canaries hang, with glass balls filled with different coloured waters. The reverberation of the light affords as pleasing a prospect in the day-time as it does at night. The extensive walk in the enclosure formed by the wooden structures offers to the sight various well-designed edifices, such as pyramids, towers, and floral bowers set up in different places.
>
> Art creates illusion, harmony makes such lovely places live, and one imagines oneself suddenly transported to the palace of one's dreams.

The Sultan's kiosk, or pavilion, is in the centre. It is there that the presents sent by the Court grandees are displayed. They are pointed out to his Highness, the source of origin being explained in each case. It is a good opportunity to show one's anxiety to please. Ambition and rivalry strive to create something new. At any rate, whatever may be lacking in originality and rarity is balanced in richness and magnificence.

When all is ready the Grand Seigneur causes *kalvet* [the state of complete privacy, either alone or with the *harēm*] to be announced. All the gates of the Serail leading to the garden are closed. The *Bostanchis* stand on guard outside, and the black eunuchs inside. All the Sultanas come there from the *Karem* after the Sultan. The *Keslar Aga*, at the head of the other eunuchs, officiates. The women rush out on all sides, like a swarm of bees settling on the flowers and stopping continually at the honey they find. There are numbers of them of every kind and sort. The *Keslar Aga* has assured me several times that the gaiety of these occasions seems to bring out any skill they claim to possess, or arts which they display in anything they do to amuse. Those little games that the poets invented for Cupid and the nymphs may give some slight idea. Each tries to distinguish herself; they are all a mass of charms; each has the same object to accomplish. One has never seen elsewhere to what lengths the resources of the intellect can go with young women who want to seduce a man they love through vanity, and especially by natural inclination. The grace of the dance, the melody of the voice, the harmony of the music, the elegance of the dresses, the wit of the conversation, the ecstasies, the effeminacy, and love—the most voluptuous, I may add, that the cleverest coquetry has invented—all unite in this delightful spot under the eyes of the Sultan.

The *Kiahia Caden* finally presents to him the girl that most takes his fancy. No pains have been spared to ensure her success. She hastens to exhibit every pleasing talent she possesses. The handkerchief that he throws to her signifies his wish to be alone with her.

The curtain which covers the sofa on which he is sitting is made to fall. The *Keslar Aga* remains to pull it aside again at the first signal, and the other women, who have scattered here and there, all occupied —some with dancing, others with singing, these with playing on their instruments, and those with partaking of refreshments—all come to the kiosque in a moment to pay their respects to the Sultan and congratulate the new favourite. The *fête* continues some time longer, and terminates by the distribution which the *Keslar Aga* makes of jewels, stuffs, and trinkets, following the wishes of his master. The presents are proportional to the pleasure received. But Mahamout always saw to it that they were of sufficient value for the girls to return to the Karem with an air of gratitude and contentment.

The Sultan's evening is spent in receiving the compliments of the chief officers of the Court and all the Grandees of the Empire. Each arranges himself in the room according to his rank, and the entire Serail is illuminated.[1]

As Flachat got most of his information direct from his friend the *Kislar Agha* we can conclude that the account is reliable, and if so this is further evidence of the existence of the custom of 'throwing the handkerchief' in the selecting of a concubine.

Passing out of the garden through the Third Gate, the visitor will soon find himself opposite the Goths' Column, which stands there as if to remind him of the ancient glories of this unsurpassable promontory.

[1] *Observations sur le commerce*, vol. ii, pp. 20–24.

KEY

1. Central Gate (*Ortakapi*).
2. Tomb(?) and ruined fountain.
3. Small iron door leading under the wall to the waterworks.
4. Two wells, connected with the large one behind.
5. Well, with spiral stone stairs, steel bridge, and hydraulic engine (*Dolap Ocaği*).
6–17. The kitchens and quarters of the cooks, confectioners, porters, scullions, etc. (*Mutfaklar ve Müştemilâti*):
   6. Entrance into kitchen quarters for produce, etc.
   7. Quarters of the food porters (*Tablakâr Koğuşu*).
   8. Kitchen Superintendent (*Mutfaklar Mubassir*).
   9. Storerooms (*kilcr*).
   10. Cooks' quarters (*Aşçi Koğuşu*).
   11. Cooks' mosque (*Aşçi Camii*).
   12. Store for kitchen utensils (*Mutfaklar Fdevat*).
   13. Tinning shop (*Kalaylik*) for kitchen utensils.
   14. Quarters of assistant cooks, confectioners, and various other kitchen attendants.
   15. Kitchen corridor (*yol*).
   16a–16l. The kitchens:
      16a. Sultan.
      16b. Sultan Valide.
      16c. Kadins.
      16d. Kapi Agha.
      16e. Members of the Divan.
      16f. Iç-oghlans, or Sultan's pages.
      16g. Humbler members of the Seraglio.
      16h. Other women.
      16j. Less important members of the Divan.
      16k. Confectioners.
      16l. Anteroom or pantry to confectioners' kitchen. Possibly also used as a coffee-room for the staff.
   17. Confectioners' mosque (*Şekerci Camii*).
18. Gate of the Dead (*Meyyit Kapi*).
19. Mosque and bath of Beşir Ağa.
20. Privy Stables and harness store (*Raht Hazinesi*).
21. Quarters of the halberdiers (*Zülüflü Baltacilar Koğuşu*).
22. Divan Tower (*Kule*).
23. Hall of the Divan (*Kubbealti*).
24. Registry for the preparation and storing of Divan documents (*Defterhane*).
25. Private office of the Grand Vizir.
26. Inner Treasury (*Içhazine*), now the Arms Museum (*Silâh Müzesi*).
27. Quarters of the white eunuchs (*Akağalar Koğuşu*).
28. Suite of the Chief White Eunuch (*Kapiağası Dairesi*).
29. Gate of Felicity (*Bab-i-Sa'adet*), or Gate of the White Eunuchs (*Akağalar Kapisi*).
30. Carriage Gate (*Araba Kapisi*).
31. Domed Anteroom with Cupboards (*Dolapli Kubbe*).
32. Vestibule with fountain (*Şadirvan*), leading on the south side to the tower steps and the secret grille window of the Hall of the Divan; and on the north side to the

Curtain or Shawl Gate (*Perde Kapisi*), the name being also given to the exit gate at the far end of the narrow passage (see No. 62).
33. Mosque of the black eunuchs (*Karaağalar Camii*).
34. Courtyard of the black eunuchs (*Karaağalar Taşliği*).
35. Quarters of the black eunuchs (*Haremağalar Dairesi*).
36. Princes' School (*Şehzadegân Mektebi*).
37. Suite of the Chief Black Eunuch (*Kislarağasi Dairesi*).
38. Suite of the Treasurer (*Hazinedar Dairesi*).
39. Suite of the Chamberlain (*Musahiban Dairesi*).
40. Gate of the Aviary (*Kuşhane Kapisi*).
41. Main harêm gate (*Harêm Çümlekapisi*).
42. Guard-room (*Nöbetyeri*).
43. Quarters of the harêm slaves (*Cariyeler Dairesi*).
44. Courtyard of the harêm slaves (*Cariyeler Taşliği*).
45. Harêm slaves' kitchen (*Cariyeler Mutfaklar*).
46. Harêm slaves' bathrooms (*Cariyeler Hamami*).
47. Stairway leading to bedrooms.
48. Commissariat department (see also No. 51).
49. Harêm laundry (*Harêm Çamaşirlik*).
50. Clothes store, or part of the laundry.
51. Lower, or ground-floor, part of harêm slaves' bedrooms. These are chiefly on the first floor and, with the entrance at No. 47, stretch over Nos. 48 and 51, there being a rectangular well through which the ground floor of No. 51 can be seen.
52. Suite of the Head Laundress (*Çamaşirci Usta Dairesi*).
53. Suite of the harêm mistress (*Ketkhuda* or *Kiaya Dairesi*).
54. Suite of the Head Nurse (*Dadi Usta Dairesi*).
55. Flight of fifty-three steps to lower terrace.
56. Hospital of harêm slaves (*Cariyeler Hastanesi*).
57. Hospital bedrooms or sitting-rooms, etc.
58. Hospital baths (*Hastanesi Hamami*).
59. Hospital cooks' quarters (*Hastanesi Aşçi Koğuşu*).
60. Hospital kitchen (*Hastanesi Mutfaklar*).
61. Hospital lavatories.
62. Shawl Gate (*Perde Kapisi*), the name being also applied to the gate at the other end of the long passage leading into No. 32.
63. Kiosk of Sultan Ahmed (*Sultanahmet Köşkü*).
64. Courtyard of the Sultan Valide (*Valde Taşliği*).
65. Reception-rooms (*sofasi*) of the Sultan Valide.
66. Corridor (*koridoru*) of the Sultan Valide.
67. Dining-room (*yemek odasi*) of the Sultan Valide.
68. Bedroom (*yatak odasi*) of the Sultan Valide.

Key continued on pg. 260D

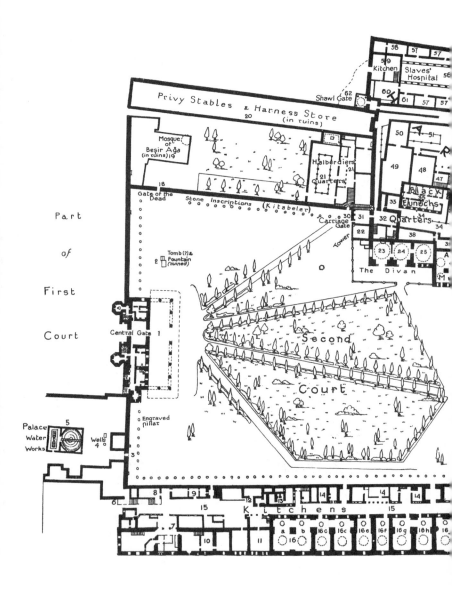

Part

of

First

Court

Privy Stables & Harness Store
(in ruins)
20

Mosque of Beşir Ağa (in ruins) 19

Gate of the Dead
18

Stone Inscriptions (Kitabeler)

Tomb (?) & Fountain (ruined)
2

Central Gate 1

Engraved Niñat

Palace Water Works
5

Wells
4

3

8   9

6

15

7   10   11

Kitchens

Shawl Gate
62

Kitchen
59

Slaves' Hospital
56

58   57   57

61   57   57

60

50

49   48

A   51

47

33   35   Eunuchs
Quartiers   34

Halberdiers Quarters
21   21

Carriage Gate
30   31   32
22   38

Tower

23   24   25

The Divan

Second

Court

12   13   14   14   4   14

15

a   b   16a   16b   16c   16d   16e   16f   16g   16h   16

N

85 Osman Kiosk
85

Courtyard of
84 Osman III

83

82
77
89 88
78
80 79 81
Royal Saloon
77
87

81
71 S
86
E
64 69
L
72
90 The
Urtyard
70 68
Cage
f Sultan
74 73 76
alide
75 Road
den 75
91 A M L I K
92
93
Hall of 94 Circumcision 115
Baghdad Kiosk
114
Pool
95
116
Pool
95
100
98 New Library
Sili
Pavilion of
110
of Holy Mantle
Royal Chamber
Revan Kiosk
113
99
Gate of the Fountain
117
Marble Mounting Block
109
Kiosk of Mustafa Pasha 118
Throne 96 Room
97
Library of Ahmed III
Third
Court
108 Hall of the Treasury
Pool
119
Chamber of Chief Physician
The Third Gate 125
Fourth Court
107 Hall of the Pantry
121
Kiosk of Abd ul-Mejid
120
101
Treasury
106
105
122 Mosque
103
M U s e u M
105
105
Baths of Selim II 104
M U s e u m 105

Scale: 0 30 60 90 120 feet
Approximately

Key continued

69. Gate of the Throne (*Taht Kapisi*).
70. Vestibule of the Hearth (*Ocakli Sofa*).
71. Vestibule of the Fountain (*Çeşmeli Sofa*).
72. Harēm treasury (*Hazine*).
73. Suite of the *kadins* (*Kadinlar Dairesi*).
74. Suite of the Head Kadin (*Başkadin Dairesi*).
75. Golden Road (*Altinyol*).
76. Place of Consultation of the Jinn (*Jin Müşaveret Mahalle*).
77. Royal Saloon (*Hünkâr Sofasi*).
78. Corridor of the Bath (*Hamam Yolu*).
79. Sultan's bath (*Hünkâr Hamami*)
80. Bath of the Sultan Validé (*Valde Hamami*).
81. Storerooms, boiler-rooms to Royal baths, etc.
82. Bedroom of Abd ul-Hamid I (*Hamit I Yatak Odasi*).
83. Room of Selim III (*Selim III Odasi*).
84. Courtyard of Osman III with vine trellis (*Asma Bahice ve Havuzlu Taşlik*).
85. Wall kiosk of Osman III (*Osman III Köşkü*).
86. Anteroom (*geçit yeri*) of Murad III.
87. Bedroom (*yatak odasi*) of Murad III.
88. Library (*Kütüphanesi*) of Ahmed I.
89. Dining-room (*yemek odasi*) of Ahmed III.
90. The Cage (*Kafes*), suite of the heir (*Veliaht Dairesi*).
91. Courtyard of the Cage (*Kafes Taşliği*).
92. Reception-room of the *selâmlik* (*Mabeyin Hümayun*).
93. Terrace enclosed by a glass partition (temporary).
94. Hall of Circumcision (*Sünnet Odasi*).
95. Pillared Hall of the Holy Mantle suite.
96. Throne Room (*Arzodasi*).
97. Library (*Kütüphanesi*) of Ahmed III.
98. New Library (*Yeni Kütüphane*), formerly the Mosque of the Palace School.

99. Reading-room for students (*Mütalea Salonu*), formerly the Mosque of Ahmed.
100. Harēm mosque (*Harēm camii*).
101. Courtyard (*taşlik*).
102. Director's quarters; boilers to Selim II baths were once here.
103. Hall of Campaign (*Seferli Koğuşu*), now the Porcelain collection (*Çini Hazinesi*).
104. Baths of Selim II, now the glass and silver collection (*Gümüş ve Billûr Salonu*).
105. Treasury (*Hazine*), now the Seraglio Museum.
106. Ambassador's Treasury (*Elçi Hazinesi*), also part of the Museum.
107. Hall of the Pantry (*Kiler Koğuşu*), now the Museum Directorate (*Müze Müdiriyet Dairesi*). Underneath the Hall, in the south side near the Treasury, runs a narrow passage (*kemeralti*) connecting the Third and Fourth Courts.
108. Hall of the Treasury (*Hazine Koğuşu*) now the Museum store.
109. Treasury deposit (*Emanat Hazinesi*).
110. Pavilion of the Holy Mantle (*Hirkai Sa'adet Dairesi*).
111. Royal Chamber (*Hasodalilar Koğuşu*), now used for official purposes.
112. Former suites for the higher members of the Royal Chamber.
113. Revan Kiosk (*Revan Köşkü*).
114. Baghdad Kiosk (*Bağdat Köşkü*).
115. Terrace (*Sultan Ibrahim kameriyesi*).
116. Pool (*havuz*).
117. Former tulip garden (*Lâle Bahçesi*).
118. Kiosk of Mustafa Pasha (*Mustafapaşa Köşkü*).
119. Chamber of the Chief Physician (*Hekimbaşi Odasi*).
120. Kiosk of Abd ul-Mejid (*Mecidiye Köşkü*).
121. Chamber of Robes (*Esvap Odasi*).
122. Mosque of Holy Mantle attendants (*Sofa Camii*).
123. The Third Gate (*Üçüncü Kapi*).

INDEX

A CATALOG OF SELECTED
DOVER BOOKS
IN ALL FIELDS OF INTEREST

A CATALOG OF SELECTED DOVER
BOOKS IN ALL FIELDS OF INTEREST

CONCERNING THE SPIRITUAL IN ART, Wassily Kandinsky. Pioneering work by father of abstract art. Thoughts on color theory, nature of art. Analysis of earlier masters. 12 illustrations. 80pp. of text. 5⅜ x 8½. 23411-8

ANIMALS: 1,419 Copyright-Free Illustrations of Mammals, Birds, Fish, Insects, etc., Jim Harter (ed.). Clear wood engravings present, in extremely lifelike poses, over 1,000 species of animals. One of the most extensive pictorial sourcebooks of its kind. Captions. Index. 284pp. 9 x 12. 23766-4

CELTIC ART: The Methods of Construction, George Bain. Simple geometric techniques for making Celtic interlacements, spirals, Kells-type initials, animals, humans, etc. Over 500 illustrations. 160pp. 9 x 12. (Available in U.S. only.) 22923-8

AN ATLAS OF ANATOMY FOR ARTISTS, Fritz Schider. Most thorough reference work on art anatomy in the world. Hundreds of illustrations, including selections from works by Vesalius, Leonardo, Goya, Ingres, Michelangelo, others. 593 illustrations. 192pp. 7⅛ x 10¼. 20241-0

CELTIC HAND STROKE-BY-STROKE (Irish Half-Uncial from "The Book of Kells"): An Arthur Baker Calligraphy Manual, Arthur Baker. Complete guide to creating each letter of the alphabet in distinctive Celtic manner. Covers hand position, strokes, pens, inks, paper, more. Illustrated. 48pp. 8¼ x 11. 24336-2

EASY ORIGAMI, John Montroll. Charming collection of 32 projects (hat, cup, pelican, piano, swan, many more) specially designed for the novice origami hobbyist. Clearly illustrated easy-to-follow instructions insure that even beginning papercrafters will achieve successful results. 48pp. 8¼ x 11. 27298-2

THE COMPLETE BOOK OF BIRDHOUSE CONSTRUCTION FOR WOODWORKERS, Scott D. Campbell. Detailed instructions, illustrations, tables. Also data on bird habitat and instinct patterns. Bibliography. 3 tables. 63 illustrations in 15 figures. 48pp. 5¼ x 8½. 24407-5

BLOOMINGDALE'S ILLUSTRATED 1886 CATALOG: Fashions, Dry Goods and Housewares, Bloomingdale Brothers. Famed merchants' extremely rare catalog depicting about 1,700 products: clothing, housewares, firearms, dry goods, jewelry, more. Invaluable for dating, identifying vintage items. Also, copyright-free graphics for artists, designers. Co-published with Henry Ford Museum & Greenfield Village. 160pp. 8¼ x 11. 25780-0

HISTORIC COSTUME IN PICTURES, Braun & Schneider. Over 1,450 costumed figures in clearly detailed engravings—from dawn of civilization to end of 19th century. Captions. Many folk costumes. 256pp. 8⅜ x 11¾. 23150-X

STICKLEY CRAFTSMAN FURNITURE CATALOGS, Gustav Stickley and L. & J. G. Stickley. Beautiful, functional furniture in two authentic catalogs from 1910. 594 illustrations, including 277 photos, show settles, rockers, armchairs, reclining chairs, bookcases, desks, tables. 183pp. 6½ x 9¼. 23838-5

AMERICAN LOCOMOTIVES IN HISTORIC PHOTOGRAPHS: 1858 to 1949, Ron Ziel (ed.). A rare collection of 126 meticulously detailed official photographs, called "builder portraits," of American locomotives that majestically chronicle the rise of steam locomotive power in America. Introduction. Detailed captions. xi+ 129pp. 9 x 12. 27393-8

AMERICA'S LIGHTHOUSES: An Illustrated History, Francis Ross Holland, Jr. Delightfully written, profusely illustrated fact-filled survey of over 200 American lighthouses since 1716. History, anecdotes, technological advances, more. 240pp. 8 x 10¾. 25576-X

TOWARDS A NEW ARCHITECTURE, Le Corbusier. Pioneering manifesto by founder of "International School." Technical and aesthetic theories, views of industry, economics, relation of form to function, "mass-production split" and much more. Profusely illustrated. 320pp. 6⅛ x 9¼. (Available in U.S. only.) 25023-7

HOW THE OTHER HALF LIVES, Jacob Riis. Famous journalistic record, exposing poverty and degradation of New York slums around 1900, by major social reformer. 100 striking and influential photographs. 233pp. 10 x 7⅞. 22012-5

FRUIT KEY AND TWIG KEY TO TREES AND SHRUBS, William M. Harlow. One of the handiest and most widely used identification aids. Fruit key covers 120 deciduous and evergreen species; twig key 160 deciduous species. Easily used. Over 300 photographs. 126pp. 5⅜ x 8½. 20511-8

COMMON BIRD SONGS, Dr. Donald J. Borror. Songs of 60 most common U.S. birds: robins, sparrows, cardinals, bluejays, finches, more–arranged in order of increasing complexity. Up to 9 variations of songs of each species.
Cassette and manual 99911-4

ORCHIDS AS HOUSE PLANTS, Rebecca Tyson Northen. Grow cattleyas and many other kinds of orchids–in a window, in a case, or under artificial light. 63 illustrations. 148pp. 5⅜ x 8½. 23261-1

MONSTER MAZES, Dave Phillips. Masterful mazes at four levels of difficulty. Avoid deadly perils and evil creatures to find magical treasures. Solutions for all 32 exciting illustrated puzzles. 48pp. 8¼ x 11. 26005-4

MOZART'S DON GIOVANNI (DOVER OPERA LIBRETTO SERIES), Wolfgang Amadeus Mozart. Introduced and translated by Ellen H. Bleiler. Standard Italian libretto, with complete English translation. Convenient and thoroughly portable–an ideal companion for reading along with a recording or the performance itself. Introduction. List of characters. Plot summary. 121pp. 5¼ x 8½. 24944-1

TECHNICAL MANUAL AND DICTIONARY OF CLASSICAL BALLET, Gail Grant. Defines, explains, comments on steps, movements, poses and concepts. 15-page pictorial section. Basic book for student, viewer. 127pp. 5⅜ x 8½. 21843-0

THE CLARINET AND CLARINET PLAYING, David Pino. Lively, comprehensive work features suggestions about technique, musicianship, and musical interpretation, as well as guidelines for teaching, making your own reeds, and preparing for public performance. Includes an intriguing look at clarinet history. "A godsend," *The Clarinet,* Journal of the International Clarinet Society. Appendixes. 7 illus. 320pp. 5⅜ x 8½. 40270-3

HOLLYWOOD GLAMOR PORTRAITS, John Kobal (ed.). 145 photos from 1926-49. Harlow, Gable, Bogart, Bacall; 94 stars in all. Full background on photographers, technical aspects. 160pp. 8⅜ x 11¼. 23352-9

THE ANNOTATED CASEY AT THE BAT: A Collection of Ballads about the Mighty Casey/Third, Revised Edition, Martin Gardner (ed.). Amusing sequels and parodies of one of America's best-loved poems: Casey's Revenge, Why Casey Whiffed, Casey's Sister at the Bat, others. 256pp. 5⅜ x 8½. 28598-7

THE RAVEN AND OTHER FAVORITE POEMS, Edgar Allan Poe. Over 40 of the author's most memorable poems: "The Bells," "Ulalume," "Israfel," "To Helen," "The Conqueror Worm," "Eldorado," "Annabel Lee," many more. Alphabetic lists of titles and first lines. 64pp. 5$\frac{3}{16}$ x 8¼. 26685-0

PERSONAL MEMOIRS OF U. S. GRANT, Ulysses Simpson Grant. Intelligent, deeply moving firsthand account of Civil War campaigns, considered by many the finest military memoirs ever written. Includes letters, historic photographs, maps and more. 528pp. 6⅛ x 9¼. 28587-1

ANCIENT EGYPTIAN MATERIALS AND INDUSTRIES, A. Lucas and J. Harris. Fascinating, comprehensive, thoroughly documented text describes this ancient civilization's vast resources and the processes that incorporated them in daily life, including the use of animal products, building materials, cosmetics, perfumes and incense, fibers, glazed ware, glass and its manufacture, materials used in the mummification process, and much more. 544pp. 6⅛ x 9¼. (Available in U.S. only.) 40446-3

RUSSIAN STORIES/RUSSKIE RASSKAZY: A Dual-Language Book, edited by Gleb Struve. Twelve tales by such masters as Chekhov, Tolstoy, Dostoevsky, Pushkin, others. Excellent word-for-word English translations on facing pages, plus teaching and study aids, Russian/English vocabulary, biographical/critical introductions, more. 416pp. 5⅜ x 8½. 26244-8

PHILADELPHIA THEN AND NOW: 60 Sites Photographed in the Past and Present, Kenneth Finkel and Susan Oyama. Rare photographs of City Hall, Logan Square, Independence Hall, Betsy Ross House, other landmarks juxtaposed with contemporary views. Captures changing face of historic city. Introduction. Captions. 128pp. 8¼ x 11. 25790-8

AIA ARCHITECTURAL GUIDE TO NASSAU AND SUFFOLK COUNTIES, LONG ISLAND, The American Institute of Architects, Long Island Chapter, and the Society for the Preservation of Long Island Antiquities. Comprehensive, well-researched and generously illustrated volume brings to life over three centuries of Long Island's great architectural heritage. More than 240 photographs with authoritative, extensively detailed captions. 176pp. 8¼ x 11. 26946-9

NORTH AMERICAN INDIAN LIFE: Customs and Traditions of 23 Tribes, Elsie Clews Parsons (ed.). 27 fictionalized essays by noted anthropologists examine religion, customs, government, additional facets of life among the Winnebago, Crow, Zuni, Eskimo, other tribes. 480pp. 6⅛ x 9¼. 27377-6

FRANK LLOYD WRIGHT'S DANA HOUSE, Donald Hoffmann. Pictorial essay of residential masterpiece with over 160 interior and exterior photos, plans, elevations, sketches and studies. 128pp. 9¼ x 10¾.   29120-0

THE MALE AND FEMALE FIGURE IN MOTION: 60 Classic Photographic Sequences, Eadweard Muybridge. 60 true-action photographs of men and women walking, running, climbing, bending, turning, etc., reproduced from rare 19th-century masterpiece. vi + 121pp. 9 x 12.   24745-7

1001 QUESTIONS ANSWERED ABOUT THE SEASHORE, N. J. Berrill and Jacquelyn Berrill. Queries answered about dolphins, sea snails, sponges, starfish, fishes, shore birds, many others. Covers appearance, breeding, growth, feeding, much more. 305pp. 5¼ x 8¼.   23366-9

ATTRACTING BIRDS TO YOUR YARD, William J. Weber. Easy-to-follow guide offers advice on how to attract the greatest diversity of birds: birdhouses, feeders, water and waterers, much more. 96pp. 5³⁄₁₆ x 8¼.   28927-3

MEDICINAL AND OTHER USES OF NORTH AMERICAN PLANTS: A Historical Survey with Special Reference to the Eastern Indian Tribes, Charlotte Erichsen-Brown. Chronological historical citations document 500 years of usage of plants, trees, shrubs native to eastern Canada, northeastern U.S. Also complete identifying information. 343 illustrations. 544pp. 6½ x 9¼.   25951-X

STORYBOOK MAZES, Dave Phillips. 23 stories and mazes on two-page spreads: Wizard of Oz, Treasure Island, Robin Hood, etc. Solutions. 64pp. 8¼ x 11. 23628-5

AMERICAN NEGRO SONGS: 230 Folk Songs and Spirituals, Religious and Secular, John W. Work. This authoritative study traces the African influences of songs sung and played by black Americans at work, in church, and as entertainment. The author discusses the lyric significance of such songs as "Swing Low, Sweet Chariot," "John Henry," and others and offers the words and music for 230 songs. Bibliography. Index of Song Titles. 272pp. 6½ x 9¼.   40271-1

MOVIE-STAR PORTRAITS OF THE FORTIES, John Kobal (ed.). 163 glamor, studio photos of 106 stars of the 1940s: Rita Hayworth, Ava Gardner, Marlon Brando, Clark Gable, many more. 176pp. 8⅜ x 11¼.   23546-7

BENCHLEY LOST AND FOUND, Robert Benchley. Finest humor from early 30s, about pet peeves, child psychologists, post office and others. Mostly unavailable elsewhere. 73 illustrations by Peter Arno and others. 183pp. 5⅜ x 8½.   22410-4

YEKL and THE IMPORTED BRIDEGROOM AND OTHER STORIES OF YIDDISH NEW YORK, Abraham Cahan. Film Hester Street based on *Yekl* (1896). Novel, other stories among first about Jewish immigrants on N.Y.'s East Side. 240pp. 5⅜ x 8½.   22427-9

SELECTED POEMS, Walt Whitman. Generous sampling from *Leaves of Grass*. Twenty-four poems include "I Hear America Singing," "Song of the Open Road," "I Sing the Body Electric," "When Lilacs Last in the Dooryard Bloom'd," "O Captain! My Captain!"–all reprinted from an authoritative edition. Lists of titles and first lines. 128pp. 5³⁄₁₆ x 8¼.   26878-0

THE BEST TALES OF HOFFMANN, E. T. A. Hoffmann. 10 of Hoffmann's most important stories: "Nutcracker and the King of Mice," "The Golden Flowerpot," etc. 458pp. 5⅜ x 8½. 21793-0

FROM FETISH TO GOD IN ANCIENT EGYPT, E. A. Wallis Budge. Rich detailed survey of Egyptian conception of "God" and gods, magic, cult of animals, Osiris, more. Also, superb English translations of hymns and legends. 240 illustrations. 545pp. 5⅜ x 8½. 25803-3

FRENCH STORIES/CONTES FRANÇAIS: A Dual-Language Book, Wallace Fowlie. Ten stories by French masters, Voltaire to Camus: "Micromegas" by Voltaire; "The Atheist's Mass" by Balzac; "Minuet" by de Maupassant; "The Guest" by Camus, six more. Excellent English translations on facing pages. Also French-English vocabulary list, exercises, more. 352pp. 5⅜ x 8½. 26443-2

CHICAGO AT THE TURN OF THE CENTURY IN PHOTOGRAPHS: 122 Historic Views from the Collections of the Chicago Historical Society, Larry A. Viskochil. Rare large-format prints offer detailed views of City Hall, State Street, the Loop, Hull House, Union Station, many other landmarks, circa 1904-1913. Introduction. Captions. Maps. 144pp. 9⅜ x 12¼. 24656-6

OLD BROOKLYN IN EARLY PHOTOGRAPHS, 1865-1929, William Lee Younger. Luna Park, Gravesend race track, construction of Grand Army Plaza, moving of Hotel Brighton, etc. 157 previously unpublished photographs. 165pp. 8⅞ x 11¾. 23587-4

THE MYTHS OF THE NORTH AMERICAN INDIANS, Lewis Spence. Rich anthology of the myths and legends of the Algonquins, Iroquois, Pawnees and Sioux, prefaced by an extensive historical and ethnological commentary. 36 illustrations. 480pp. 5⅜ x 8½. 25967-6

AN ENCYCLOPEDIA OF BATTLES: Accounts of Over 1,560 Battles from 1479 B.C. to the Present, David Eggenberger. Essential details of every major battle in recorded history from the first battle of Megiddo in 1479 B.C. to Grenada in 1984. List of Battle Maps. New Appendix covering the years 1967-1984. Index. 99 illustrations. 544pp. 6½ x 9¼. 24913-1

SAILING ALONE AROUND THE WORLD, Captain Joshua Slocum. First man to sail around the world, alone, in small boat. One of great feats of seamanship told in delightful manner. 67 illustrations. 294pp. 5⅜ x 8½. 20326-3

ANARCHISM AND OTHER ESSAYS, Emma Goldman. Powerful, penetrating, prophetic essays on direct action, role of minorities, prison reform, puritan hypocrisy, violence, etc. 271pp. 5⅜ x 8½. 22484-8

MYTHS OF THE HINDUS AND BUDDHISTS, Ananda K. Coomaraswamy and Sister Nivedita. Great stories of the epics; deeds of Krishna, Shiva, taken from puranas, Vedas, folk tales; etc. 32 illustrations. 400pp. 5⅜ x 8½. 21759-0

THE TRAUMA OF BIRTH, Otto Rank. Rank's controversial thesis that anxiety neurosis is caused by profound psychological trauma which occurs at birth. 256pp. 5⅜ x 8½. 27974-X

A THEOLOGICO-POLITICAL TREATISE, Benedict Spinoza. Also contains unfinished Political Treatise. Great classic on religious liberty, theory of government on common consent. R. Elwes translation. Total of 421pp. 5⅜ x 8½. 20249-6

MY BONDAGE AND MY FREEDOM, Frederick Douglass. Born a slave, Douglass became outspoken force in antislavery movement. The best of Douglass' autobiographies. Graphic description of slave life. 464pp. 5⅜ x 8½.	22457-0

FOLLOWING THE EQUATOR: A Journey Around the World, Mark Twain. Fascinating humorous account of 1897 voyage to Hawaii, Australia, India, New Zealand, etc. Ironic, bemused reports on peoples, customs, climate, flora and fauna, politics, much more. 197 illustrations. 720pp. 5⅜ x 8½.	26113-1

THE PEOPLE CALLED SHAKERS, Edward D. Andrews. Definitive study of Shakers: origins, beliefs, practices, dances, social organization, furniture and crafts, etc. 33 illustrations. 351pp. 5⅜ x 8½.	21081-2

THE MYTHS OF GREECE AND ROME, H. A. Guerber. A classic of mythology, generously illustrated, long prized for its simple, graphic, accurate retelling of the principal myths of Greece and Rome, and for its commentary on their origins and significance. With 64 illustrations by Michelangelo, Raphael, Titian, Rubens, Canova, Bernini and others. 480pp. 5⅜ x 8½.	27584-1

PSYCHOLOGY OF MUSIC, Carl E. Seashore. Classic work discusses music as a medium from psychological viewpoint. Clear treatment of physical acoustics, auditory apparatus, sound perception, development of musical skills, nature of musical feeling, host of other topics. 88 figures. 408pp. 5⅜ x 8½.	21851-1

THE PHILOSOPHY OF HISTORY, Georg W. Hegel. Great classic of Western thought develops concept that history is not chance but rational process, the evolution of freedom. 457pp. 5⅜ x 8½.	20112-0

THE BOOK OF TEA, Kakuzo Okakura. Minor classic of the Orient: entertaining, charming explanation, interpretation of traditional Japanese culture in terms of tea ceremony. 94pp. 5⅜ x 8½.	20070-1

LIFE IN ANCIENT EGYPT, Adolf Erman. Fullest, most thorough, detailed older account with much not in more recent books, domestic life, religion, magic, medicine, commerce, much more. Many illustrations reproduce tomb paintings, carvings, hieroglyphs, etc. 597pp. 5⅜ x 8½.	22632-8

SUNDIALS, Their Theory and Construction, Albert Waugh. Far and away the best, most thorough coverage of ideas, mathematics concerned, types, construction, adjusting anywhere. Simple, nontechnical treatment allows even children to build several of these dials. Over 100 illustrations. 230pp. 5⅜ x 8½.	22947-5

THEORETICAL HYDRODYNAMICS, L. M. Milne-Thomson. Classic exposition of the mathematical theory of fluid motion, applicable to both hydrodynamics and aerodynamics. Over 600 exercises. 768pp. 6⅛ x 9¼.	68970-0

SONGS OF EXPERIENCE: Facsimile Reproduction with 26 Plates in Full Color, William Blake. 26 full-color plates from a rare 1826 edition. Includes "The Tyger," "London," "Holy Thursday," and other poems. Printed text of poems. 48pp. 5¼ x 7.	24636-1

OLD-TIME VIGNETTES IN FULL COLOR, Carol Belanger Grafton (ed.). Over 390 charming, often sentimental illustrations, selected from archives of Victorian graphics—pretty women posing, children playing, food, flowers, kittens and puppies, smiling cherubs, birds and butterflies, much more. All copyright-free. 48pp. 9¼ x 12¼.	27269-9

PERSPECTIVE FOR ARTISTS, Rex Vicat Cole. Depth, perspective of sky and sea, shadows, much more, not usually covered. 391 diagrams, 81 reproductions of drawings and paintings. 279pp. 5⅜ x 8½. 22487-2

DRAWING THE LIVING FIGURE, Joseph Sheppard. Innovative approach to artistic anatomy focuses on specifics of surface anatomy, rather than muscles and bones. Over 170 drawings of live models in front, back and side views, and in widely varying poses. Accompanying diagrams. 177 illustrations. Introduction. Index. 144pp. 8⅜ x11¼. 26723-7

GOTHIC AND OLD ENGLISH ALPHABETS: 100 Complete Fonts, Dan X. Solo. Add power, elegance to posters, signs, other graphics with 100 stunning copyright-free alphabets: Blackstone, Dolbey, Germania, 97 more–including many lower-case, numerals, punctuation marks. 104pp. 8⅛ x 11. 24695-7

HOW TO DO BEADWORK, Mary White. Fundamental book on craft from simple projects to five-bead chains and woven works. 106 illustrations. 142pp. 5⅜ x 8. 20697-1

THE BOOK OF WOOD CARVING, Charles Marshall Sayers. Finest book for beginners discusses fundamentals and offers 34 designs. "Absolutely first rate . . . well thought out and well executed."–E. J. Tangerman. 118pp. 7¾ x 10⅝. 23654-4

ILLUSTRATED CATALOG OF CIVIL WAR MILITARY GOODS: Union Army Weapons, Insignia, Uniform Accessories, and Other Equipment, Schuyler, Hartley, and Graham. Rare, profusely illustrated 1846 catalog includes Union Army uniform and dress regulations, arms and ammunition, coats, insignia, flags, swords, rifles, etc. 226 illustrations. 160pp. 9 x 12. 24939-5

WOMEN'S FASHIONS OF THE EARLY 1900s: An Unabridged Republication of "New York Fashions, 1909," National Cloak & Suit Co. Rare catalog of mail-order fashions documents women's and children's clothing styles shortly after the turn of the century. Captions offer full descriptions, prices. Invaluable resource for fashion, costume historians. Approximately 725 illustrations. 128pp. 8⅜ x 11¼. 27276-1

THE 1912 AND 1915 GUSTAV STICKLEY FURNITURE CATALOGS, Gustav Stickley. With over 200 detailed illustrations and descriptions, these two catalogs are essential reading and reference materials and identification guides for Stickley furniture. Captions cite materials, dimensions and prices. 112pp. 6½ x 9¼. 26676-1

EARLY AMERICAN LOCOMOTIVES, John H. White, Jr. Finest locomotive engravings from early 19th century: historical (1804–74), main-line (after 1870), special, foreign, etc. 147 plates. 142pp. 11⅜ x 8¼. 22772-3

THE TALL SHIPS OF TODAY IN PHOTOGRAPHS, Frank O. Braynard. Lavishly illustrated tribute to nearly 100 majestic contemporary sailing vessels: Amerigo Vespucci, Clearwater, Constitution, Eagle, Mayflower, Sea Cloud, Victory, many more. Authoritative captions provide statistics, background on each ship. 190 black-and-white photographs and illustrations. Introduction. 128pp. 8⅞ x 11¾. 27163-3

LITTLE BOOK OF EARLY AMERICAN CRAFTS AND TRADES, Peter Stockham (ed.). 1807 children's book explains crafts and trades: baker, hatter, cooper, potter, and many others. 23 copperplate illustrations. 140pp. $4\frac{5}{8}$ x 6. 23336-7

VICTORIAN FASHIONS AND COSTUMES FROM HARPER'S BAZAR, 1867–1898, Stella Blum (ed.). Day costumes, evening wear, sports clothes, shoes, hats, other accessories in over 1,000 detailed engravings. 320pp. $9\frac{3}{8}$ x $12\frac{1}{4}$. 22990-4

GUSTAV STICKLEY, THE CRAFTSMAN, Mary Ann Smith. Superb study surveys broad scope of Stickley's achievement, especially in architecture. Design philosophy, rise and fall of the Craftsman empire, descriptions and floor plans for many Craftsman houses, more. 86 black-and-white halftones. 31 line illustrations. Introduction 208pp. $6\frac{1}{2}$ x $9\frac{1}{4}$. 27210-9

THE LONG ISLAND RAIL ROAD IN EARLY PHOTOGRAPHS, Ron Ziel. Over 220 rare photos, informative text document origin (1844) and development of rail service on Long Island. Vintage views of early trains, locomotives, stations, passengers, crews, much more. Captions. $8\frac{7}{8}$ x $11\frac{3}{4}$. 26301-0

VOYAGE OF THE LIBERDADE, Joshua Slocum. Great 19th-century mariner's thrilling, first-hand account of the wreck of his ship off South America, the 35-foot boat he built from the wreckage, and its remarkable voyage home. 128pp. $5\frac{3}{8}$ x $8\frac{1}{2}$. 40022-0

TEN BOOKS ON ARCHITECTURE, Vitruvius. The most important book ever written on architecture. Early Roman aesthetics, technology, classical orders, site selection, all other aspects. Morgan translation. 331pp. $5\frac{3}{8}$ x $8\frac{1}{2}$. 20645-9

THE HUMAN FIGURE IN MOTION, Eadweard Muybridge. More than 4,500 stopped-action photos, in action series, showing undraped men, women, children jumping, lying down, throwing, sitting, wrestling, carrying, etc. 390pp. $7\frac{7}{8}$ x $10\frac{5}{8}$. 20204-6 Clothbd.

TREES OF THE EASTERN AND CENTRAL UNITED STATES AND CANADA, William M. Harlow. Best one-volume guide to 140 trees. Full descriptions, woodlore, range, etc. Over 600 illustrations. Handy size. 288pp. $4\frac{1}{2}$ x $6\frac{3}{8}$. 20395-6

SONGS OF WESTERN BIRDS, Dr. Donald J. Borror. Complete song and call repertoire of 60 western species, including flycatchers, juncoes, cactus wrens, many more–includes fully illustrated booklet. Cassette and manual 99913-0

GROWING AND USING HERBS AND SPICES, Milo Miloradovich. Versatile handbook provides all the information needed for cultivation and use of all the herbs and spices available in North America. 4 illustrations. Index. Glossary. 236pp. $5\frac{3}{8}$ x $8\frac{1}{2}$. 25058-X

BIG BOOK OF MAZES AND LABYRINTHS, Walter Shepherd. 50 mazes and labyrinths in all–classical, solid, ripple, and more–in one great volume. Perfect inexpensive puzzler for clever youngsters. Full solutions. 112pp. $8\frac{1}{8}$ x 11. 22951-3

PIANO TUNING, J. Cree Fischer. Clearest, best book for beginner, amateur. Simple repairs, raising dropped notes, tuning by easy method of flattened fifths. No previous skills needed. 4 illustrations. 201pp. 5⅜ x 8½. 23267-0

HINTS TO SINGERS, Lillian Nordica. Selecting the right teacher, developing confidence, overcoming stage fright, and many other important skills receive thoughtful discussion in this indispensible guide, written by a world-famous diva of four decades' experience. 96pp. 5⅜ x 8½. 40094-8

THE COMPLETE NONSENSE OF EDWARD LEAR, Edward Lear. All nonsense limericks, zany alphabets, Owl and Pussycat, songs, nonsense botany, etc., illustrated by Lear. Total of 320pp. 5⅜ x 8½. (Available in U.S. only.) 20167-8

VICTORIAN PARLOUR POETRY: An Annotated Anthology, Michael R. Turner. 117 gems by Longfellow, Tennyson, Browning, many lesser-known poets. "The Village Blacksmith," "Curfew Must Not Ring Tonight," "Only a Baby Small," dozens more, often difficult to find elsewhere. Index of poets, titles, first lines. xxiii + 325pp. 5⅜ x 8¼. 27044-0

DUBLINERS, James Joyce. Fifteen stories offer vivid, tightly focused observations of the lives of Dublin's poorer classes. At least one, "The Dead," is considered a masterpiece. Reprinted complete and unabridged from standard edition. 160pp. 5³⁄₁₆ x 8¼. 26870-5

GREAT WEIRD TALES: 14 Stories by Lovecraft, Blackwood, Machen and Others, S. T. Joshi (ed.). 14 spellbinding tales, including "The Sin Eater," by Fiona McLeod, "The Eye Above the Mantel," by Frank Belknap Long, as well as renowned works by R. H. Barlow, Lord Dunsany, Arthur Machen, W. C. Morrow and eight other masters of the genre. 256pp. 5⅜ x 8½. (Available in U.S. only.) 40436-6

THE BOOK OF THE SACRED MAGIC OF ABRAMELIN THE MAGE, translated by S. MacGregor Mathers. Medieval manuscript of ceremonial magic. Basic document in Aleister Crowley, Golden Dawn groups. 268pp. 5⅜ x 8½. 23211-5

NEW RUSSIAN-ENGLISH AND ENGLISH-RUSSIAN DICTIONARY, M. A. O'Brien. This is a remarkably handy Russian dictionary, containing a surprising amount of information, including over 70,000 entries. 366pp. 4½ x 6⅛. 20208-9

HISTORIC HOMES OF THE AMERICAN PRESIDENTS, Second, Revised Edition, Irvin Haas. A traveler's guide to American Presidential homes, most open to the public, depicting and describing homes occupied by every American President from George Washington to George Bush. With visiting hours, admission charges, travel routes. 175 photographs. Index. 160pp. 8¼ x 11. 26751-2

NEW YORK IN THE FORTIES, Andreas Feininger. 162 brilliant photographs by the well-known photographer, formerly with *Life* magazine. Commuters, shoppers, Times Square at night, much else from city at its peak. Captions by John von Hartz. 181pp. 9¼ x 10¾. 23585-8

INDIAN SIGN LANGUAGE, William Tomkins. Over 525 signs developed by Sioux and other tribes. Written instructions and diagrams. Also 290 pictographs. 111pp. 6⅛ x 9¼. 22029-X

ANATOMY: A Complete Guide for Artists, Joseph Sheppard. A master of figure drawing shows artists how to render human anatomy convincingly. Over 460 illustrations. 224pp. 8⅜ x 11¼. 27279-6

MEDIEVAL CALLIGRAPHY: Its History and Technique, Marc Drogin. Spirited history, comprehensive instruction manual covers 13 styles (ca. 4th century through 15th). Excellent photographs; directions for duplicating medieval techniques with modern tools. 224pp. 8⅜ x 11¼. 26142-5

DRIED FLOWERS: How to Prepare Them, Sarah Whitlock and Martha Rankin. Complete instructions on how to use silica gel, meal and borax, perlite aggregate, sand and borax, glycerine and water to create attractive permanent flower arrangements. 12 illustrations. 32pp. 5⅜ x 8½. 21802-3

EASY-TO-MAKE BIRD FEEDERS FOR WOODWORKERS, Scott D. Campbell. Detailed, simple-to-use guide for designing, constructing, caring for and using feeders. Text, illustrations for 12 classic and contemporary designs. 96pp. 5⅜ x 8½.
25847-5

SCOTTISH WONDER TALES FROM MYTH AND LEGEND, Donald A. Mackenzie. 16 lively tales tell of giants rumbling down mountainsides, of a magic wand that turns stone pillars into warriors, of gods and goddesses, evil hags, powerful forces and more. 240pp. 5⅜ x 8½. 29677-6

THE HISTORY OF UNDERCLOTHES, C. Willett Cunnington and Phyllis Cunnington. Fascinating, well-documented survey covering six centuries of English undergarments, enhanced with over 100 illustrations: 12th-century laced-up bodice, footed long drawers (1795), 19th-century bustles, 19th-century corsets for men, Victorian "bust improvers," much more. 272pp. 5⅜ x 8¼. 27124-2

ARTS AND CRAFTS FURNITURE: The Complete Brooks Catalog of 1912, Brooks Manufacturing Co. Photos and detailed descriptions of more than 150 now very collectible furniture designs from the Arts and Crafts movement depict davenports, settees, buffets, desks, tables, chairs, bedsteads, dressers and more, all built of solid, quarter-sawed oak. Invaluable for students and enthusiasts of antiques, Americana and the decorative arts. 80pp. 6½ x 9¼. 27471-3

WILBUR AND ORVILLE: A Biography of the Wright Brothers, Fred Howard. Definitive, crisply written study tells the full story of the brothers' lives and work. A vividly written biography, unparalleled in scope and color, that also captures the spirit of an extraordinary era. 560pp. 6⅛ x 9¼. 40297-5

THE ARTS OF THE SAILOR: Knotting, Splicing and Ropework, Hervey Garrett Smith. Indispensable shipboard reference covers tools, basic knots and useful hitches; handsewing and canvas work, more. Over 100 illustrations. Delightful reading for sea lovers. 256pp. 5⅜ x 8½. 26440-8

FRANK LLOYD WRIGHT'S FALLINGWATER: The House and Its History, Second, Revised Edition, Donald Hoffmann. A total revision–both in text and illustrations–of the standard document on Fallingwater, the boldest, most personal architectural statement of Wright's mature years, updated with valuable new material from the recently opened Frank Lloyd Wright Archives. "Fascinating"–*The New York Times*. 116 illustrations. 128pp. 9¼ x 10¾. 27430-6

PHOTOGRAPHIC SKETCHBOOK OF THE CIVIL WAR, Alexander Gardner. 100 photos taken on field during the Civil War. Famous shots of Manassas Harper's Ferry, Lincoln, Richmond, slave pens, etc. 244pp. 10⅝ x 8¼. 22731-6

FIVE ACRES AND INDEPENDENCE, Maurice G. Kains. Great back-to-the-land classic explains basics of self-sufficient farming. The one book to get. 95 illustrations. 397pp. 5⅜ x 8½. 20974-1

SONGS OF EASTERN BIRDS, Dr. Donald J. Borror. Songs and calls of 60 species most common to eastern U.S.: warblers, woodpeckers, flycatchers, thrushes, larks, many more in high-quality recording. Cassette and manual 99912-2

A MODERN HERBAL, Margaret Grieve. Much the fullest, most exact, most useful compilation of herbal material. Gigantic alphabetical encyclopedia, from aconite to zedoary, gives botanical information, medical properties, folklore, economic uses, much else. Indispensable to serious reader. 161 illustrations. 888pp. 6½ x 9¼. 2-vol. set. (Available in U.S. only.)
Vol. I: 22798-7
Vol. II: 22799-5

HIDDEN TREASURE MAZE BOOK, Dave Phillips. Solve 34 challenging mazes accompanied by heroic tales of adventure. Evil dragons, people-eating plants, bloodthirsty giants, many more dangerous adversaries lurk at every twist and turn. 34 mazes, stories, solutions. 48pp. 8¼ x 11. 24566-7

LETTERS OF W. A. MOZART, Wolfgang A. Mozart. Remarkable letters show bawdy wit, humor, imagination, musical insights, contemporary musical world; includes some letters from Leopold Mozart. 276pp. 5⅜ x 8½. 22859-2

BASIC PRINCIPLES OF CLASSICAL BALLET, Agrippina Vaganova. Great Russian theoretician, teacher explains methods for teaching classical ballet. 118 illustrations. 175pp. 5⅜ x 8½. 22036-2

THE JUMPING FROG, Mark Twain. Revenge edition. The original story of The Celebrated Jumping Frog of Calaveras County, a hapless French translation, and Twain's hilarious "retranslation" from the French. 12 illustrations. 66pp. 5⅜ x 8½. 22686-7

BEST REMEMBERED POEMS, Martin Gardner (ed.). The 126 poems in this superb collection of 19th- and 20th-century British and American verse range from Shelley's "To a Skylark" to the impassioned "Renascence" of Edna St. Vincent Millay and to Edward Lear's whimsical "The Owl and the Pussycat." 224pp. 5⅜ x 8½. 27165-X

COMPLETE SONNETS, William Shakespeare. Over 150 exquisite poems deal with love, friendship, the tyranny of time, beauty's evanescence, death and other themes in language of remarkable power, precision and beauty. Glossary of archaic terms. 80pp. 5³⁄₁₆ x 8¼. 26686-9

THE BATTLES THAT CHANGED HISTORY, Fletcher Pratt. Eminent historian profiles 16 crucial conflicts, ancient to modern, that changed the course of civilization. 352pp. 5⅜ x 8½. 41129-X

THE WIT AND HUMOR OF OSCAR WILDE, Alvin Redman (ed.). More than 1,000 ripostes, paradoxes, wisecracks: Work is the curse of the drinking classes; I can resist everything except temptation; etc. 258pp. 5⅜ x 8½.   20602-5

SHAKESPEARE LEXICON AND QUOTATION DICTIONARY, Alexander Schmidt. Full definitions, locations, shades of meaning in every word in plays and poems. More than 50,000 exact quotations. 1,485pp. 6½ x 9¼. 2-vol. set.

Vol. 1: 22726-X
Vol. 2: 22727-8

SELECTED POEMS, Emily Dickinson. Over 100 best-known, best-loved poems by one of America's foremost poets, reprinted from authoritative early editions. No comparable edition at this price. Index of first lines. 64pp. 5³⁄₁₆ x 8¼.   26466-1

THE INSIDIOUS DR. FU-MANCHU, Sax Rohmer. The first of the popular mystery series introduces a pair of English detectives to their archnemesis, the diabolical Dr. Fu-Manchu. Flavorful atmosphere, fast-paced action, and colorful characters enliven this classic of the genre. 208pp. 5³⁄₁₆ x 8¼.   29898-1

THE MALLEUS MALEFICARUM OF KRAMER AND SPRENGER, translated by Montague Summers. Full text of most important witchhunter's "bible," used by both Catholics and Protestants. 278pp. 6⅝ x 10.   22802-9

SPANISH STORIES/CUENTOS ESPAÑOLES: A Dual-Language Book, Angel Flores (ed.). Unique format offers 13 great stories in Spanish by Cervantes, Borges, others. Faithful English translations on facing pages. 352pp. 5⅜ x 8½.   25399-6

GARDEN CITY, LONG ISLAND, IN EARLY PHOTOGRAPHS, 1869–1919, Mildred H. Smith. Handsome treasury of 118 vintage pictures, accompanied by carefully researched captions, document the Garden City Hotel fire (1899), the Vanderbilt Cup Race (1908), the first airmail flight departing from the Nassau Boulevard Aerodrome (1911), and much more. 96pp. 8⅞ x 11¾.   40669-5

OLD QUEENS, N.Y., IN EARLY PHOTOGRAPHS, Vincent F. Seyfried and William Asadorian. Over 160 rare photographs of Maspeth, Jamaica, Jackson Heights, and other areas. Vintage views of DeWitt Clinton mansion, 1939 World's Fair and more. Captions. 192pp. 8⅞ x 11.   26358-4

CAPTURED BY THE INDIANS: 15 Firsthand Accounts, 1750-1870, Frederick Drimmer. Astounding true historical accounts of grisly torture, bloody conflicts, relentless pursuits, miraculous escapes and more, by people who lived to tell the tale. 384pp. 5⅜ x 8½.   24901-8

THE WORLD'S GREAT SPEECHES (Fourth Enlarged Edition), Lewis Copeland, Lawrence W. Lamm, and Stephen J. McKenna. Nearly 300 speeches provide public speakers with a wealth of updated quotes and inspiration–from Pericles' funeral oration and William Jennings Bryan's "Cross of Gold Speech" to Malcolm X's powerful words on the Black Revolution and Earl of Spenser's tribute to his sister, Diana, Princess of Wales. 944pp. 5⅜ x 8⅜.   40903-1

THE BOOK OF THE SWORD, Sir Richard F. Burton. Great Victorian scholar/adventurer's eloquent, erudite history of the "queen of weapons"–from prehistory to early Roman Empire. Evolution and development of early swords, variations (sabre, broadsword, cutlass, scimitar, etc.), much more. 336pp. 6⅛ x 9¼.

25434-8

CATALOG OF DOVER BOOKS

AUTOBIOGRAPHY: The Story of My Experiments with Truth, Mohandas K. Gandhi. Boyhood, legal studies, purification, the growth of the Satyagraha (nonviolent protest) movement. Critical, inspiring work of the man responsible for the freedom of India. 480pp. 5⅜ x 8½. (Available in U.S. only.) 24593-4

CELTIC MYTHS AND LEGENDS, T. W. Rolleston. Masterful retelling of Irish and Welsh stories and tales. Cuchulain, King Arthur, Deirdre, the Grail, many more. First paperback edition. 58 full-page illustrations. 512pp. 5⅜ x 8½. 26507-2

THE PRINCIPLES OF PSYCHOLOGY, William James. Famous long course complete, unabridged. Stream of thought, time perception, memory, experimental methods; great work decades ahead of its time. 94 figures. 1,391pp. 5⅜ x 8½. 2-vol. set.
Vol. I: 20381-6 Vol. II: 20382-4

THE WORLD AS WILL AND REPRESENTATION, Arthur Schopenhauer. Definitive English translation of Schopenhauer's life work, correcting more than 1,000 errors, omissions in earlier translations. Translated by E. F. J. Payne. Total of 1,269pp. 5⅜ x 8½. 2-vol. set. Vol. 1: 21761-2 Vol. 2: 21762-0

MAGIC AND MYSTERY IN TIBET, Madame Alexandra David-Neel. Experiences among lamas, magicians, sages, sorcerers, Bonpa wizards. A true psychic discovery. 32 illustrations. 321pp. 5⅜ x 8½. (Available in U.S. only.) 22682-4

THE EGYPTIAN BOOK OF THE DEAD, E. A. Wallis Budge. Complete reproduction of Ani's papyrus, finest ever found. Full hieroglyphic text, interlinear transliteration, word-for-word translation, smooth translation. 533pp. 6½ x 9¼. 21866-X

MATHEMATICS FOR THE NONMATHEMATICIAN, Morris Kline. Detailed, college-level treatment of mathematics in cultural and historical context, with numerous exercises. Recommended Reading Lists. Tables. Numerous figures. 641pp. 5⅜ x 8½.
24823-2

PROBABILISTIC METHODS IN THE THEORY OF STRUCTURES, Isaac Elishakoff. Well-written introduction covers the elements of the theory of probability from two or more random variables, the reliability of such multivariable structures, the theory of random function, Monte Carlo methods of treating problems incapable of exact solution, and more. Examples. 502pp. 5⅜ x 8½. 40691-1

THE RIME OF THE ANCIENT MARINER, Gustave Doré, S. T. Coleridge. Doré's finest work; 34 plates capture moods, subtleties of poem. Flawless full-size reproductions printed on facing pages with authoritative text of poem. "Beautiful. Simply beautiful."–*Publisher's Weekly.* 77pp. 9¼ x 12. 22305-1

NORTH AMERICAN INDIAN DESIGNS FOR ARTISTS AND CRAFTSPEOPLE, Eva Wilson. Over 360 authentic copyright-free designs adapted from Navajo blankets, Hopi pottery, Sioux buffalo hides, more. Geometrics, symbolic figures, plant and animal motifs, etc. 128pp. 8⅜ x 11. (Not for sale in the United Kingdom.) 25341-4

SCULPTURE: Principles and Practice, Louis Slobodkin. Step-by-step approach to clay, plaster, metals, stone; classical and modern. 253 drawings, photos. 255pp. 8⅛ x 11.
22960-2

THE INFLUENCE OF SEA POWER UPON HISTORY, 1660–1783, A. T. Mahan. Influential classic of naval history and tactics still used as text in war colleges. First paperback edition. 4 maps. 24 battle plans. 640pp. 5⅜ x 8½. 25509-3

THE STORY OF THE TITANIC AS TOLD BY ITS SURVIVORS, Jack Winocour (ed.). What it was really like. Panic, despair, shocking inefficiency, and a little heroism. More thrilling than any fictional account. 26 illustrations. 320pp. 5⅜ x 8½.
20610-6

FAIRY AND FOLK TALES OF THE IRISH PEASANTRY, William Butler Yeats (ed.). Treasury of 64 tales from the twilight world of Celtic myth and legend: "The Soul Cages," "The Kildare Pooka," "King O'Toole and his Goose," many more. Introduction and Notes by W. B. Yeats. 352pp. 5⅜ x 8½.
26941-8

BUDDHIST MAHAYANA TEXTS, E. B. Cowell and others (eds.). Superb, accurate translations of basic documents in Mahayana Buddhism, highly important in history of religions. The Buddha-karita of Asvaghosha, Larger Sukhavativyuha, more. 448pp. 5⅜ x 8½.
25552-2

ONE TWO THREE . . . INFINITY: Facts and Speculations of Science, George Gamow. Great physicist's fascinating, readable overview of contemporary science: number theory, relativity, fourth dimension, entropy, genes, atomic structure, much more. 128 illustrations. Index. 352pp. 5⅜ x 8½.
25664-2

EXPERIMENTATION AND MEASUREMENT, W. J. Youden. Introductory manual explains laws of measurement in simple terms and offers tips for achieving accuracy and minimizing errors. Mathematics of measurement, use of instruments, experimenting with machines. 1994 edition. Foreword. Preface. Introduction. Epilogue. Selected Readings. Glossary. Index. Tables and figures. 128pp. 5⅜ x 8½.   40451-X

DALÍ ON MODERN ART: The Cuckolds of Antiquated Modern Art, Salvador Dalí. Influential painter skewers modern art and its practitioners. Outrageous evaluations of Picasso, Cézanne, Turner, more. 15 renderings of paintings discussed. 44 calligraphic decorations by Dalí. 96pp. 5⅜ x 8½. (Available in U.S. only.)
29220-7

ANTIQUE PLAYING CARDS: A Pictorial History, Henry René D'Allemagne. Over 900 elaborate, decorative images from rare playing cards (14th–20th centuries): Bacchus, death, dancing dogs, hunting scenes, royal coats of arms, players cheating, much more. 96pp. 9¼ x 12¼.
29265-7

MAKING FURNITURE MASTERPIECES: 30 Projects with Measured Drawings, Franklin H. Gottshall. Step-by-step instructions, illustrations for constructing handsome, useful pieces, among them a Sheraton desk, Chippendale chair, Spanish desk, Queen Anne table and a William and Mary dressing mirror. 224pp. 8⅛ x 11¼.
29338-6

THE FOSSIL BOOK: A Record of Prehistoric Life, Patricia V. Rich et al. Profusely illustrated definitive guide covers everything from single-celled organisms and dinosaurs to birds and mammals and the interplay between climate and man. Over 1,500 illustrations. 760pp. 7½ x 10⅛.
29371-8

Paperbound unless otherwise indicated. Available at your book dealer, online at **www.doverpublications.com**, or by writing to Dept. GI, Dover Publications, Inc., 31 East 2nd Street, Mineola, NY 11501. For current price information or for free catalogues (please indicate field of interest), write to Dover Publications or log on to **www.doverpublications.com** and see every Dover book in print. Dover publishes more than 500 books each year on science, elementary and advanced mathematics, biology, music, art, literary history, social sciences, and other areas.